Think on These Things

Ernest H. Streets

ISBN: 978-1-78364-484-1

The Open Bible Trust
Fordland Mount, Upper Basildon,
Reading, RG8 8LU, UK.

www.obt.org.uk

Contents

****

Foreword

It was in the late sixties that I first met Ernest Streets and his wife. I was living in Reading at the time, some 40 miles west of London, and had become friendly with his daughter and her family who had moved from Scotland to the area. He spoke at a meeting and he was such a dynamic speaker that I can still remember his subject, Paul's letter to the Philippians.

I had read a number of his leaflets and booklets prior to that occasion and after it sought out the rest. This book contains those leaflets and booklets, written over many years but now collected into this book.

It was obvious that here was a man who could find no rest with the *status quo*. The driving force in his life was the Living Word, Christ Jesus, his risen and exalted Saviour, and the guiding force was the Written Word, the Bible, the Scriptures, the inspired Word of God.

In what follows the reader will be challenged time and time again to go back to the Bible. Ernest Streets believed that, "To be effective, faith must always rest upon a *personal* understanding of the Scriptures rather than on the teaching of men." He also taught that "Our faith and consequent practise must rest upon the scripture of truth, not on tradition, church history, custom or sentiment."

He applied this principle in his own life and teaching and, as the reader progresses through this work, he will discover that in the last chapter (the last pamphlet written by Mr. Streets) he disagrees with one theme which recurs in the earlier writings; namely the date of writing of John's Gospel. He looked upon the study of the scriptures as a voyage of discovery and his hope and prayer was that his writings would start those that read them upon a voyage of discovery also.

Mr. Streets' daughter and family moved back to Scotland in the seventies and each time I visited that lovely country I called to see them, and as a result got to know Mr. and Mrs. Streets much better. In due course I had the pleasure of discussing many subjects with him and had the privilege of speaking at the Cowdenbeath Gospel Mission. It was clear that here was a man of generous spirit and an open mind, a man who deeply loved the Lord and who was well acquainted with the Bible. It puzzled me as to why he had written so little.

In the fifties he had published six separate leaflets under the general title of *Think on These Things,* and these constitute the first six chapters of this book. He had also brought out four Study Booklets, those which make up chapters 7 – 10. But why had there been no more in the intervening twenty to twenty five years? I asked him, but he avoided the subject.

In the eighties I had been studying the writings of John and had concluded that the traditional view (that John had written his gospel, letters and Revelation in the last decade of the first century) did not fit in with the testimony of Scripture. This caused some controversy in the circles in which I moved and when Earnest Streets got to hear of this, he sent me a manuscript of what constitutes the last chapter of this book, *Another look at the Gospel of John.* It was published as a booklet by the Open Bible Trust in 1985, many years after the rest of his writings.

It would appear that some thirty years earlier Mr. Streets had come to similar conclusions to myself about John, but when the manuscript had been sent to the publishers not only was it rejected, but so, too, was he. Yet throughout the many years I had known him, he said nothing of the situation. This is a testimony to the man's graciousness towards others.

So in the earlier chapters of this book the reader will find the traditional view expounded, that John wrote his Gospel towards the end of the first century. In the last chapter, you will find that Mr. Streets has John's Gospel written much earlier, before the destruction of Jerusalem and the Temple (A.D. 70) and before the final quotation of Isaiah 6 at Acts 28:25–28. My views on this subject appear in Appendix 2 of *Approaching the Bible* and in my book *John: His life and writings*; for more details see 'Further Reading' at the end of this book. The English theologian J A T Robinson also came to the same conclusion. See his *Redating the New Testament* and especially his last book the *Primacy of John*, published by SCM.

I have not taken the liberty of changing anything that Mr. Streets has written in his earlier works to make them conform to his later views. Having pointed this out, I ask the reader to keep it in mind. I did take the liberty of changing the note referring to "the place of John's Gospel". There Mr. Streets' directed the reader to see his views on John as expressed in the booklet *Understandest thou what thou readest?*, chapter 2. I have directed the reader the last chapter instead.

It gives me great pleasure to see all of Mr. Streets' writings available together in one book for the first time. I do commend this work to the reader. This does not mean to say that I concur with all that follows, but I do heartily endorse the spirit in which it is written. The Scriptures are the final authority on all matters, or, as the doctrinal basis of the Open Bible Trust:

> Whilst acknowledging the Lord's gift of teachers to His people (Ephesians 4:11) we maintain that Scripture is the sole arbiter in matters of Christian doctrine and practice and that received traditions and opinions, however widespread or ancient and however vigorously supported by men of whatever eminence, learning and godliness, are of no binding authority except in so far as they are clearly demonstrable from the Word of God (Romans 10:17; 1 Peter 1:24).

Michael Penny

Paul's Ministry

Are you missing something in the Scriptures?

The risen Christ appeared to Paul – for what purpose?

*Paul is the only person called **the Apostle of the Gentiles**.*
You are a Gentile. What message had he for you which was independent
of anything the Twelve had to proclaim?

During his testimony before King Agrippa, Paul made a significant statement which you will find reported at Acts 26:22-23; "Having therefore obtained help of God, I continue unto this day, witnessing both to small and great, **saying none other things than those which the prophets and Moses did say should come:** that Christ should suffer, and that He should be the first that should rise from the dead, and should shew light unto the people – (i.e. the people of Israel, the covenant people) – and to the Gentiles". A reading and study of Paul's ministry as recorded and reported in the Acts, from chapter 13 onwards, and a similar reading and study of the epistles written during the time of his missionary activities, the epistles to the Galatians, Thessalonians, Corinthians and Romans (also to the Hebrews, which was most likely written by Paul about that same time), will make quite plain that his statement was absolutely true.

All his ministry, preaching or writing, during this time was wholly founded on the general testimony and teaching of the Old Testament scriptures. He was not inspired to add one little bit of teaching that could be called new, fresh revelation. Even though he did receive wonderful revelations during the experience about which he writes at 2 Corinthians 12:1-4, he states that such revelations were of the nature of "unspeakable words which it was not lawful for a man to utter". Therefore his claim at Acts 26:22 stands. He said and wrote, "**none other things than those which the prophets and Moses did say should come**", nothing else at all but that had been previously set forth, or prepared for in the sacred writings of the prophets and Moses. Paul's usage of the phrase "the prophets and Moses" immediately brings to mind the similar phrases recorded at Luke 24:27 and 44, where we read, (verse 27) that the Lord "beginning at Moses and all the prophets expounded unto them in all the Scriptures the things concerning Himself", further (at verse 44) "He said unto them, these are the words which I spake unto you while I was yet with you, that all things must be fulfilled which were written in the law of Moses, and the prophets, and in the psalms, concerning me".

Concerning these verses with the statement at Acts 26:22 it is clear that Paul kept right in line with the teaching of the Lord, in that he continued, (at least to the end of the period covered by the Acts, which historically extends to within a few years of the destruction of Jerusalem in 70 A.D.), to expound and teach from the very same scriptures as used by the Lord, those things which had been set forth by Moses, - whose writings cover the beginning of the world as well as the early history of the covenant people, Israel and the prophets, whose ministries cover the remainder of the history of Israel to the close of the Old Testament.

From this it should be quite clear that nothing but Old Testament teaching was expounded, explained and amplified right to the end of the Acts – **"none other things than those which the prophets and Moses did say should come"**, nothing outside that scope, nothing intrinsically new was introduced. What is reported in the historical records of the birth, life, death, resurrection and ascension of Christ in the Gospels, and the proclamations and teaching of those who ministered and wrote through the period covered by the Acts, is nothing else than a setting forth of "the gospel preached before unto Abram" (Galatians 3:8), which gospel promised signal blessing to Abram and to his seed, and that through Abram and his seed "all families of the earth" should be blessed. (for details of these promises read Genesis, chapters 12 to 25, also the repeated promises to Isaac and Jacob etc.).

In complete accord with this is the clearly recorded fact that the proclamation of the gospel in the New Testament, up to the end of the Acts, was "to the Jew first" (Romans 1:16 etc.). In the promises made to Abraham, Isaac and Jacob and through the ministries of the prophets, it is made quite clear that the chosen people, Israel, were to be the channel through whom the world-wide blessing was to flow. The Old Testament Scriptures, and the New Testament Scriptures up to the end of the Acts, show no salvation for Gentiles apart from Israel. Even as stated by Christ, "Salvation is of the Jews" (John 4:22). They were chosen to be God's "key" people. Of necessity the message had to be to them "first", to prepare them for their national ministry. This is what Peter says as reported at Acts 3:25, 26; "Ye are the children of the prophets and of the covenant which God made with our fathers, saying unto Abraham, 'And in thy seed shall all the kindreds of the earth be blessed.' *Unto you first* God, having raised up His Son Jesus, sent Him to bless you, in turning away every one of you from his iniquities."

So we find it recorded that Christ "was a minister of the circumcision to confirm the promises made unto the Fathers" (Romans 15:8, the fathers being Abram, Isaac and Jacob). Moreover, the Lord Himself declared, "I am not sent but unto the lost sheep of the house of Israel" (Matthew 15:24), and He instructed the twelve apostles "Go not into the way of the Gentiles, and into any city of the Samaritans enter ye not: but go rather to the lost sheep of the house of Israel" (Matthew 10:5, 6).

At Pentecost the message was given to "*Jews*, devout *men out of every nation under heaven*", as we read at Acts 2:5. We further read that some years later "they which were scattered ... by persecution ... travelled ... *preaching the word to none but unto the Jews only*" (Acts 11:19). Acts 10 records that a special vision was necessary before Peter would take the message to the Gentile Cornelius, and although Paul, throughout all his missionary ministry was careful to give his message "to the Jew first", yet he was harried and persecuted by those very same Jews because he dared give his message to the Gentiles after his own compatriots had refused it. But remember, this message given "to the Jew first", and then to the Gentiles, was wholly consistent with, indeed solely and solidly founded on, "**those things which the prophets and Moses did say should come**".

The close of the Acts sees Paul in Prison in Rome. His missionary journeyings were concluded. The teaching and truth as set forth in the epistles to the Galatians, Thessalonians, Corinthians, Romans (and Hebrews) had been received, and was known by those believers for whom it was originally and primarily intended. The ministry "to the Jew first", and to those Gentiles who, as stated by Paul in Romans 11, were "wild olive branches graffed into ... the olive tree" (read Romans 11:11-26) and thus became "partakers of Israel's spiritual things" (Romans 15:27), was almost concluded. From a reading of Acts 28:16-21 we learn that the leaders of the Jewish community in Rome were called together to hear what Paul had to say to them. He expounds, testifies and persuades "out of the law of Moses and out of the prophets", all day. Note that he is still saying "none other things than those which the prophets and Moses did say should come", but alas, all his exposition, testimony and persuasion fails, and finally (Acts 28:25-28), he is inspired to pass sentence, not only on those Jews in Rome, but a sentence which affected all of the chosen people wherever they might be, namely, that because of their spiritual deafness, blindness and hardness of heart and their consequent refusals of the salvation which "first" had been "sent" specially to them (Acts 3:26; 13:26), that such "salvation of God is sent unto the Gentiles" (28:28). From this point it could no longer be said that "Salvation is of the Jews", for the opportunity of receiving that salvation in the national sense, which would fit them to be the channel through whom the blessed message could flow out to the other nations, was taken from them.

"The salvation of God is sent unto the Gentiles."

In connection with this unexpected, unpredicted movement, Paul, though still in prison, writes more epistles: - to the Ephesians, Philippians, Colossians, 1st and 2nd Timothy and Titus as well as the small personal letter to Philemon. In these epistles, written after the end of the Acts, Paul, whilst repeating the items of truth relating to the doctrines of redemption – salvation by blood, justification by faith etc., now sets forth truth which had not previously been made known or even hinted at. Whereas in his ministry *up to the end of the Acts,* as we have already seen, he spoke and wrote "**none other things** than those which the prophets and Moses did say should come", *after the end of the Acts*, from prison, he writes about aspects of truth which had been made known to him by revelation (Ephesians 3:3). By revelation, not through the Old Testament prophets, or Moses' writings, for he claims that the truth he then makes known, "in other ages was not made known unto the sons of men, as it is now revealed" (Ephesians 3:5), therefore the prophets and Moses could have known nothing of it, neither could Paul himself have previously said or written anything about it. He also emphasises the same thing a little lower down in the same passage (Ephesians 3:9) writing that the revelation he was then making known "hath been hid in God from the beginning of the world", and in the Colossians epistle he declares that this same truth "hath been hid from ages and generations but now is made manifest" (Colossians 1:26). Add to these the further statement that this revelation of truth was given "to fulfil – or complete – the Word of God" (Colossians 1:25).

If the Scriptures are the inspired, infallible, unbreakable Word of God that they claim to be (2 Timothy 3:16; 1 Peter 1:10-12; 2 Peter 1:20, 21; John 10:35; Matthew 5:17, 18; Luke 21:33, etc.), and if inspired words mean anything at all, then it is quite evident that while *up to the end of the Acts* Paul declared **"none other things"** than were set forth in the Old Testament writings, and that *after the end of the Acts* he sets forth truth which he unmistakably claims had previously been hidden in God and not at all made known to the sons of men, then such truth must indeed be a completely new, fresh revelation, touching on part of the great redemptive purpose of God which He had in His wisdom seen fit to keep back until "the salvation of God' had been taken from Israel and "sent unto the Gentiles".

For whom was this new revelation given? "For *you Gentiles*" (Ephesians 3:1). "That *the Gentiles* should be fellow-heirs etc.". (Ephesians 3:6). "Unto me," writes Paul, "is this grace given, that I should preach among *the Gentiles* the unsearchable riches of Christ, and to make all men see what is the fellowship – dispensation or administration – of the mystery"

(Ephesians 3:8, 9). "God would make known the riches of the glory of this mystery among *the Gentiles*" (Colossians 1:27). No longer is it true that "Salvation is of the Jews"; no longer is "the Jew first"; no longer are Gentile believers being graffed into Israel's olive tree, for these truths, the foundations of which are laid in the writings of "**the prophets and Moses**" are for the present suspended and superseded. The new message – and remember it must be new if it had been "hid in God" and thus not even hinted at by the Old Testament writers – is sent to *the Gentiles*, through Paul the Apostle of the Gentiles (Romans 11:13; 1 Timothy 2:7; 2 Timothy 1:11 etc.).

What is the content of this new revelation? We can answer only briefly, and point only to the salient features. By an operation of God, called "the dispensation – or administration – of the grace of God" (Ephesians 3:2), He is making known a previously well-kept mystery – or secret part of His great redemptive plan (Ephesians 3:3-5; 3:11) – and is forming a called out company designated "the church, which is His body" (Ephesians 1:22, 23) and "the body of Christ" (Ephesians 4:12; Colossians 1:18). This "body of Christ" is not to be thought of as being illustrated by the human body with its many differing unequal members, as in 1 Corinthians 12 where the human body illustrates the church of the Acts period, in which the Jewish believer had advantage and profit (Romans 3:1, 2) over the Gentile believer, and the various members had differing miraculous gifts but rather as when we refer to "a fine body of men" – policemen or soldiers let us say – in which "body", or company, each man is equally a policeman, or soldier. Likewise, in "the body of Christ" each member is on an equality with all other members. (Ephesians 3:6, where "fellow-heirs, of the same body, and partakers etc. "is literally, "equal-heirs, of the equal-body, and equal-partners").

The members of this "body of Christ" are seen by God to be "Seated together with Christ in the heavenly places far above all principality and power and might and dominion" (Ephesians 1:20, 21; 2:6), and are "being built together unto an holy temple – inner shrine – in the Lord, for an habitation of God through the Spirit" (Ephesians 2:21, 22). No hint of the foregoing truths can be found in the Scriptures before the close of the Acts.

What is the purpose of this new revelation? Scripture answers that it was (1) "to the intent *that now* unto the principalities and powers in the heavenly places might be known by the church the manifold wisdom of God" (Ephesians 3:10), and further (2) "*that in the ages to come* He might shew the exceeding riches of His grace in His kindness toward us through

Christ Jesus" (Ephesians 2:7). No hint of such a purpose can be found in the Scriptures before the close of the Acts.

"Think on these things" – then search the scriptures and see whether these things are as we declare them to be (Acts 17:11). We affirm most strongly that an appreciation of this truth of "the mystery" (Ephesians 3:3) will be the key to a fuller understanding of the whole plan and purpose of God as revealed through the Scriptures, and thus will lead to the reception of untold blessing.

The Churches and the Church

A Church is a called out company

For what purpose?

Under what conditions?

How many churches in the scriptures?

"Then had the churches rest ... and were multiplied" (Acts 9:31) "The church which is His body" (Ephesians 1:22, 23)

'The churches' and 'the church' – just what is the distinction here? Most Bible teachers and preachers would answer somewhat in the following manner. "The distinction is that the plural, 'the churches', refers to the many local companies of believers, - gathered each in their different towns and cities wheresoever they may be, most often designated according to their geographical position, for instance "the church in thy house" (Philemon verse 2, Romans 16:5), "the church ... at Corinth" (1 Corinthians 1:2), 'the churches of Galatia" (Galatians 1:2), "the churches of God which in Judea are in Christ Jesus" (1 Thessalonians 2:14), and to bring it up to date, the churches in London, Manchester, New York, Bombay etc., etc.; all the many and varied denominational, inter-denominational and undenominational groups and gatherings all around the world, - composing Christendom at any particular time, whilst the singular 'the church', (Matthew 16:18; Ephesians 1:22, 23; Colossians 1:18, 24), is the designation of the spiritual mystical body, composed of all the true believers in Christ who have lived and died, all true believers now living, and all those who will yet embrace the truth in Christ. The local 'churches' and the mystical 'church' commenced in Jerusalem at Pentecost time, a few weeks after the crucifixion and resurrection of Christ, as recorded at Acts Chapter 2."

On the face of it, and without bothering to study further, that seems to be a likely explanation. Is it really just as simple as that? What do you make of Matthew 18:17; to what did Christ refer when He said "tell it to the church"? His hearers did not question what he said or ask what He meant.

There must have been a 'church' then in existence, a church before the crucifixion, before Pentecost!!

We intend this pamphlet to be a brief scriptural and historical survey of the whole subject, and first we need to determine the meaning of the word rendered 'church'. This we shall find by reference to the Old Testament.

"The Old Testament" we can hear some exclaim, "Why the Old Testament? The Word 'church' does not occur there at all!" Nevertheless, will you look at Psalm 22:22. What do you read? "in the midst of *the congregation* I will praise Thee". Now turn to Hebrews 2:12, where Psalm 22:22 is quoted and rendered "In the midst of *the church* will I sing praise unto Thee". In the epistle to the Hebrews the Greek word *ekklesia*, nearly always translated 'church' in the New Testament, is used as the equivalent of the Hebrew word *qahal*, which is translated 'congregation', 'assembly', 'company' or 'multitude'. Thus these two words are used interchangeably by the Holy Spirit, and their absolute identity, as far as their use in Scripture is concerned, is determined and established. The Hebrew word *qahal* is used many times throughout the Old Testament Scriptures, and in its verbal form always means 'to call together', 'to assemble', and in its noun form means 'a company, congregation or assembly called together, or called out, for some specific purpose'. The equivalent Greek word *ekklesia* also means 'a called out company', 'an assembly'. The English word 'church' is in reality but a poor translation, and has been the foundation of much confusion of thought on this subject, but we use it for the time being because it is the popular term.

At Deuteronomy 23:3 it is stated that "no Ammonite or Moabite shall enter into the congregation (*qahal*) of the Lord", and this law was acted upon after the return from Babylon, as can be seen by reading Nehemiah 13:1-3, where the phrase "congregation of God" is used. From these and many other references it is clear that the nation of Israel, as a nation, was reckoned to be "the congregation or church, of God" throughout its Old Testament history, even as Stephen is reported as saying when he spoke of Moses being "in the church in the wilderness" (Acts 7:37, 38).

We have already referred to Nehemiah 13, in which chapter is the record of the separation of the mixed multitude from "the congregation, or church, of God". According to the Talmudic writings it was at this juncture that the famous Council known as The Great Synagogue was called into being, to reorganize the religious and spiritual life of the people lately returned from Babylon. References to its good work are to be found in the books of Ezra and Nehemiah. 'Synagogue' is the Greek word *sunagoge* which means 'the place of assembly', but like our usage of the English word 'church', it was employed to signify the company gathered in the place, as well as the place of gathering itself. The Great Synagogue, at first comprising 120 members, was composed of: - (1) the princes and nobles, (2) the leading priests (3) the chief Levites, (4) the doctors of the Law, and (5) some delegates of the populace. It was an assembly representative of "the whole congregation of Israel" or 'church of God'. After several years its numbers were reduced to 70. Having discharged its original commission it continued as the Sanhedrin, the Council of the nation which judged both the Lord and the apostles. (Matthew 26:59; Acts 4:15 etc.).

Amongst many far-reaching reforms and institutions, the Great Synagogue organised the synagogue system, which provided for the formation of local representative 'assemblies' wherever sufficient Jews should be found living or working. The local 'assemblies' or 'churches' met in the synagogues and were responsible for passing on the instruction of the Mosaic Law, as well as for the continuation of the corporate worship of their community. So they taught and practised the ordinances of the Law, Sabbaths, Passover and other yearly feasts, circumcision, various 'washings' or baptisms and enforced a host of manmade Pharisaic regulations which gradually accumulated. Thus the synagogues became schools for the instruction of the young, minor courts of Law with disciplinary powers of excommunication and scourging, as well as being places of worship. It is easy to see how many synagogues became politico-religious bodies, whilst the Sanhedrin at Jerusalem became more and more involved in civil and political matters, to the exclusion of the spiritual requirements for which the Great Synagogue and the synagogue system had been originally evolved. There were differences of opinion and of Scriptural interpretation which resulted in a variety of Judaistic parties and sects, and these have their echo in the many denominations and shades of opinion within present-day Christendom has a large measure grown out of the synagogue system.

So far we have pointed out, (1) that the nation of Israel, as a nation, was spoken of as 'the congregation, or church of God'. It was 'called out' and separated from the other nations and destined to be "a priestly kingdom" (Exodus 19:5, 6), to mediate between God and the other peoples of the earth. This role it will one day fulfil (Isaiah 61:6). Further, we have pointed out (2) that there was instituted a system whereby 'assemblies' were to be found, not only throughout Palestine, but also in all places to which the Jews had travelled or been dispersed. It was to these synagogues that the Lord customarily resorted (Luke 4:16). Let us turn again to the Scriptural record.

Although it is possible that the Lord Himself had other matters in mind and in view when He instructed His hearers to "tell" their difficulties "unto the church" (Matthew 18:17), it is certain that they would understand Him to be directing them to the local synagogue.

But about this very time, as recorded at Matthew 16, a new development was introduced by the Lord. In reply to Peter's confession "Thou art the Christ, the Son of the living God" verse 16, Christ says "Blessed art thou ... thou art Peter, and upon this rock – (the established truth that He was the Christ, the Son of God) – I will build my church" verse 18. As we have seen there were already many "called out companies", synagogues or assemblies, locally representing the whole congregation or church of God, and now Christ says "I will build *my assembly, my church*". This "church" as indicated in verse 19 in this same chapter, was to be linked with the kingdom of heaven, the preaching and teaching of which had been the occupation of the Lord and His apostles from the time of His temptation (see Matthew 4:11). It was this church which was commenced at Pentecost time in Jerusalem seven weeks after the crucifixion. The original place of assembly was most likely the same upper room in which the historic Passover celebration had taken place (Luke 22:12; Acts 1:13), and for some time the whole multitude of those who responded to Peter's appeals for repentance (Acts 2:38; 3:19), assembled daily in the Temple (Acts 2:46; 5:12, 42). When eventually these believers in Christ were scattered by persecution (Acts 8:1; 11:19), they would undoubtedly either join themselves to the synagogues in the places where they went, or set up synagogues of their own, according to their requirements. Many such synagogues throughout Judea became "the churches of God which in Judea are in Christ Jesus" (1 Thessalonians 2:14). From Acts 9:2; 22:19 and 26:11, we see that Saul sought out the believers in Christ who were found worshipping in the synagogues, and when he was later called and commissioned by Christ, he always went first to the synagogues to proclaim his particular gospel (Acts 9:20; 13:5, 14; 14:1 etc.).

This church, "My church", which largely grew up in the synagogues was at first composed wholly of Christian Jews and proselytes to the Jewish faith, and according to the particular teachings and practices of the synagogues in which they had been brought up, or which they had joined as proselytes, they continued such Mosaic and Judaistic teaching and practice.

When, as the result of the preaching of Paul and his companions, Gentiles were joined to the believing companies, most of these Christianised synagogues, or assemblies which had more or less adopted the synagogue system, insisted upon treating the incomers as proselytes, and subjected them to circumcision and water baptism, and included them in the observances of Sabbaths, Passover (with its New Covenant implications as indicated by Christ), and also the other feasts, observances and rites which were of purely Jewish origin.

The great differences of opinion that arose because of these things, and the great stand for the freedom of the Gentile believers taken by Paul (read the epistle to the Galatian churches) – were in very large measure brought to a head in the open controversy respecting circumcision. The subsequent Council of the apostles and other leaders at Jerusalem formulated certain decrees or rules, (read Acts 15), which doubtless brought much relief and joy to many Gentile believers, but also emphasised the cleavage between "Circumcision" and "Uncircumscision" (Galatians 2:7-9), between those who kept the Law of Moses and those who were free from Mosaic and Judaistic observances (Acts 21:20, 25). These major differences, along with a host of other differences of interpretation and practice, continued amongst those who went to make up "my church", who were "blessed with faithful Abraham ... Abraham's seed and heirs according to the promise" (Galatians 3).

This church which the Lord had promised to build, connected with the kingdom of heaven, is seen to be "the city which hath foundations" for which Abraham looked (Hebrew 11:10); the city founded upon Peter and the other apostles of the circumcision, called in Revelation "the twelve apostles of the Lamb"; the city clearly seen as "the Bride, the Lamb's wife" (Revelation chapters 19 and 21).

Eventually came the end of the period covered by the book of Acts. Israel, as a nation, failed to respond to the continued offers of blessing; failed to put into practice their obligations as "the congregation or church of God". Therefore Paul was inspired to pronounce the fatal words that "the salvation of God is sent unto the Gentiles" (Acts 28:28). These words presaged the bringing to pass of the Lord's prophecy that "Jerusalem should be trodden down until the times of the Gentiles be fulfilled" (Luke 21:24). This meant that the purposes and promises of God relating to "my church", the Bride of Christ, connected with the kingdom of heaven, fell into abeyance, and will continue in abeyance "until the times of the Gentiles be fulfilled", which times have not yet run their course.

'Assembly', 'synagogue' or 'church' life, with all the varieties of Mosaic, Judaistic and Pharisaic teachings and practices, continued for a few years, during which Paul was inspired to write the epistles from his prison in

Rome, containing the new revelation of "the church which is His body" (see Ephesians, Philippians, Colossians and 2nd Timothy). This was a revelation of truth which, if received and acknowledged, writes Paul, would deal with the schisms and differences between 'circumcision' and 'uncircumscision' and bring to an end "the law of commandments contained in decrees", bringing together the different companies of believers into "one new man" (Read Ephesians 2:11-18). But this fresh revelation, which "fulfilled or completed the word of God" (Colossians 1:25), was unheeded and refused, as it is even at this present day. Paul, "the prisoner of Christ" (Ephesians 3:1; 4:1), was spurned and neglected. He writes "all they which are in Asia be turned away from me" (2 Timothy 1:15).

The majority were ashamed of him and of the testimony of the Lord which he bore (2 Timothy 1:8). Demas and others who had been former fellow-labourers, forsook him (2 Timothy 4:10, 16), and the wonderful message of super-heavenly blessing (Ephesians 1:3 etc.), and of the "edifying – or building up – of the body of Christ" (Ephesians 4:11-16), which in completion would be "an holy temple ... for the habitation of God through the Spirit" (Ephesians 2:19-22), was largely, almost completely hidden under the continuing Judaistic teaching of the Christianised synagogues and the Christian assemblies which had more or less adopted the synagogue system.

In 70 A.D. the city of Jerusalem and the Temple were destroyed, confirming the Lord's prophecies and also Paul's announcement that the salvation of God had been sent to the Gentiles. The Temple cult ceased. The Sanhedrin could no longer operate from Jerusalem, and the scattered priests, scribes and doctors of the law turned to a closer study of the Torah, which led to Talmudism. We have no space to develop the outcome in that direction.

The Christian Jews and the believing Gentiles, having refused Paul's message of "the church which is His body" continued the synagogue based assembly life as best they could, and remained more or less faithful to the teaching of the twelve apostles of the circumcision, many still retaining the hope of the early return of Christ to set up the promised earthly kingdom, but still divided as 'circumcision' and 'uncircumscision' and by the many other differences of belief and practice. In the ground of such a torn and divided company, serious errors and difficulties took root and developed. Really authentic records of these torn and divided groups, from 70 A.D., through the second and into the third century are very scanty. It is certain, that, being much misunderstood, they suffered under successive persecutions, and from the writings of the early 'Fathers' who ruled various assemblies and communities, we can gather that there was a move along the line of ceremonial clericalism. The bishops and deacons etc. of the Christianised synagogue system gradually gave place to a priesthood. The Old Testament pattern of the Levitical priesthood became the model for a so called 'Christian priesthood'. Then the Emperor Constantine, in order to help consolidate his empire, took to himself the right to rule in ecclesiastical matters and became 'Pontifex Maximus'. Later the Emperor Theodosius compelled his subjects to accept the 'catholic faith'.

From this point 'church' history can be fairly easily followed. Reformers of, and dissenters from the 'catholic faith', for the most part ignoring Paul's revelation of "the church which is His body", and failing to "rightly divide the word of truth", have but revived and continued much of the Judaism of the synagogues, often mixing with it some of the clericalism or priestcraft of the "catholic faith" and producing some very strange results. Thus on to today's Christendom with its many hundreds of denominations, sects and assemblies, each claiming to be right.

Believer, where do you stand in relation to all this? The writer feels sure that the teaching to sweep away the accumulated schisms and differences of the past and the present, is the truth revealed to Paul, who after the end of the Acts, as "the prisoner of Jesus Christ for you Gentiles" and "the apostle and teacher of the Gentiles" (1 Timothy 2:7; 2 Timothy 1:11), made known "the mystery" concerning "the church which is His body", which in every way is distinct from the "church" of Israel as a nation, and also distinct from "the churches" of the Acts period, who formed "my church", "the Bride, the Lamb's wife".

To sum up, it can be seen that the subject of the Church, or the Churches in the Scriptures, has three main parts. If we are going to "test the things that differ" (Philippians 1:10) we will recognise this threefold outworking of the redemptive plan of God, as shown on the enxt page.

A.	Israel, the nation, the church of God relating to the *earthly, kingdom sphere.*
B.	"My church", the Bride, relating to the *heavenly sphere,* connected with the kingdom of, or 'out from' heaven. The Bride, the Holy city, New Jerusalem "comes down from God out of heaven" (Revelation 21:2, 9, 10).
C.	The church – "His body" relating to the "far above all" heavenlies (Ephesians 1:20, 21; 2:6) the *super heavenly sphere.*

Only by an acknowledgement of our Lord Jesus Christ in His exalted position, seated in the heavenlies far above all, as Lord and Head over the church which is His body, can any measure of true spiritual unity, peace and blessing be enjoyed (see Ephesians 1:17-23; 4:8-16).

"The gospel of *your* salvation" (Ephesians 1:13)

Do you really know the biblical meaning of salvation?

*Is this gospel on **resurrection** good news?*

Can this gospel have a message for you in this life – today?

When the phrase "the gospel of your salvation" is read, if you care to take note, you will usually find that no particular emphasis is placed upon, or even thought as being necessary in relation to any one of the words. It is, unfortunately, a case where 'familiarity breeds contempt'. The present day almost world-wide proclamation of the message of the love of God for sinners; dulls our appreciation of the historical facts that form the background upon which the progressive revelation concerning salvation by redemption was built up and made known.

The words "the gospel of your salvation" in Ephesians 1:13, were penned by the Apostle Paul to believers in a part of what we now know as Asia Minor. That these believers were *Gentiles* is quite clear from the words of Ephesians 2:11, 12, 3:1, 8; and 4:17. "Well", you ask, "what has that got to do with it?" Quite a lot! Paul writes to these Gentiles about "the word of truth, the glad tidings of *your* salvation". They had lately been "far off" (2:13) "without Christ, having no hope and without God" being "aliens from the common wealth of Israel and strangers from the covenants of promise" (2:12). As Gentiles, they had no part in, nor could they lay claim to, any of the privileges or salvation which were Israel's promised and covenanted portion. But now, for them, all this had been changed. They had heard, and believed, a certain "word", or message "of truth" (1:13) which was to them "the good news of *your* salvation", as a result of which they had been "made nigh" to God "by the blood of Christ" (2:13). This was, as Paul states "*Your* salvation"; *Gentile* salvation, as distinct from the salvation which had for centuries earlier been extended to Israel practically exclusively. Put the emphasis well and truly on that word "*your*", that is where it belongs. Although we may be a trifle vague as to the true meaning of the word 'Salvation', we have become so familiar with the idea of what is loosely termed "the offer of salvation for all", that we miss certain distinctions, and as a consequence, misapply certain out workings of truth, taking matters in connection with the message of salvation respecting Israel, and applying such matters to ourselves.

The truth is that the good news of salvation for the Gentiles is distinct and different in its outworking along certain lines, from the good news of salvation promised and covenanted to Israel. It is this particular aspect of truth that we desire to study and briefly set out.

First, it would be advantageous if we could find out a little more about the word 'salvation' itself. As occurring many times in the Old Testament Scriptures it is the rendering of three Hebrew words, which as well as 'salvation', are also rendered 'deliverance, health, help, safety, saving, welfare and victory'. The primary meaning and thought behind the words employed is that of deliverance, and then the resulting ease, or lifting away of any burden, trouble, stress or strain. In the Old Testament we read of individual, family, tribal and national salvation.

The first usage of the word is found in Genesis 49, where Jacob, rehearsing the characteristics of his sons and prophesying concerning them in relation to the future (49:1), in the midst of it all, at verse 18, seems impatiently to cry "I have waited for Thy salvation, O Lord" – as much as to say, "I know from the characters of my sons, that in the future, in the last days in particular, their descendants will fail and have much trouble, therefore on their behalf, I wait for, I look forward to and earnestly desire Thy salvation. Oh Jehovah". These words, - coming from the man who wrestled at the ford Jabbok, and who, as a consequence had received the indication of a much needed change of character, "No more Jacob, but Israel" (see Genesis 32:22-30) – can point only to one conclusion. Jacob's deliverance from himself and his fears; his deliverance into a new life; his 'salvation' on that notable occasion, was wrought through his personal contact with the "Man" (verse 24) Who was none other than "God" (verse 30). Thus 'salvation' to Jacob was not *a thing*; was not only *an experience* but primarily a person, even God Himself. From his prophetic utterances concerning his sons in Genesis 49, it would appear that Jacob foresaw, however dimly, that "all Israel shall be saved" even as he himself had been delivered. So it is written "there shall come from Zion the Deliverer Who shall turn away ungodliness from Jacob" (Isaiah 59:20; Romans 11:26).

This personification of salvation is repeated over and over again. At the time of Israel's deliverance from the pursuing Egyptians, Moses sang "The Lord ... is become my salvation" (Exodus 15:2). Psalmist and prophet add their voices in testimony as to be seen at Psalm 52:1-2; Isaiah 12:2, and a host of other similar occurrences. *Jehovah was salvation,* and the presence of Jehovah in the midst of His chosen people, whether pictured and manifested by the pillar of cloud and fire, or in the Ark of the Covenant, or as stated in various ways, guaranteed for them such deliverances as they needed from time to time. In a peculiar sense and in differing ways and circumstances, God revealed Himself to His chosen people as their Deliverer, their Salvation. Commencing with the deliverance from the burdens and bondage of Egypt, there are many occasions in which Israel, as a nation, proved that having Jehovah as their God, and in their midst, gave deliverance and made all the difference between defeat and victory. This gives special point and significance to the repeated statements and promises "I will be your God and ye shall be My people" (Exodus 6:7; Leviticus 26:12 etc.) and "I will dwell with them", "I will be amongst Israel" (Exodus 29:45; Deuteronomy 7:21; Jeremiah 14:8-9 etc.).

Advancing to the study of the word rendered 'salvation' in the New Testament, it is found that, as the Hebrew words of the Old Testament, so also the Greek word used in the New means 'deliverance, soundness, ease and health'. Moreover, the truth that salvation was the possession of God's chosen people by reason of the fact that He, their Salvation, was their God and dwelt in their midst, is continued without break. In the Old Testament, as we have already noted, Israel had the visible tokens of God's presence in the fiery, cloudy pillar, and in the ark of the testimony as the very central feature of all the priestly functions in tabernacle or temple ritual. On the first pages of the New Testament a more vivid and direct setting forth of this same truth is to be found. Prior to the birth of the long promised Messiah, the angel messenger proclaimed "Thou shalt call His name Jesus ... as spoken by the prophet who said 'They shall call His name Emmanuel'" (Matthew 1:21-23). "Jesus" is the rendering of the Greek *Iesous* which is the equivalent of *Yeshuah* the principal Old Testament Hebrew word rendered 'salvation'. "Emmanuel", as interpreted in verse 23, means "God with us". In effect therefore, the message of the angel was "Thou shalt call His name *Yeshuah Emmanuel* – God our Salvation with us – for He shall save His people ... "Shall save "His people", who are "His people"? Why, of course "His people" are the people of Israel, according to the promise "Ye shall be *my* people", (Leviticus 26:12). They "His people", are later spoken of by John, "He came unto *His own* but His own received Him not" (John 1:11).

The Jehovah of the Old Testament, Who was Israel's Salvation, is the Jesus of the New Testament, still set forth as being the Salvation of His own People Israel. Read the touching and impressive account found in

Luke 2:25-35, when the aged Simeon – (who had, with others, been "waiting for the consolation of Israel") – took and held the baby Jesus in his arms, and contentedly exclaims "... mine eyes have seen Thy salvation ... the glory of Thy people Israel" (verses 30, 32). More than half a century later, the Spirit, through the apostle Paul, confirms all this by the statement at Romans 15:8 "... Jesus Christ was a minister of the circumcision" – i.e. of Israel – "to confirm the promises made unto the fathers". "But He was not successful in that ministry" you say "for His own people Israel, the circumcision, received Him not – in fact they rejected and crucified Him".

Yes! That is true. They rejected Him, *but he did not reject them*. He still continued to work with them, so that about twenty-five years after the crucifixion Paul emphatically declares "God *hath not* cast away – rejected – His people whom He foreknew" (Romans 11:2). It is indeed a serious mistake to suppose, as many do, that God cast away His own chosen people Israel at the time of the crucifixion of His Son on Calvary. The rejection and consequent crucifixion of Christ, the Salvation of God, had been foreseen and prepared for in every way. In John, chapters 13-16 is recorded what the Lord had to say to those of "His own" (John 13:1), who had believed and received Him.

We will summarise and paraphrase some of His statements thus: - "I have been present with you in the flesh, Jehovah your salvation, strengthening and helping you, but now I am going away from you for a short time. Nevertheless, I will not leave you without a strengthener and helper, for I will come to you in another form. I will pray My Father and He will send Me back to You as the strengthening, delivering Spirit of truth. He, the Spirit of truth, is my other self, and through my strengthening Spirit I will constantly stay at your side, indeed I will come and make my home within each one of you."

So Christ, the Salvation of God for Israel returned, being in the lives of those who believed. He thus returned to the very people who had rejected and crucified Him. From Pentecost and onward through that period as covered by the record of the Acts, He was manifestly still among them, giving signs, miracles, and gifts of the Spirit to prove His presence. These confirming, attesting signs and spiritual gifts are to be seen in operation right to the last chapter of the Acts, (see Acts 28:8), making evident the fact that from the commencement of Israel's nationhood, (when signs and miracles were constant occurrences, see Exodus, Numbers etc.), right through to the end of the Acts, Jehovah Jesus, the Salvation of God was with – in the midst of – His chosen people Israel.

From the beginning of the ministry of John Baptist and of Christ, there was proclaimed "the gospel of the kingdom" (Matthew 4:23), which is later also called "the gospel of the circumcision" (Galatians 2:7). *This "gospel", accompanied and confirmed by signs, miracles, healings and gifts of the Spirit was a message of good news concerning Christ the Salvation of God as king over the promised and covenanted kingdom of Israel, which was also called "the kingdom of the heavens".* Whilst this message was being proclaimed it was signally true, as Christ Himself declared, that "Salvation is of – or belongs to and comes through – the Jews" (John 4:22).

Towards the end of this long period – (from the calling into being the nation of Israel, through to the end of Acts, during which time the chosen people held the central place in the purpose of God) – some Gentiles, beginning with Cornelius (Acts 10), and continuing with the many Gentiles who believed as a result of the missionary ministry of Paul and his associates (Acts 13-28), were brought into blessing. Such Gentiles, says James at Acts 15:14, were the result of a "visit" by God, - (a visit being of a temporary nature, not a permanency) – a visit, a temporary movement "to take out of the Gentiles a people for His name". In order that this might be accomplished, there was the proclamation of "the gospel of the uncircumscision" (Galatians 2:7, and please read carefully verses 1-9 here).

That this "gospel of the uncircumscision" was different from "the gospel of the circumcision" as preached by Peter and the eleven, is evident from the fact that Paul went to Jerusalem to explain, he says, "that gospel *which I preach* among the Gentiles" (Galatians 2:2). The gospel of the uncircumscision resulted in Gentiles being grafted into Israel's olive tree (Romans 11:17-24) and thus being constituted "Abraham's seed and heirs according to the promise" (Galatians 3:29). This good news recognised that Christ, the Salvation of God, really belonged to Israel, but that as a temporary measure, and to accomplish one phase of the purpose of God, Israel was sharing her blessings, and Gentiles were thus "partakers of Israel's spiritual things" (Romans 15:27).

While we do not want to cloud the issue here by including too much detail, we feel that we must point out that "the gospel of the uncircumscision" was the message connected with Paul's "ministry of reconciliation" (2 Corinthians 5:18-20), and that it was being proclaimed by Paul to the Gentiles in conjunction with "the ministry of the new covenant" (2 Corinthians 3:6) which Paul at that same time was exercising amongst his Jewish compatriots. (The content of the "ministry of the new covenant" is clearly set forth in the epistle to the Hebrews). Some of the people of Israel

– "the remnant" – and some of the Gentiles were brought together by these ministries, and miracles, gifts of the spirit, healings, etc. were still in evidence amongst them because Israel still held the important place in the purpose of God, and it was then still then true that "Salvation was of the Jews".

To sum up this section let us say that the *"gospel of the uncircumscision" and the ministries of "the reconciliation" and "the new covenant", were messages of good news concerning Christ the Salvation of God, set forth as the heavenly Bridegroom and Husband (2 Corinthians 11:2) and spoke of the believers of these messages as the Bride and Wife, who should occupy the heavenly city, the New Jerusalem, that some "city" and "heavenly country" for which Abraham looked (Hebrews 11:8-16; Revelation 19:7-9; 21:2, 10-27).*

But the long period of Israel's prominence in the purpose of God temporarily came to an end. Temporarily? Yes, of course: For "God is not a man that He should lie" (Numbers 23:19), further His "gifts and calling are without repentance" (Romans 11:29). He has not lied, neither has He changed His mind concerning the calling of His people Israel, and will eventually implement all His promises to them and completely fulfil all His covenant with them. But meantime their prominent place in His purpose has been suspended. How do we know this? Look at Acts 28, and read what happened when Paul reached Rome, as stated in verses 17-29. Have you read those verses, and have you grasped the importance of what happened? After quoting the portentous words from Isaiah, 6:9-10 Paul utters what was a judicial sentence in verse 28, "Be it known unto you, that Salvation of God is sent unto the Gentiles". Nothing so drastic as this had ever been said before. It just means that Christ, Israel's Salvation; the King of their long awaited kingdom; the heavenly Bridegroom Who with His Bride was to minister such blessing to Israel, and through Israel to all the other nations (Israel 60:18, 22; 61:10-11 etc.); Christ, Israel's Salvation, was withdrawn from them!! Withdrawn, after all those centuries. Withdrawn, and for the time at least, not to return, for "the Salvation of God is sent" to others, sent "to the Gentiles". Not many years after this fateful announcement Jerusalem was reduced to rubble, and the majority of the Jews who remained after a terrible time of war and siege, were transported. There was no deliverance for them, for their Salvation, their Deliverer, was no longer in their midst.

Israel's loss was the Gentiles gain. From that time until and including the present time, Christ, the Salvation of God, has been and is "among you Gentiles", and is for us Gentiles "the hope of glory" (Colossians 1:27). It was not until after the event of Acts 28:28 that John was inspired to write his Gospel in which Christ is shewn to be "the Saviour of the world" (John 4:42), offered in wondrous grace to "whosoever". More-over, in connection with the eventful movement of "the Salvation of God" from Israel and "to the Gentiles", Paul, earlier called to be the apostle of the Gentiles, received by revelation an aspect of redemptive truth which had previously been kept hidden in God (Ephesians 3:8-9; Colossians 1:25-26). It is this previously hidden purpose, in conjunction with the 'whosoever' message of John, that constitutes "the gospel of *your* salvation", Gentile salvation that is to be believed and embraced in this present time. Paul, as the preacher, apostle and teacher of the Gentiles (1 Timothy 2:7; 2 Timothy 1:11) disclosed this previously hidden phase of the redemptive eternal purpose, in his epistles written *after* the close of the Acts. He reveals it as being the calling out and formation of a company called "the church which is His body" (Ephesians 1:22-23) and "the body of Christ" (Ephesians 4:12). This company is to be the spiritual temple for "an habitation of God, through the Spirit" (Ephesians 2:19-22), when the eternal purpose is brought to fulfillment.

Thus "the gospel of your salvation", *Gentile salvation after the pronouncement of Acts 28:28,* is a message entirely unrelated to Israel in any way. Gentile believers of the present day have no part in Israel's earthly kingdom "the kingdom of heaven". They are not *now* "being blessed with faithful Abraham", - or being made "Abraham's seed"; they are not *now* being grafted into Israel's olive tree: neither are they gifted with miraculous spiritual gifts of tongues, healings, etc.. No, those phases of the redemptive purpose ceased or were suspended when "the salvation of God was sent to the Gentiles".

Now, *"the gospel of your salvation" is a proclaiming of the good news of the grace and love of God for all, which carries with it the opportunity for all who will receive it, to enjoy "the secret of the gospel" (Ephesians 6:19), which is the truth that Christ, the salvation of God, is not only the Savior of the "whosoever" believer, but is also the Head of the church which is His body.*

This is the gospel for today, the gospel "for you Gentiles", "the gospel of *your* salvation". May God give us such grace that we may believe and embrace it fully.

"The Eternal Purpose ... in Christ Jesus our Lord" (Ephesians 3:11)

How does the purpose affect you?

Do you know your place in it?

Are you co-operating as you should?

Can we find in the Scriptures any guiding lines that will help us determine just what "the eternal purpose", (more correctly rendered in the *Revised Version* margin "the purpose of the ages") really is, and what part in it, or in its outworking, God has allotted to us?

Let us first observe the words of the statement in their relationship to the context. Have a look at Ephesians 3, and read again the portion from verse 8. In verse 8 Paul writes that to him, in a particular sense, had been committed a ministry of grace, to be exercised among the Gentiles. He indicates that a certain body of truth, which he calls "the unsearchable riches of Christ", had previously been "hid in God", verse 9; hid throughout all past time, for he also states in verse 9, that "from the beginning of the world" it had been kept as a "mystery", or secret part of God's great purpose. But, he says in verses 8, 9 and 10, this secret is now to be disclosed, and to him was first given the privilege of proclaiming this particular body of truth, in order that all might have the opportunity to appreciate God's present intention.

The present aim – and this is the crux of the matter so far as our little study is concerned – is that the church should be used *now*, to display the manifold wisdom of God to super-heavenly intelligences, named "principalities and powers", verse 10; that church, which earlier in the epistle he calls "the church which is His body" Ephesians 1:22-23; that church, which in Ephesians 2:19-22 he states is to be "an holy temple ... an habitation" – or home "for God through the Spirit". This present aim, i.e. the calling and formation of the Body of Christ, says Paul, is "according to" – in harmony with, or is an integral part of "the purpose of the ages which God purposed in Christ Jesus our Lord". Read those four verses in Chapter 3, i.e. verses 8-11, over and over again, until you really grasp what it is Paul says is "in harmony with the purpose of the ages". Surely it is, that the church *now*, - (at the time when Paul wrote the words, and so far as we can see, the time continuing from, that juncture and including the present time) – that the church which is His body – is *now* the channel through which God is ministering and testifying His many sided wisdom to and before the super-heavenly intelligences. This much we learn by taking note of the context in which the words "the eternal purpose", or the purpose of the ages, occur.

We can learn a little more by studying the actual words used in the statement, "The purpose of the ages which He purposed in Christ". The two words "purpose" and "purposed" are not as similar as our *Authorised Version* would lead us to suppose. The word that is rendered 'purpose' means something set down beforehand, a pre-determined plan, such as an architects plan. The word that is rendered 'purposed', means did, or wrought, or made, so that the whole statement could read "In harmony with the pre-determined plan of the ages which God is making – working out or accomplishing – through Christ Jesus our Lord". Now the fact that God is working out and perfecting this purpose "through Christ Jesus our Lord", gives us the clue as to the nature of the overall predetermined plan, for He, our Lord, had such names as truly expressed both His character and career, His worth and His work. If this is so it must give the clue to what we seek.

1. The plan is being wrought out in and through "Christ". Christ – this we might say is an official title, and is synonymous with the Hebrew Messiah, both of them meaning "the Anointed", a term which gathers up all the Hebrew expectation of the one who should come, having the authority and ability of God Who would send Him. The pre-determined plan is being wrought through the only one Who has Divine authority and ability.

2. The plan is being wrought out in and through "Christ Jesus". Jesus – some would say this is merely the personal human name, but oh! What a wealth of significance attaches to it! We only have space for the barest note as to its meaning. It certainly was a common name among Jews. It is the Greek equivalent of the Hebrew Yeshuah "Jehovah is Salvation". As applied to, and joined with the term Christ, "the anointed", it becomes a name expressive of faith in God and in His purpose of salvation, to be wrought by the one Who also has the authority and ability. Through the prophetic statement of Isaiah 7:14, as quoted in connection with the babe Jesus at the time of His birth, (Matthew 1:21-23), an added significance is impressed upon us, namely that "Jesus", the anointed, the One with the authority and ability to save, or deliver, was none other than God Himself

in the likeness of human flesh, "God with us". The pre-determined plan is being wrought through the One Who is personally the Divine salvation.

3. The plan is being wrought out in and through "Christ Jesus our Lord". Lord – the Greek word had a wide range of application – in a legal sense it means 'owner', 'master'; it was also used as a term of respect and by way of courtesy; it is used rightly in acknowledging a superior. It was applied to the newborn babe of Bethlehem by the angel who proclaimed to the wondering shepherds "Unto you is born ... Christ the Lord" (Luke 2:11). In Acts 10, Peter proclaims Christ's indisputable Lordship, verse 36, as being proved by His death and resurrection, verses 37-43. This same truth is repeated by Paul in Romans 14:9, "To this end Christ died, and rose and revived, that He might be Lord ..." His Lordship is displayed through death and resurrection. The pre-determined plan is wrought through One, Who with authority and ability accomplished the act of deliverance or salvation, which He had come expressly to bring – that salvation which He was Himself personally, and the accomplishment is manifested in His triumphant Lordship over death, when He rose from the tomb.

But we must proceed one step more in order to appreciate the real link between this truth and the predetermined plan. We must ask, "Why was the death and resurrection necessary?" The forfeiture of life was necessary in order that the justly required "Ransom", the redemption price to effect deliverance, might be paid to the full; the rising from death was necessary in order that those who were ransomed by the death, might, in the power of newness of life, enjoy the acquittal and release obtained for them (see Romans 4:25). Thus we can come to the very pith and marrow of this matter. The pre-determined plan is being "wrought through Christ Jesus our Lord", and if the names are truly indicative of His character and career, His worth and His work, then their use can only mean that the great purpose of the ages must be *a redemptive purpose.*

Before we seek to trace a little of the pattern of this redemptive purpose of the ages, let us quickly look forward to its consummation. Ephesians 1:10 gives a glimpse of this in brief grand phrases. "That in the dispensation of the fulness of times God might gather together in one all things in Christ, both which are in heaven and which are on earth; even in Him ..." The "beginning" of the purpose of the ages was Christ, (Colossians 1:15-18; John 1:1-3; Hebrews 1:1-2, the word rendered "worlds" should be "ages"). The outworking of the details are "through Christ Jesus our Lord" (Ephesians 3:11), and as we see from Ephesians 1:10, the consummation is "even in Him ...". How true it is that "Christ is all, and in all" (Colossians

3:11). What are the principal parts of this great pre-determined plan? We believe that the key is near the door, in other words, that the words given at the very commencement of the Scriptures, give us, in very broad outline, the answer to our question. Look at Genesis 1:1. "In the beginning God created the heaven and the earth". We have not space to go into grammatical details but would ask the reader to accept the following as being reliable. The words with which Genesis 1:1 opens, "In the beginning", whilst certainly indicating a point of time, can with greater accuracy be understood as pointing out what happened at the commencing point, and so we think of them as "In beginning", or "To begin with", "As a first fruits", "As a foregleam", or "As a thumbnail sketch". As this is so, we ask "What did God do as a foregleam?. What was the thumbnail sketch which He drew at the beginning?"

In His first action – "In beginning" – He revealed that what He had in mind, what He was going to work out in detail through the succeeding ages, would be connected and concerned with the three great spheres of operations indicated, viz: -

> (1). "God", which points to the sphere of His being and dwelling, the *super heavenly place* of His abode, "for behold, heaven and the heaven of heavens cannot contain Him" (2 Chronicles 6:18).

> (2) "The heaven" (or heavens, for the word is plural) – all the sphere between God's exalted dwelling place and the earth, (which is man's more humble abode) – *the heavenly sphere*. And
> ...

> (3) "the earth" – the sphere in which the drama of human reaction to the Divine plan would be enacted, in preparation for "the life that is to come" –*the earthly sphere*.

We believe that God's wondrous redemptive purpose of the ages is being worked out, through time, in those three spheres, therefore in the opening words of the scriptures, we have the indication of the all-inclusive *sphere* of redemption, embracing super heavens, heavens and earth. The statement at Ephesians 1:10, which discloses the consummation of the purpose of the ages, bear this out. There we read "in the dispensation of the fulness of times, God will: -

1. "gather together in one all things in Christ", i.e. He will cause all things to come under the headship of Christ, Who being "set at God's right hand ... far above all" (Ephesians 1:20, 21), operates

in and from the *super-heavenly sphere*.

2.   The unity under the headship of Christ in the super heavens will extend and embrace "even the things which are in the heavens", i.e. the *heavenly sphere*.

3.   "also the things which are on the earth", i.e. *the earthly sphere*. So again let us state that the opening words of the Scriptures are the key to the understanding of the all-inclusive **sphere** of redemption, embracing super heavens, heavens and earth.

As we read on in the Scriptures, other truths relating to the purpose of the ages are illustrated. In Genesis 6, for instance, Noah receives instruction concerning the Ark – (which pointed forward to Christ the Deliverer from judgment) – the Ark in which eight humans and a large representation of the lower animal creation were to find deliverance from the all-engulfing waters of destruction. We see at verse 16 in Genesis 6 that this place of refuge was to consist of three compartments, "lower, second and third", which compare with "earth", "heavens" and "God" of Genesis 1:1. From this illustration of the Ark we surely learn of the *fact* of redemption – deliverance from the judgment that falls upon sin, operating in three spheres.

In the book of Exodus we have the details of the Tabernacle, the pattern of which Moses saw on Mt. Sinai. Like the Ark, the Tabernacle also points forward to Christ. Here again are three main features "outer court" "holy place" and "the most holy" or "holy of holies". The tabernacle sets forth (1) the fact of God's approach to, and desire to dwell among men, and (2) man's way of approach to God, and is mainly concerned with approach, worship and service. Therefore, in the Tabernacle we see the *result* of redemption approach to God, worship of God, and service for God, again operating in three spheres.

Let us point to one other illustration. In the books of Kings and Chronicles we can read the account of the preparations for, and the building and dedication of the Temple at Jerusalem. Though on a much larger scale, and with innumerable additions and embellishments, the overall pattern was virtually the same as that of the Tabernacle, and it too, points forward to Christ, this time in His future glory. By comparison the Tabernacle might have appeared as but the shadow in the light of reality, for 1 Chronicles 22:5 tells us "the house that is to be builded for the Lord, must be exceeding magnifical, of fame and of glory throughout all countries". The completed Temple was indeed truly magnificent, and on the day of dedication, as we can read in 2 Chronicles 7:1, 2, "the glory of the Lord filled the house, and the priests could not enter because the glory of the Lord filled the Lord's house". The Temple in its three parts, "the outer court" "the court of the Temple" and "the Temple" proper, surely displayed the *ultimate purpose* of redemption, the shewing forth of the glory of God.

We have pointed out that the purpose of the ages, as seen outlined in the words of Genesis 1:1, and as illustrated by the Ark, the Tabernacle and the Temple, was to embrace and be effective in three spheres. Which of these spheres of the outworking of this purpose affects and interests us today? Are our hopes centred in the Earthly sphere? Surely not, for Israel the nation, must be the *centre* for the outworking of that part of the plan, for to them was promised the well-defined geographical blessing of "the land", the land of Promise, on which land they are to be the Holy nation, Priestly-Kings, ministering before God, and for God to all the other nations on earth.

Are our hopes centred in the Heavenly Sphere, the Heavenly city and country for which Abraham looked, which is also called "the Bride, the Lamb's wife? No, we think not, for the Bride is composed, so the Scripture teaches, of the faith Remnant of Israel (Romans 11:5), joined by certain Gentiles whom Paul points out are "blessed with Faithful Abraham" ... and who by faith became "Abraham's seed and heirs according to the promise", Gentiles who were "grafted into" Israel's olive tree (Romans 11:17-22)". This Bride City, the Heavenly Jerusalem (Hebrews 12:22) surely will be the *centre* for the outworking of the purpose of the ages respecting the *Heavenly Sphere*.

Then where should our hopes be centred, into what part of the redemptive purpose of the ages do we fit and find our place? Will not our hopes, Gentile hopes, be set forth by Paul the "preacher, apostle and teacher of the Gentiles"? (1 Timothy 2:7; 2 Timothy 1:11). Yes, that must be so, for in those epistles written by Paul *after* the end of the Acts – (that is after "the salvation of God" had been taken from Israel and "sent unto the Gentiles", Acts 28:28) – a third, specially called out company, is revealed, not now just Jews who form the representative nation for the earthly sphere; not now the mixed Jewish-Gentile company who will form the Bride-City in the heavenly sphere, but a Gentile company, name by the Spirit through Paul "the church which is His body" and "the body of Christ" (Ephesians 1:22-3; 4:12 etc.). This company, this church, is composed of those "chosen from before the foundation of the world" (Ephesians 1:4) to receive and enjoy "the mystery of the gospel"

(Ephesians 6:19) "the mystery which in other ages was not made known unto the sons of men ... that the Gentiles should be joint-heirs, in a joint-body, and joint-partakers of God's promise in Christ by the gospel" (Ephesians 3:3-6). This "mystery" or secret, previously hidden (Ephesians 3:9; Colossians 1:26) was first revealed to Paul (Ephesians 3:2, 3, 7, 8 etc.), and in the Scriptures is made known only through the Epistles which Paul wrote *after* the end of the Acts.

This Gentile company, the body of Christ, has "every blessing that is spiritual in the heavenly places" (Ephesians 1:3), being "seated with Christ" (Ephesians 2:6) "far above all" (Ephesians 1:21). This church, the body of Christ, must surely be the *centre* for the outworking of the purpose of the ages in the third and highest of the spheres – the super-heavenly.

For fear that our conclusions might appear to be rather restrictive we would request the reader to note that we have stated we are of the opinion that (1) Israel the nation, (2) the bride-city, and (3) the church which, is His body, are the *centres* or focal points in respect of the outworking of the purpose of the ages in each of the spheres indicated. We believe that they are the *principled features*. There are other features of the eternal purpose, supporting and in measure subsidiary, which perhaps leads up to, or flow out from these principal features.

For instance, though Paul's ministry to the Gentiles, with its revelation of "the mystery", "the body of Christ", is, we believe, the outstanding feature relative to the present phase of the purpose of the ages, and that it is connected with the super-heavenly sphere, in most cases the appreciation of the mystery and membership in the body of Christ is preceded by an appreciation of the "whosoever" gospel, as set forth in the Gospel of John, with its calling of "as many as receive Him" to be "children of God", (John 1:12 Greek), or "other sheep" (John 10:15-17), and with its blessing of "everlasting life" (John 3:16 etc.), or "life through His name" (John 20:30-31), in line with the great teaching of justification by faith, as presented by Paul in the Epistle to the Romans. Therefore we believe we are right in conceiving that the "whosoever" ministry is part of the eternal purpose supporting or leading up to the principal feature of the super-heavenly sphere, and that those of the "whosoever" calling who do not receive the revelation of "the mystery" or appreciate membership in "the church which is His body", nevertheless have a specific place in the finally completed purpose.

Similarly, "guests" at the wedding of the King's Son (Matthew 22:1-10) will find their place in conjunction with the "bride-city", at the time of the marriage of the Lamb (Revelation 19:5-9; 21:2-17); and "the nations of them which are saved" (Revelation 21:24) will have their place alongside the chosen nation Israel during the time of that peoples coming superiority (Deuteronomy 28:13 etc.).

The purpose of the ages is an outcome of "the manifold wisdom of God" (Ephesians 3:10), and we must bear in mind the significant words of our Lord "in my Father's house", i.e. the completed spiritual temple of God, of which the body of Christ is to be the inner shrine (Ephesians 2:20-22) ... "in my Father's house are many resting places" (John 14:2), and that each of the many and varied specially called companies will find their "prepared" resting place (John 14:2, 3) when the great purpose is brought to its perfecting.

May God give us grace, wisdom and revelation to see, acknowledge and appreciate our particular place in His all-inclusive redemptive purpose, that we, as members of His body, might be used now to make known to principalities and powers the manifold wisdom of God (Ephesians 3:10), and be used in the ages to come to shew the exceeding riches of His grace (Ephesians 2:7), and so add our little quota to the ultimate glory which shall be His when the far-reaching redemptive purpose is completed.

"The mystery of the Gospel" (Ephesians 6:19)

Which gospel?

What is the mystery?

No doubt you will have met with those who express themselves something like this: - "There's no need to waste time by delving into deep Bible study – just have childlike faith in, be satisfied with, and preach if you feel you must, the simple gospel, that's really all that's needed." But is it? We may be accused of 'splitting hairs', or of 'trying to be clever', but we must ask "Which of the New Testament Scriptural messages, each called 'gospel', is 'the simple gospel'?" Is it "the gospel of the kingdom" (Matthew 4:23), or "the gospel of the uncircumscision" (Galatians 2:7), or "the gospel of the circumcision" (Galatians 2:7). Is it "the gospel of the grace of God" (Acts 20:24) or "the everlasting gospel" (Revelation 14:6)? These, and the other Scriptural messages called "gospels" are not all the same, indeed some are widely divergent, and we are certainly not 'splitting hairs' if we seek to determine which of them is the gospel for today.

We have stated that some of these "gospel" messages are widely divergent. You don't believe that? Then look, for instance at the terms and offers of the two messages spoken of at Matthew 4:23 and Revelation 14:6. According to the record of Matthew, "the gospel of the kingdom" was a proclamation *to the people of Israel* (Matthew 10:5-7; 15:24; see also Romans 15:8). It was the proclamation that "the kingdom of heaven is at hand", coupled with the request or command "Repent", and accompanied by the miraculous healing "of all manner of sickness and disease among the people". Notice specially that there was no mention of the death of Christ as Savior, no teaching of redemption by blood or of justification by faith – nevertheless it was a "gospel". It was 'good news' for the nation Israel, had they but received it. Is it the "gospel" for today?

Now look at Revelation 14:6-7. John the seer, witnessing "things to come", sees an angel preacher proclaiming the terms of "the everlasting gospel", exhorting those of every kindred, tongue, people and nation on the earth to "Fear God, and give glory to Him, for the hour of His judgment is come

... worship Him ...". Here the straight forward message of "the everlasting-gospel" is seen to be an exhortation, not just to Israel, but to all peoples who will then be upon the earth, to acknowledge and give glory and worship to the Creator "Him that made heaven and earth, and the sea, and the fountains of waters".

This time there is no request for repentance, no mention of a kingdom having come near, or being set up, nor any mention of miraculous healings. As in the case of "the gospel of the kingdom", there is again no mention of the sacrifice of Christ, of redemption, forgiveness or justification. What a strange "gospel"! Would you preach that "gospel" now? Are we 'splitting hairs' then, when we ask "Which of these, or of the other Scriptural "gospel" messages, is "the simple gospel" for today? Are we not right to try and determine just what it is we are asked to accept and believe?

As a matter of fact none of the varied Scriptural messages called "gospels" can in any sense be said to be "simple". The terms used to proclaim them may be fairly straightforward and plain, but there are matters in connection with the reasonable understanding and reception of any one of them, which necessitate a background knowledge that can only be gained by an acquaintance with some of the history and teaching of the Old Testament, as well as some of the doctrine of the New Testament Scriptures. It is this fact which makes evangelizing such a difficult task today, when the Bible is so sadly neglected and its truths entirely unknown by the vast majority. The title of this section, culled from Paul's Epistle to the Ephesians, speaks of the "mystery of the gospel". Let us first of all ask "With what particular gospel is this mystery connected?", and secondly "What is the mystery, can we understand it and share in it?

The word "gospel" occurs four times in the Epistle to the Ephesians. We cannot learn a great deal from the immediate contexts of these occurrences, only that: -

1. this 'good news', whatever its content, was a message which, when believed, brought a deliverance of some kind, spoken of as "salvation", while the believer was "sealed with that holy Spirit of promise" (Ephesians 1:13);

2. that there was a specific "promise" of God "in Christ" in connection with it (Ephesians 3:6);

Think on These Things   36

3. that it was good news which ministered "peace" (Ephesians 6:15); and

4. there was a "mystery" or secret, connected with it (Ephesians 6:19).

If we would learn the details of this gospel with which a 'secret' is connected, it is evident that we must cast the net for study beyond the Epistle to the Ephesians. But what shall we study? Shall we link the "gospel" mentioned in Ephesians with Matthew's "gospel of the kingdom" as proclaimed to Israel, a gospel, as we have seen, which had no mention of redemption or justification, and which pointed to an earthly kingdom? Surely Paul, the great protagonist of justification by faith alone, was not referring to that? Then shall we link it with "the everlasting gospel", with its call for fear of the Creator, the "gospel" which is to be proclaimed by the angel messenger in the future? That certainly doesn't seem to be the likely link. What then will help us? What shall we study? Would it not be logical and rational to study those other portions of Scripture written by Paul, and others, at about the same time, and as a result of similar circumstances to those which occasioned the writing of the Epistle to the Ephesians? Surely in those related parts of the Scripture, the references to "the gospel" might give us the information we seek – do you not agree?

The first thing we must take account of is that Ephesians was written by Paul *after* the conclusion of the events recorded in the Acts. He wrote it from a prison in Rome (Ephesians 3:1; 4:1), the prison about which Acts 28:30 tells us. (Even though it was his own hired house it nevertheless was "prison" to him for he was never without a military guard to whom he was evidently chained). The second thing we must take account of is that because it was penned *after* the end of the Acts, Ephesians was written in connection with that part of the purpose of God which was brought into operation as a result of the very important statement at Acts 28:28, that "the salvation of God" – which salvation had for the many centuries been Israel's special privilege – was taken from them and was "sent unto the Gentiles".

Now we must find out what other parts of the Scripture were (1) written after the end of the Acts, and (2) written in connection with, or in the light of, the stated fact that at the end of the Acts "the salvation of God is sent unto the Gentiles". A little thought and examination will reveal that those portions of the Scripture which were written *after* the Acts had closed, and which, by their internal evidence are seen to be written in the light of the statement of Acts 28:28, are the Epistles of Paul to the Ephesians (as we have already noted), to the Philippians and the Colossians, the two Epistles to Timothy, the shorter letters to Titus and Philemon, and the Gospel of John. (In relation to John's Gospel see John 1:11-12, and note further the insistence upon "whosoever" and "the world", factors not apparent in the synoptic Gospels). A careful reading and comparison of these parts of Scripture will, we believe, make plain to us the content of that "gospel" which Paul, in Ephesians 6:19 speaks of as having a "secret" issue.

If we study carefully along the line indicated, we find that this "gospel" was the gospel of Gentile or world-wide salvation, or as popularly stated today, "full and free salvation for all men everywhere, through faith in the sacrifice of Christ". It is not generally realized that until the setting forth of this "whosoever" message by Paul and John *after* the end of The Acts, the outworking of the promises, and the proffered blessings of all the previous "gospel" messages, were dependent upon an obedient response by Israel, who were, until Acts 28:28, the chosen key people of God. Up to Acts 28:28 "salvation was of the Jews", as stated by Christ (John 4:22), but *from* and *after* Acts 28:28 "salvation" became the possession of all peoples and nations, without any reference to Israel, and its promises are to be fully enjoyed quite apart from Israel's national repentance as was formerly necessary (Acts 3:19-21 etc.). Accordingly, *after* Acts 28:28, John was able to write "God so loved *the world* that ...*whosoever* believeth ... "(John 3:16 etc.). Never before had the world-embracing love of God been stated. Not until *after* the end of the Acts, with its concluding statement that the "salvation of God" was to be taken from Israel and "sent unto the Gentiles", was it possible for that world-embracing message of love to be sounded out, and for salvation to be offered on an equality to "whosoever will".

In similar vein, *after* Acts 28:28, Paul as "the preacher, apostle and teacher of the Gentiles" (1 Timothy 2:7; 2 Timothy 1:11) writes to the Gentile believers about "the gospel of *your* salvation", i.e. the gospel of Gentile, world-wide salvation, distinct from the previous "gospels", such as "the gospel of the kingdom" to Israel as a nation, in respect of their promised earthly kingdom, or as the "gospel of the uncircumcision" (Galatians 2:7) to the Gentile *during* the Acts period, who were called out as "a people for His name" (Acts 15:14), and who had definite connection with and were dependent upon Israel, being "blessed with faithful Abraham" (Galatians 3:7-10), and thus by faith were constituted "Abraham's seed and heirs according to the promise" (Galatians 3:29; Genesis 12:1-3; 17:5-8, etc.), or as illustrated in Romans 11:17-24, were the "wild olive branches" grafted into Israel's "good olive tree", - in other words, dependent upon Israel, being partakers of Israel's spiritual things (Romans 15:27).

We only have space to give a few of the references and note a few of the indications which point to the fact that the "gospel" referred to in Paul's last seven letters (Ephesians, Philippians, Colossians, Titus, 1 Timothy, 2 Timothy, Philemon), was the same as the "whosoever" message of John's Gospel. Study the following: - Paul's "gospel" (2 Timothy 2:8) *after* Acts 28:28, was an offer and promise of life in Christ (2 Timothy 1:1; Titus 1:2; Colossians 3:4), as also was John's (John 1:4; 3:15-16, 36; 5:40; 20:31 etc.). Paul's "gospel" had "the world" and "all" men in view (Colossians 1:5-6, 23; Ephesians 3:9), so also had John's (John 1:29; 3:16; 4:42; 6:51 etc.). "Salvation" from sin and sins, and the experience of "forgiveness" were the prime issues for those who believed either of these "gospels" of Paul and John, revealed, and written about in fulness, *after* Acts 28:28 (Ephesians 1:7; Colossians 1:14; John 3:17; 5:24, 34; 10:9; Ephesians 2:8; 4:32; Colossians 2:13; 3:13; 1 Timothy 1:15; 2:14; 2 Timothy 1:9; Titus 3:5; John 1:29 etc.).

We are not is a position to answer the first of the two questions we asked earlier, "With what particular gospel is the mystery of Ephesians connected?". It is certainly not "the gospel of the kingdom", not "the gospel of the circumcision", nor yet "the gospel of the uncircumscision", or "the everlasting gospel", but it is connected with "the gospel of the grace of God". For that gospel, "the gospel of the grace of God", Paul willingly suffered as "an ambassador in bonds" (Ephesians 6:20), in order that he "might finish his course with joy" (see Acts 20:22-24), even though it meant "the loss of all things" (Philippians 3:8). It is the gospel of "redemption through His blood, the forgiveness of sins, according to the riches of His grace" (Ephesians 1:7), which involves the believer being "quickened together with Christ ... raised up together ... and made to sit together ... in Christ Jesus" (Ephesians 2:5-6). No other scriptural "gospel" message lifts the believer to that exalted position at God's own "right hand in the heavenly places, far above all ..." (Ephesians 1:20-21). It is the 'gospel' of "life through His name" (John 20:31); "Life" actually "in Christ", for "Christ is our Life" (Colossians 3:3-4; 2 Timothy 1:1 etc.).

The second of the two questions to which we sought an answer asks "what is the mystery – or secret – and can we understand and share in it?". A brief answer must suffice as the subject is really very far-reaching. The "secret" of this gospel of redemption and forgiveness which makes known "Life in Christ", is that God is calling out and forming the believers who receive and acknowledge this truth, as "joint-heirs, in a joint-body, as joint-partakers of His promise in Christ by the gospel" (Ephesians 3:6). There had previously been other called out companies, other "churches" (Matthew 16:18; Acts 7:38; Romans 16:16; 1 Thessalonians 2:14; Romans

16:4 etc.), but none like this, the composition of which God had kept secretly "hid from the beginning of the world" (Ephesians 3:9), "the mystery which in other ages was not made known unto the sons of men" (Ephesians 3:3-5; Colossians 1:26). It is "the church which is His body" (Ephesians 1:22-23), or "the body of Christ" (Ephesians 4:12), *in which all the members are on an absolute equality*, "joint-heirs, a joint-body, joint-partakers, (or equal heirs, an equal body, etc.) – this had never been known, or even envisaged before. It is the church which in completion will be "an holy temple ... (the true spiritual Holy of Holies) ... in the Lord, for an habitation of God through the Spirit" (Ephesians 2:21-22).

"The mystery of, or belonging to, the gospel", is this, that previously "far off" sinners of the Gentiles, who had been "without Christ, having no hope, and without God", not even having *any* connection with the people who had been called "the holy nation", for, says Paul they were "aliens from the commonwealth of Israel and strangers from covenants of promise", are, by the wondrous work which this gospel reveals, "made nigh" to God "by the blood of Christ" (Ephesians 2:12-13); they are brought together in the unity of the Spirit and made equal "members of His body" (Ephesians 4:11-16; 5:30), in order that God might satisfy His desire, as illustrated right from the beginning (Genesis 3:8 etc.; Exodus 25:8 etc.), that He should be able to enjoy "fellowship" in a "home". This place for real fellowship will be His when "the body" is completed and becomes the "holy temple", the inner shrine, the heavenly Holiest of all, for His eternal habitation. (Ephesians 2:19-22).

May "the eyes of our understanding be enlightened", and "the spirit of wisdom and revelation" be granted (Ephesians 1:17-18) that we may fully embrace the gospel for today, and acknowledge and appreciate its mystery (secret).

"The Body of Christ" (Ephesians 4:12)

What is it like?

What is its function?

"The mystery ... that the Gentiles should be fellowheirs, and of the same body and partakers of His promise in Christ by the gospel whereof I (Paul) was a minister" (Ephesians 3:3-7).

"The church, which is His body" (Ephesians 1:22-23).

"Christ is the head of the body, the church" (Colossians 1:18).

"One body" (Ephesians 4:4; Colossians 3:15).

There are many who are 'mystified' by some of the very foundation truths relating to "the mystery", that truth concerning "the church, which is His body" as revealed initially to Paul, the apostle of the Gentiles. Those 'mystified' ones often ask such questions as the following: - "Just what is this 'church', this 'body of Christ' really like?"; "Is not the word 'body' simply used as an illustrating term, to portray the spiritual truth of the union which exists between Christ the Saviour, and those who believe in Him?"; or "Is not the word 'body' in Ephesians and Colossians used in just the same way as it is used in Romans 12 and 1 Corinthians 12?". Again some ask "In the coming ages will the completed 'body of Christ' always be manifestly joined with Christ its 'Head', so that, for instance, when He comes to earth to reign, 'the body' will come back to earth with Him?". We will endeavour to give possible answers to such questions.

Three Greek words are rendered 'body' in the *Authorized Version.*

> (1) *chros*, which signifies the surface of the body, is rendered 'body' in Acts 19:12.
>
> (2) *ptoma*, which literally means 'a fall', is rendered 'body' in Matthew 14:12 and Mark 15:45, where it signifies 'a fallen body', a 'dead body' or 'corpse'. (In other verses *ptoma* is rendered 'carcass', 'corpse' and 'dead bodies').

(3) *soma* which occurs over 140 times.

- It is used of the body as a whole, the instrument of life, the medium for the expression of being, whether of man living, or dead; or in resurrection.
- It is used of the physical existence as distinct from the spiritual existence.
- It is used of beasts, of grain, and of celestial bodies.
- It is used of companies of believers each in their separate geographical locations, i.e. the "body in Christ" at Rome (Romans 12:5) or "the body of Christ" at Corinth (1 Corinthians 12:27).
- It is used metaphorically of believers of different companies, in different places, separated not only geographically but also in point of time historically, yet reckoned as together constituting "the body of Christ" spiritually or mystically – secretly (Ephesians 1:23; 3:6; 4:4, 12; Colossians 1:18, 24).
- Only once in the *Authorized Version* is *soma* rendered by anything other than 'body' or 'bodily', when it is rendered 'slaves' at Revelation 18:13, where the meaning, 'captive bodies' is intended.

We can only determine the truth that the Spirit is seeking to impart in His use of the word 'body', if we study the context in which the word occurs and give due place to the words among which it appears. For the purposes of this little paper we need only give consideration to the use of *soma* as it is rendered 'body' in Romans 12 and 1 Corinthians 12, in Ephesians and in Colossians.

Take a look at, and read Romans 12:3-8 and 1 Corinthians 12 – the whole chapter. It is quite apparent from the employment of the words "as" and "so" in Romans 12:4, 5 and 1 Corinthians 12:12, that the physical human body, as we all know it with its many "members" limbs or organs, **is most certainly being used as the illustration** of the method for the manifestation of the Spirit in His diversities of operations through the many believers in the local churches at Rome and Corinth, where each believer, says Paul "had differing gifts" (Romans 12:6) or was each one the possessor of some gift of the Spirit (1 Corinthians 12:7, 11).

Thus it logically follows that the members, limbs or organs of these bodies "in Christ" at Rome and Corinth were, **for the purposes of practical service**, each one different from the other: some strong, some, by comparison, frail; some comely, some uncomely; some easily and plainly seen, others hidden and obscure. 1 Corinthians 12 tells us distinctly that within the church of God during the Acts period, as exemplified by the assemblies at Rome and Corinth, there were many differences and diversities. The varying members were not on an equality in respect of functional activity, though each one was activated by the same Spirit. There were within those churches not only "differences of administration" i.e. the ministries of "Apostles, prophets, teachers, helps and governments", but there were also "diversities of operations" i.e. some had "the word of wisdom", some "the word of knowledge", others "faith, gifts of healing, the working of miracles, the discerning of spirits, diversities of tongues, and the interpretation of tongues", etc.

Further in 1 Corinthians 7, Paul refers to the two major parties within the assemblies at that time: (1) "the Circumcision", being Jews, some of whom, though they had embraced Christ as their promised Messiah, were nevertheless zealous for, and rigidly kept the law of Moses with all its ceremonial, and (2) "the Uncircumscision", being Gentiles, some of whom had become believers in Christ, but as Gentiles were free from the requirements of Moses' Law. This national difference, between Jews and Gentiles, carried with it a distinct religious cleavage, and was the cause of open dissension in the church of God during the Acts period.

Moreover, in 1 Corinthians 1, Paul reveals that there were groups within the assembly at Corinth, calling themselves "the Paul party", "the Apollos party and "the Christ party". Thus it was that, while *for the practical purposes of the manifestation of the Spirit through service, they* were "the body of Christ and members in particular", (1 Corinthians 12:27), or "one body in Christ, and every one members one of another" (Romans 12:5), they were by no means experiencing or enjoying unity, but openly manifested and recognised wide differences of faith and practice. These differences and divergences characterised "the church of God" in any particular place during the Acts period. In each place the company of believers was a 'body' of many differing and unequal members, for which the human body with its variety of limbs and organs, each with their **differing practical functions**, was a fitting figure and illustration.

When we come to study the contexts of the word "body" in relation to the revelation of "the mystery" (Ephesians 3:3) "the church which is His body" (Ephesians 1:22-23) the "same body" (Ephesians 3:6) or the "one body" (Ephesians 2:16; 4:4; Colossians 3:15) we find that a very significant and remarkable characteristic is brought before us, which marks this church, relating to "the mystery", as being utterly distinct and entirely different from the churches which existed during the Acts. Indeed it is this distinctive characteristic that constitutes "the mystery".

The "churches of God" during the Acts, as exemplified by the companies at Rome and Corinth, formed separate "bodies" each in their different geographical districts; "bodies" which could be accurately illustrated by the physical human body because each member, or limb or organ, was adding his or her different function of outward practical service – miracles, tongues, wisdom, knowledge, healings, discerning of spirits etc. – as activated by the Spirit – and thus supplying the "confirmation" as promised by Christ, and necessary in those early days (Mark 16:16-20); 1 Corinthians 1:6; Hebrews 2:3, 4).

"The church which is His body", the fresh revelation given to Paul, and written about in his epistles penned after the end of the Acts, does not need, or partake of, the outward confirming miraculous signs to aid acts of outward practical service, for it is entirely **a spiritual entity**; its "members" are "blessed with every blessing that is spiritual" (Ephesians 1:3). This does not mean that the individual believers in this present dispensation, who comprise 'the body of Christ', can be slack in respect of "practical Christianity" on earth – no indeed. The 'practical' sections of the epistle written by Paul after the end of Acts give the lie to that attitude. The point is that the churches of God during the Acts period were separate "bodies" each in their own place geographically **on earth**, and were exercising **an earthly ministry** in the purpose of God, while "the church which is His body", revealed after Acts 28:28, is "the **one** body", not now many separate "bodies", but a **spiritual body, in the heavenlies**; its principal function being **spiritual ministry** of witness to spiritual intelligencies, as it "now makes known the manifold wisdom of God to principalities and powers in the heavenlies" (Ephesians 3:10).

Moreover, from Ephesians 3:3-7, we learn that the "mystery", or secret, is concerned with the composition of "the body of Christ", for Paul reveals that the secret is "that the Gentiles should be fellow-heirs and of the same body and partakers of God's promise in Christ" brought to light by that particular gospel of which he (Paul) had been made a minister (Ephesians 3:6-7). It is difficult to express or convey the truth contained in the words translated "Fellow-heirs ... same body ... and partakers". There is in these words a triple use of the Greek prefix *sun* which indicates a "together-witness", or identity, or unity, betokening equality and uniformity. Paul reveals that the members of "the church which is His body" are "fellow or joint or equal heirs, in a fellow or joint or equal body, being fellow or joint or equal partakers" of God's promise. No member has any priority of place, or superiority of advantage, or greatness of responsibility over any other, or more than any other member, for, says Paul in Ephesians 4, the identity of "the one body" is realized in the unity of the Spirit (verses 3-6), and the members of the perfected "body of Christ" will fully enter into "the unity of the faith and of the knowledge of the Son of God" and will express and display the "perfect man, in the measure of the stature of the fulness of Christ" (verse 12-13), and he goes on to say that "the whole body" is "equally jointed and united by that which every joint, (on an equality) supplieth ..." (verse 16, see also Colossians 2:19).

It is impossible to miss the sense of unity, equality or identity of membership here. Such an equality of construction and function cannot be illustrated by reference to the physical human body, whose many varied members, limbs and organs are unequal in size, construction and function.

So we ask, just what kind of 'body' is this "body of Christ", of which He is the "Head"? If we cannot illustrate it by the use of the human head and body, what figure or illustration can we use to help us understand? We have seen a Chinese puzzle – a 'mystery', in which three dozen very intricately carved but equally shaped inter-locking pieces of wood have to be fitted together to form a cube. Equal "members" forming "one body". A company of well-trained, smartly turned out soldiers may be spoken of as "a fine body of men", each one in the company, as a soldier, being on an equality with all the others in the company. Such illustrations display the idea of identity within "the body", but they do not take us far enough.

Perhaps the composition of the British Commonwealth of Nations will supply us with a more fitting illustration. The Commonwealth is a community or 'body' of states and nations within the whole number of the states, nations and peoples of the world, yet in some ways separate from the other states and peoples by reason of a particular common allegiance or tie.

Each member state and country within the Commonwealth has equal status, and at the Commonwealth Conferences, each state, as represented by its Prime Minister or other senior state or governmental representative, has equal functions, opportunities and responsibilities, so far as determining united policy, and so far as giving witness to the other states and peoples of the world of what is thought by the united Commonwealth "body" of nations, to be true democratic, freedom-loving government and interdependence. (The withdrawal of South Africa from the Commonwealth because of conflicting racial policies gives point to this).

Further, this identity of belief, function and responsibility is unified by the recognition and acceptance of the Queen as "Head" of the Commonwealth. Not all the participating member states recognise her as "Queen", for some are republics, but each recognises and accepts her a the symbolic unifying "Head" over the free association of member nations. There is no written or formal Constitution of the Commonwealth, so we might conceive of it as a spiritual unity of peoples unified under one "Head". (Much of what we have written concerning the Commonwealth is also applicable to the United States of America as unified under their President.)

An application of this illustration might supply the answer to the question as to whether the completed "body of Christ", after "manifestation with Him in Glory", will always be openly joined with Christ throughout succeeding ages. "The church, the body of Christ", is a spiritual unity of believers who each acknowledge the Headship of Christ. As the legally constituted representatives of the member nations within the Commonwealth 'body' do not constantly stay with, or remain in the presence of their accepted 'Head', so today, those members of 'the body of Christ' on earth cannot actually be in the presence of, and so be with their 'Head' who is "in the heavenlies". In the time to come it is surely possible that the "Head" of the church may be present on earth, whilst the completed 'body', which will perhaps by then have taken its place as "the inner sanctuary ... for the habitation of God through the Spirit" (Ephesians 2:19-22), will continue its appointed function in the heavenlies.

We trust that this brief consideration of so vast a subject may prove helpful to some who may have been 'mystified' by the truth of "the mystery", and like Paul, we too would request that "if there be any points upon which we think differently, these also may God make plain to us, Only let our conduct be consistent with the revelation of truth we have already received and grasped" (Philippians 3:15, 16).

Understandest thou what thou readest?

A key to Bible study

"Understandest thou what thou readest?" This question was asked by Philip the Evangelist of the Ethiopian eunuch who was reading the Old Testament scriptures. With candour he replied "How can I except some man should guide me?" (Acts 8:26-35). Even from a cursory reading of the scriptures it is evident that some guidance is necessary, else the sincere seeker after truth would be in danger of being lost in a maze of difficulties and discouraged from serious study by many seeming contradictions. For instance, consider the following. The commandment in respect of circumcision is explicit as being obligatory for the 'seed' of Abraham, and also for servants, some of whom would not be of the family of Abraham, but who would come within the orbit of the covenant made by God with Abraham (Genesis 17:9-14). Yet Paul, who himself had been circumcised (Philippians 3:5) discounts the rite completely and tells those who, he says "are by faith children of Abraham" (Galatians 3-7) and are "blessed with faithful Abraham" (Galatians 3:9) and whom he says definitely are "Abraham's seed and heirs according to the promise" (Galatians 3:29; 4:28) and thus plainly qualify for circumcision, that "If ye be circumcised Christ shall profit you nothing" (Galatians 5:2, 3), and again he says "neither circumcision availeth anything, nor uncircumscision" (Galatians 5:6; 6:15). Can you really understand this?

Similarly, the commands for Sabbath keeping are strictly enjoined – (we have not space to give references, teaching about the Sabbath has its roots in Genesis 2:1-9), yet Paul, who himself made full use of the Sabbaths, (Acts 13:14, 44; 16:13; 17:2; etc.), discounts Sabbath or other special day observances in Galatians 4:9-11, and Colossians 2:16, 17. So again we ask, "Understandest thou?"

Then there is the absolutely contradictory advice given by Paul, first, to the widows at Corinth that they should not re-marry (1 Corinthians 7:8), whilst not long afterwards he advised the young widows at Ephesus that they should remarry (1 Timothy 5:3-14). Do you understand and know the reason for the giving of such contrary advice? "Understandest thou what thou readest?"

The purpose of this chapter

This chapter does not set out the answers to these and other similar questions that arise from a close study of the scriptures, but does endeavor to make plain a general line of guidance that it would be wise to follow, and which, when followed and applied, will the better enable the reader and student of the scriptures to understand the message which they hold for us at this time.

Coverdale's rules for Bible Study[1]

More than four centuries ago an eminent student and translator of the scriptures, named Miles Coverdale, whose good work reached its apex in the production of the first complete English Bible in 1535, wrote "It will greatly help you understand scripture if you mark, not only 1) What is spoken or written, but 2) Of, (or about) whom, 3) To whom, 4) At what time, 5) With what intent, 6) With what words, 7) With what circumstances, 8) Where, and 9) Considering what goeth before and what followeth".

These are wise words and we cannot do better than follow out these directions as we study the sacred page, for an application of these rules will most assuredly aid us toward an understanding of what we read.

Some of Coverdale's rules applied

We can commence by applying some of the foregoing rules to the scriptures as a whole, and would reverently ask "*of whom* and *to whom* are the scriptures written?" Some, unthinkingly, would at once answer "Why surely they are *about* (*or of*) and *to* all of us. But "what saith the scripture" itself? Let us search and may grace be given us that we may abide by the conclusions to which we shall be led.

A. Is the Old Testament *about* and *to* us?

A little reading and a moment or two of consideration will result in making plain that:

---

[1] For more details about Coverdale and his rules for Bible Study see *Approaching the Bible* by Michael Penny, listed in Further Reading at the back of this book.

1. *The Pentateuch*, Genesis to Deuteronomy was written in the main *about,* and *to* Israel, the chosen people; the injunctions and laws were given *to* that people (Romans 3:2; 9:1-5).

2. *The Historical Books*, Joshua to Esther are all *about* and *to* Israel.

3. *The Wisdom Literature*, Job to the Song of Solomon is the repository of the wisdom *of* Israel.

4. *The Prophets*, whose ministry is recorded in the books from Isaiah to Malachi, stated *to* Judah and Israel, (except in small degree when other nations or peoples affected, or were associated with Israel in some way, and again, also in small measure, some prophetic messages are directed to nations and peoples who will yet be associated with, or affected by, the chosen peoples who will get be associated with, or affected by, the chosen people during the "time of the end" – yet to come), thus we find that the Old Testament is *not about* or *to* us of this present day.

An important definition of some words used

As we shall be employing the words "*about*" "*to*" and "*for*" many times throughout this study, it is really important for the reader to be absolutely certain of the implications of these particular words in the sense in which we are using them.

1. We have pointed out that the Old Testament is not *about* us and in so saying we are using the word *about* as meaning '*concerning*', '*in relation to*', '*connected to or with*' Thus the histories and incidents recorded in the Old Testament are concerning, in relation to, connected to or with Israel and *not* concerning, etc., us of this present time.

2. We have stated that the Old Testament is not *to* us, and in so saying we are using the word *to* as meaning '*directed to*', particularly in order that obedience may be given. Thus the requirements and commandments of the Old Testament (respecting worship, sacrifice etc.) are 'directed to' Israel and are not 'directed to' us, that we should obey them in this present time. (That some of the Ten Commandments have become the basis for laws governing human behaviour in most civilized nations does not make this any less than true).

3. When we come to the word '*for*', as we shall in the next paragraph, it is being used in the sense of '*for our use*', this we believe will be evident from the quotations we cite.

All of the Old Testament *for* us

Whilst the Old Testament scriptures are not *about* us, or directed *to* us, yet according to 1 Corinthians 10:11 "These things (concerning Israel as stated in verses 1-10) happened unto them for ensamples: they are written *for* our admonition upon whom the ends of the age are come". Or again, in 2 Timothy 3:16, 17, "All scripture is given by inspiration of God, and is profitable *for* doctrine, *for* reproof, *for* correction, *for* instruction in righteousness, that the man of God may be thoroughly furnished". These two statements refer to course to the Old Testament writings, for when Paul wrote these words, the books of our present New testament were either being written, or had not then been written, and such parts as had been produced had not in any way been brought together to form the volume we now know as the New Testament.

Both Old Testament and New Testament should be approached in the same way

The large majority of present-day Bible readers recognise that the Old Testament, though not *about* them or *to* them, is nevertheless most useful *for* them: *for* admonition *for* instruction etc., and whilst that same majority would not think of trying to impose the rigid dictates of the Mosaic Code, Sacrifices, Priesthood etc., upon themselves or others in these days, yet unfortunately they fail to apply to the New Testament scriptures the same kind of test that they almost instinctively apply to the Old Testament; they fail to ask "Is this, or that part of the New Testament *about* and *to* me?" and "Have *I* to obey these injunctions and requirements?"

Unfortunately, we repeat, the great number of Bible readers assume that the whole of the New Testament is definitely directed *to* them and that it is incumbent upon them to try to keep and observe all the injunctions and requirements that were voiced by the Lord Jesus during his earthly ministry, as well as such further requirements as were imposed upon what is usually called the "early church", as spoken by and mentioned in the writings of Peter, John, James, Luke, Jude and Paul. The writer considers this to be an utterly illogical and erroneous approach. To gain the true understanding of the New Testament, it is essential to apply the same rule that was applied to the Old Testament, and so we must reverently enquire "*about* and *to* whom is the New Testament written?". In seeking the answer to this question we need to disabuse our minds of preconceived notions and must be willing to face the issues squarely, for *a careful sincere unbiased study will make quite plain that only a comparatively small portion of the New Testament is about, or directed to us Gentiles of the present day.* This bold statement may startle some who read it – but no! Do not throw this book down, but read on, and be like the Berean believers, of whom it is recorded in Acts 17:11, "They were more noble than those of Thessalonica, in that they received the word with all readiness of mind, *and searched the scriptures daily* whether those things were so". Reader, would you join God's nobility? Would you "study to show yourself approved unto" Him? Then you must 'search', and you will find that what is stated above is true. Shall we 'search' and 'study' together, letting the inspired scripture be its own interpreter?

B. Is the New Testament *about* and *to* us?

To answer this question we will best cover the ground by distinguishing the various ministers and ministries recorded, written about and spoken of.

a. Ministry of John the Baptist

Let us first ask "*to* whom was John the Baptist's ministry directed?". Acts 19:4 supplies the answer that "John preached *to* all the people of Israel", so that what is reported as from his lips is certainly *not to* or *about* us.

b. Ministry of the Lord Jesus

"*To* whom did the Lord on earth speak and minister?". "Surely" you might answer "His words and ministry are *to* us all?" Are they? Listen to these words from His own lips "I am not sent but unto the lost sheep of the house of Israel" (Matthew 15:24), Moreover, He directed His chosen helpers 'the twelve' "Go *not to* the Gentiles ... but go *to* the lost sheep of the house of Israel" (Matthew 10:5, 6).

Some years after the Lord's death, resurrection and ascension Paul conclusively states "Now I say that Jesus Christ was a minister of the circumcision" (i.e. Israel) "to confirm the promises made unto the fathers" (Romans 15:8). 'The fathers' are Abraham, Isaac and Jacob; if you then, the reader, can claim 'promises' as made to your 'fathers'; can trace your genealogy back to Abraham; if you are thus of the house of Israel; if of the circumcision; then you may be able to say that the Lord's earthly ministry was *to* you, but if you are a Gentile, i.e. of a nation other than the Israelitish nation, we state with all the solemnity of scripture authority that the Lord's earthly ministry, as recorded in the Gospels of Matthew, Mark and Luke (John's ministry and Gospel are dealt with separately later) was *not to* you at all, and that for you to try to obey such commandments and requirements as He voiced in the days of His flesh, is to place yourself in an extremely difficult situation. For instance, try and work out and obey the requirements of "the sermon on the mount". Look at Matthew 5:38-42, "If any man ... will take thy coat, let him have thy cloak also ... Give to him that asketh of thee and from him that would borrow of thee turn not away". Now be candid, what would happen if you gave to everyone who asked of you, even giving more than they requested? Could you really obey this and all the other requirements of this searching sermon?

Moreover, how about Luke 12:22-40? The teaching here is pinpointed at verse 33, "Sell that ye have and give alms ..." etc. Have we Gentiles to do this? Was this teaching *to* us? If these requirements are to be applied to present day believers then the writer must admit that he is not an obedient believer, nor does he personally know any single 'Christian' who measures up to this standard.

The truth is that these requirements, setting forth the rigorous conditions for entry into "the Kingdom of Heaven" *were not* and *are not directed* to *us,* to be obeyed in these days, for we Gentiles are not being offered the "Kingdom"; these requirements were placed before Christ's disciples in preparation for the setting up of that Kingdom, which could have been set up had the people of Israel, - "the lost sheep of the house of Israel" (Matthew 10:5, 6; 15:24) – repeated and obeyed as called upon so to do by John the Baptist, Christ, by the "twelve", and by the "seventy" (Matthew 9:2; Matthew 4:17 etc. Matthew 10; Luke 10.). These requirements and conditions were given by Christ in His office and ministry as the "minister of the circumcision" (Romans 15:8) and we repeat, were not given *to* us Gentiles at all.

c. Ministries of Peter, James, Jude, John and Paul, etc.

We pass on to consider whether the ministries exercised by Peter, James, Jude, John and Paul, and the others connected with them, as reported and recorded in the Acts, the epistles written *during* the time covered by the Acts, the Gospel and the Revelation of John and the epistles written *after* the close of the Acts, were ministries *to* us.

An important digression

But let us digress for a little to observe and comment upon an important point which arises here. We have just written of the ministries "reported and recorded in the Acts, the epistles written *during* the time covered by the Acts". Note that *we purposely couple certain epistles with the historical record as given in the Acts.* Now note this specially and particularly. If you would really understand the scripture, you must, as advised by Miles Coverdale, take into consideration "*at what time*" the various parts of the scripture were written. (See Coverdale's rules for study a few pages back). For example, in the Old Testament, the utterances of the prophets can only be interpreted rightly and understood when placed upon the background of the relevant events as detailed in the historical books dealing with the same period. "*At what time*" must be considered before determining the meaning of the prophets' words. Similarly, to interpret and understand the epistles in the New Testament it is *essential* to relate them to the historical events of the time at which they were written.

Surely this is but the logical and common-sense method? To do otherwise will cause the student or reader to have a distorted view, and has resulted in many applying, or trying to apply to themselves in these days, many matters which were intended for the time now long past. It is this mis-application of scripture which has fathered the divisions and sects of Christendom all down the years.

Let us now return to our search. In order to help us to 'understand' what we read, we ask again "*to* whom" were the ministries of Peter, James, Jude, John, Paul and those who laboured with them, directed? Were they directed *to* us Gentiles of this present day?

2. Peter

We read in Matthew 16:19 that to Peter were given "the keys of the Kingdom of heaven" and at Galatians 2:7-9 Paul states clearly that "James, Cephas (Peter) and John" exercised a ministry in connection with which "*the gospel of the circumcision*" was proclaimed, and that, at that time, they should continue to minister "unto the circumcision" (i.e. Israel) whilst Paul and his companions took "the gospel of the uncircumcision" to "the Gentiles" [1]

It is thus clear that Peter's preaching ministry was *to* the circumcision and *not to* us Gentiles of this present time. The epistles of Peter were directed "*to* the strangers scattered abroad" (1 Peter 1:1; 2 Peter 3:1), The word strangers might mislead some to think that these epistles were written to Gentiles, 'strangers' so far as Israel was concerned, but this is certainly not the case, for those to whom Peter wrote were "the circumcision" – Jews who were 'strangers' in the lands and places to which they had been scattered by the persecutions of those days (Acts 8:1; 11:19).

2. James

 The epistle of James is definitely stated to be "*to* the twelve tribes scattered abroad" (James 1:1). – the same people to whom Peter wrote.

Thus the ministers and epistles of both Peter and James are *not to* you or me, for we are not "the circumcision" we are not of "the twelve tribes scattered" from Palestine by persecution, nor are we, who are Gentiles, "a chosen generation, a royal priesthood, an holy nation, a peculiar people" (1 Peter 2:9) for these descriptions belong *to* Israel (Exodus 18:5, 6).

3. Jude

The epistle of Jude is also *to* the circumcision. This is evident from its contents; its references to the events from history of the chosen people; the mention, at verse 9, of "Michael the archangel" – "the great prince which standeth for the children of thy people" says Daniel, (Daniel 12:1); the reference to the words of the apostles of the Lord Jesus, which words, says Jude, his readers had heard (verses 17, 18), these apostles being the 'twelve' whom we earlier noted were sent only "*to* the lost sheep of the house of Israel". (Matthew 10:5, 6).

4. John

Next to be considered must be John's epistles, gospel and "the Revelation of Jesus Christ which God gave unto him" (Revelation 1:1). Hint of a long period of service for John is contained in the reported words of the Lord about him as recorded at John 21:20-25, and during this long time he had more than one ministry. (like Paul, as we shall later see). As one of the 'twelve' he was initially sent "*to* the lost sheep of the house of Israel" and after the collective ministry of the 'twelve' had ceased, Paul records at Galatians 2:9, that John, along with James and Peter, continued to engage in the ministry *to* the circumcision.

a. The Epistles of John

Whilst it is admittedly difficult to fix dates for the three epistles that bear John's name, and whilst the epistles and gospel from his pen are similar, in their presentation of the Lord, and of their subject and general tone, yet the internal evidence of the first epistle, directed to some assembly of believers who had intimate knowledge of the truth (1 John 2:14; 2:21; 5:13), points to its being part of the ministry *to* the circumcision.[2] It was written we should judge, almost at the end of the Acts period, and looks forward to the impending change from the restricted ministries of that period[3] to the wider ministry of the untrammelled "whosoever" gospel to "the world" (1 John 2:2; 4:14) which perhaps most present day believers are surprised to learn was not proclaimed until the acts period was at an end.

Thus the first epistle of John was *not to* us Gentiles of the present time. The second and third epistles of John are examples of the private correspondence of that day (as also is the epistle of Paul to Philemon) and are written to specifically designated believers; the second to "the elect lady", and the third to "Gaius". So John faithfully ministered *to* the circumcision until, (as we have already briefly intimated and hope to set forth more clearly in succeeding pages) by their refusal to repent and believe their special gospel, (the gospel of the circumcision), the people of Israel temporarily forfeited their privileged position. When this happened, John was evidently entrusted with his "gospel" ministry, which has a far wider scope and appeal than any of the ministries or writings so far considered. But before turning to this we must briefly note his ministry through the "Revelation".

b. The Revelation

"The Revelation of Jesus Christ which God gave unto" John is separate from his other ministries, in that it is a prophetic ministry concerning "things which must shortly come to pass" (Revelation 1:1); concerning "The Lord's Day" or "The Day of the Lord" (Revelation 1:10); concerning "things seen, things which are, and things which shall be hereafter". It is addressed collectively *to* seven specifically names churches (Revelation 1:4-11). This 'Revelation' is an amplification of some of the 'apocalyptic' visions of the Old Testament prophets and gives glimpses of such things as are largely beyond our grasp, but which will be understood by those in the circumstances of that period immediately preceding the Lord's return to earth. It is an extremely interesting though much misunderstood book, but in face of Revelation 1:4-11 we can assuredly say that it was *not* directed *to* us.

c. The Gospel of John

It is quite clear that in his Gospel John addresses his message *to* "the World" *to* "whosoever". It is clearly written from the point of view of the needs of all men and in view of the fact intimated at chapter 1 verse 11, "He" (i.e. Christ, the Word and the Light) "came unto His own", (i.e. His own people Israel) "and they received Him not".

Because of this refusal by Israel to receive Him, the ministry to them, that is the ministry to the circumcision in which John earlier had a part, had been brought to a close, and so John proceeds, at verse 12 "But as many as received Him ... "and thereupon addresses his message to those in "the world" to "whosoever". This statement at John 1:11, 12 at once dates this gospel as being written after Israel had been temporarily set aside from being "the people of God"; after the momentous event recorded at Acts 28:23-28, where we read that the opportunity of "seeing, hearing and being converted and healed" (Acts 28:27) was taken from Israel ("His own") and that "the salvation of God" was "sent unto the Gentiles" (unto "as many as would receive Him" out of the nations of "the world"), because they will hear it" (Acts 28:28). Let us repeat that it is clear that John's message was written after Israel had failed to respond to all God's gracious dealings with them, gracious dealings and opportunities continuing more than 30 years after they had "crucified the Lord of Glory". This persistent refusal of His grace eventuated in God turning from them "until the times of the Gentiles be fulfilled" (Luke 21:24).

Thus whilst John's ministry to the circumcision was per force at an end, God gave him this wider ministry "to the world" to "whosoever". This ministry was a special "witness" (a word used 47 times in this gospel) to the Lord as the "Son of God".

The incidents recorded, the "signs" detailed, and the spoken words reported are all for one particular purpose, namely, "to manifest forth His glory" (2:11) in order that men might believe on Him as "the Lamb of God which taketh away the sin of the world" (1:29) and "the Saviour of the world" (4:42) and it is recorded several times that "many did believe". Further it is recorded that He did and said many things that the joy of those who believed "might be full" and that in Him "we might have peace".

Now we *can* say that this wider ministry of John was *to* us; *to* the world of men of which we form a part. The gracious invitations to the all-embracing "whosoever" include us, and we can rejoice in the reception of "life through His name" (20:31). We find that John really had three distinct ministries during his long period of service. (1) To the circumcision. (2) A prophetic ministry – also in connection with the circumcision. (3) The wider world-wide ministry, applicable to this present time. [Editor's note: Ernest Streets was later to change his view on this: see the later chapter *Another Look at the Gospel of John*.]

5. Paul

To complete our quest and in order that we might be able the better to "understand" what we read we must consider the ministries and epistles of Paul. At the time of Paul's conversion the Lord revealed to Ananias that this particular man was to be "a chosen vessel ... to bear my name before *the Gentiles*, and Kings, *and the children of Israel*" (Acts 9:15). These words give the *extent* of the witness to be borne by this remarkable servant of the Lord, and at the same time Paul himself was clearly told that he was to exercise *two distinct ministries.*

Paul's two distinct ministries

First see and read Acts 26:16. Paul was to be, says the risen Lord, "a minister and a witness, both" (signifying *two*)" *of these things* which thou hast seen" (the basis of his first ministry) "and *of those things* in the which I will appear unto thee" (the promise of a then future revelation of truth which was to be the basis of the second ministry).

Far too few Bible readers and students recognise that Paul was given these two distinct ministries, nor is it appreciated that he wrote seven epistles relating to each, Galatians, 1st and 2nd Thessalonians, Hebrews, 1st and 2nd Corinthians and Romans, during and relating to his first ministry, which is reported in the history of the Acts, chapters 13-28; Ephesians, Philippians, Colossians, Philemon, 1st and 2nd Timothy and Titus, during the period of his second ministry which took effect from Acts 28:28, at which time "the salvation of God" was taken from Israel and "sent unto the Gentiles".

Paul's two ministries associated with the Gentiles

That both ministries were to be associated with the Gentiles is made quite plain, in that at his conversion the Lord immediately spoke to Paul of "the Gentiles, unto whom now I send thee" (Acts 26:17). There was also the intimation of Ananias as already noted (Acts 9:15) and in addition, when writing his epistle to the Galatians – his first epistle – Paul states "It pleased God to reveal His son in me that I might preach Him among the Gentiles" (Galatians 1:15, 16) and he further refers to this fact in Romans 11:13; Ephesians 3:1; 1 Timothy 2:7; and 2 Timothy 1:11.

We have above referred to the Lord's words to Ananias (Acts 9:15) that, although Paul was called to be the apostle "to the Gentiles", he was nevertheless to bear a testimony to "the people of Israel". In fact, during his first ministry, Paul's apostleship to the Gentiles was directly related to his testimony to his own kinsmen of Israel, for during this first ministry he says he magnified his office as a means to urge Israel to repentance "I am the apostle to the Gentiles" he says, "I magnify my office if by any means I may provoke to emulation them which are my own flesh, and might save some of them" (Romans 11:13, 14).

Paul's first ministry limited

During the first ministry Paul categorically states that he said *"none other things than those which the prophets and Moses did say should come"* (Acts 26:22). This is a very important statement, giving the precise scriptural limits of his first ministry. He was limited to "the things which he had seen" (Acts 26:16) as revealed in "the prophets and Moses" i.e. the Old Testament, with which he was thoroughly conversant.

Paul's first ministry named as being "of the New Covenant"

In respect of this ministry based solely on the prophets and Moses – (Moses the human instrument in relation to the giving of the first, or old, covenant, and the prophets who pronounced the effects of Israel's failure to keep the first covenant of the law, and also revealed God's promise of the "new covenant") – Paul claims that he had been made "an able minister of the new covenant" (2 Corinthians 3:6).

Now the new covenant was made with Judah and Israel because they had broken and disobeyed the old or first covenant – see and read Jeremiah 31:31-37 – but it should be noted that the scriptures reveal that the effects of this new covenant were not to be enjoyed only by Judah and Israel, but that, according to the terms of the promises and covenant made by God with Abraham (which promises and covenant were given and made before either the covenant of the law, or the new covenant of the spirit had been made) "all nations", i.e. Gentiles, should also be blessed (Genesis 12:3; 17:2-8; Galatians 3:8). The Abrahamic promises and covenant will be fully implemented when Christ "the messenger of the covenant" (Malachi 3:1) returns to earth, or as Isaiah says "the Redeemer comes to Zion", then Gentiles also will be blessed, and through Israel receive of the fruits of both the Abrahamic and the new covenants (Isaiah 59:20, 60:3; 62:1, 2 etc.).

Paul's first ministry also "of reconciliation"

In order that the way for this world-wide blessing should be prepared, Paul's ministry of the new covenant was also a "ministry of reconciliation"

(2 Corinthians 5:18), not only to reconcile a stubborn Israel to God, but also seeking to reconcile "the world" i.e. the Gentile nations, to God (2 Corinthians 5:18) and further to reconcile Jews with Gentiles that they might be "all one in Christ Jesus" (Galatians 3:28, 29) so that the Gentile believers might become "heirs according to the promise" (Galatians 3:29) being blessed "with faithful Abraham" (Galatians 3:9) for had the people of Israel responded and repented, Christ "the messenger of the covenant" would then have returned, even as Paul *at that time* taught and expected, (1 Thessalonians 4; 2 Thessalonians) and as Peter had likewise stated (Acts 3).

Extent of, and Epistles written during, Paul's first ministry

This first of his two ministries extended from Paul's conversion up to the time of his final appeal to the Jews of the dispersion in Rome, and along with the historical events of this ministry as given in the Acts chapters 8, and 13-28, must be included in the epistles written by Paul *during that time*, which are, as before stated, Galatians, 1st and 2nd Thessalonians, Hebrews, 1st and 2nd Corinthians and Romans. These seven epistles, written whilst Paul was exercising his ministry "of the new covenant" and "reconciliation" are wholly founded upon what "the prophets and Moses did say should come"; those statements of glorious truth and intimations of wonderful blessing, are all connected with and on the basis of, God's covenants and promises with and to Abraham and Israel.

Reason for inclusion of the Gentiles during Paul's first ministry

During Paul's first ministry and the writing of the first seven epistles from his pen, believing Gentiles were as "wild olive branches" "grafted into" the good olive tree, i.e. Israel (Romans 11:17, 24; Jeremiah 11:16; Hosea 14:6).

Read all Romans 11 very carefully and you will discover that *at that time,* whilst Paul was ministering the "new covenant" and "reconciliation", (which ministry extended to the end of the Acts), Israel stood as a nation before God, for they were then still "His people" (Romans 11:1, 21, and "the people of God" (1 Peter 2:10)[4] and that had they even then, *as a nation* turned in repentance and faith God could have moved as promised and predicted by the prophets, and as expected *at that time* by Peter, Paul and the others who ministered to Israel. But they did not, as a nation, repent and turn to God. Israel in the land and Israel in dispersion, received many opportunities, as recorded throughout the Acts, and this first ministry of Paul, *including and bringing in, as it did, the Gentiles to enjoy blessing along with Israel* did not "provoke Israel to emulation" as Paul stated he had hoped (Romans 10:19; 11:11; 11:14).

At that time the Gentiles were brought into Abrahamic and new covenant blessing, in an endeavour to "provoke Israel to jealousy", but the endeavour failed. Thus, because of their stubbornness and unbelief, as prophesied (Deuteronomy 4:25-28; 28:15 – 29:28; Isaiah 6:9-12, Daniel 9:26) Israel temporarily ceased to stand as a nation before God, and at the historical period following immediately upon the end of the Acts, their city, Jerusalem, the centre of their national and religious life, was reduced to a heap of rubble, even as foretold by the Lord (Matthew 23:34-39; Luke 19:41-44; 21:20-24).

Temporarily, therefore, their national and spiritual privileges were withdrawn, and the outworking of the covenants and promises made with and to Abraham and Israel are held in abeyance until "the times of the Gentiles be fulfilled" (Luke 21:24).

The words of the prophet Isaiah, repeated by Paul (Acts 28:25-27) signalized these great and far-reaching changes, as "the Salvation of God" was taken from an unrepentant Israel and "sent unto the Gentiles", for, says Paul "they will hear it" (Acts 28:28). These words, tragic for Israel, blessed for the Gentiles, closed Paul's first ministry.

An objection stated and answered

"But surely this first ministry of Paul was *to* us" you will perhaps say "for it appears to be as much if not more, to Gentiles than to Jews, and we too are Gentiles". Yes! It is true that we are Gentiles, *but we are not Gentiles living at that time when the ministries of the "new covenant" and "reconciliation" were being exercised, and when the Jews as a people still stood before God, holding prior place in the purpose of God and having "much advantage"* (Romans 3:1, 2). It is important, as Coverdale's rule implies, to determine *at what time* this ministry was exercised.

Position of Gentiles *now,* compared with positions of Gentiles *then.*

You who thus query, are *now,* as Gentile believers, enjoying your salvation, blessings and spiritual privileges solely because you are linked with Israel, *as the Gentile believers then were?* To use the figure of the olive tree that Paul at that time used, we ask, "are you now *today* 'grafted into' Israel's olive tree?" (Romans 11:17) "Does 'the root', i.e. Israel, 'bear thee'?" (Romans 11:18) "Are you 'a partaker of the root and fatness of the olive tree'?" (Romans 11:17) "Why no!" you will answer, "for Israel's tree" (figuratively either olive or fig) "was cut down, or is withered away, as the Saviour by parable and miracle prophesied (Matthew 21:17-22; Luke 13:6-9) and for these many centuries Israel as a nation has had no standing before God, nor (until recently) amongst the other nations". That is certainly true, as both scripture and history agree. Then can you not see and appreciate that *Paul's first ministry was conditioned by Israel's response.* This first ministry of Paul, the ministry of the new covenant and reconciliation (2 Corinthians 3:6; 5:18), based wholly on "the prophets and Moses" *was effective only whilst Israel stood as a nation and people before God, and whilst there was thus the possibility of the new covenant being fully implemented and reconciliation received.*

This first ministry was certainly to Gentiles as well as Jews, - to the Jews who were a direct party to the covenant, and to such Gentiles who *at that time,* were through their faith, being linked with faithful Abraham, and thus with Israel (Galatians 3:8; Romans 11:20) to receive the fruits of covenant blessing – but these Jews and Gentiles, though "one in Christ Jesus" (Galatians 3:18) *were nevertheless not on equal terms* for the Jews *at that time* still held their privileged position in the purpose of God (Romans 3:1, 2; 9:4, 5), and note how *that then* the message of salvation had to be "to the Jew *first"* (Acts 3:25, 26; 11:19; 13:46; Romans 1:16; 2:9; 2:10)[5] Paul stating *that then* there indeed was "much profit every way ... and advantage" in being a circumcised Jew (Romans 3:1, 2). They were *then* still "the people of God", and had "the adoption, and the glory, and the covenants, and the giving of the law, and the service of God, and the promises; whose are the fathers, and of whom as concerning the flesh Christ came, Who is over all, God bless for ever" (Romans 8:4, 6), so that, *at that time* it could be truly said "Salvation is of the Jews" (John 4:22).

But such is *not* the case *now.* To be a Jew has been no 'profit' or 'advantage' these nineteen hundred years for Israel is *not now* the vehicle and channel through which God is seeking to bless mankind, and we Gentile believers today are not in any way dependent upon the Jews as a nation or people, for our blessings.

Paul's first ministry *for* us, though not *to* us

This we conclude that the first ministry of Paul (the history and record of which is found in Acts, chapter 8, and chapters 13-18, and in the epistles which Paul wrote during that time, namely Galatians, 1st and 2nd Thessalonians, Hebrews, 1st and 2nd Corinthians and Romans) was not and is not specifically *to* us Gentiles of this present time, though of course as we pointed out to be the case with the Old Testament, and as is the case with all the other ministries and epistles so far considered, such ministries and their message are all *for* us, for our use in the sense that they are "profitable *for* doctrine ... *for* instruction" (2 Timothy 3:16, 17). Profitable indeed, as in the case of the Old Testament books they given the foundations of the great and unchanging doctrines of redemption by blood, justification by faith etc., and in the case of the New Testament ministries so far considered, in particular the statements in the epistles of Galatians and Romans, where these great doctrines of our salvation are so clearly set forth, and form the background and basis upon which the higher and more glorious truths in Paul's second ministry are built.

These great doctrines of salvation and grace remain unchanged whilst the various ministries of the truth of God may be directed *to* different sets of people and believers at different times, whose "callings" and ultimate "hopes" are likewise different.

Close of Paul's first ministry

The first ministry of Paul drew to its close with his apprehension at Jerusalem (Acts 21:33) and actually ceased when his appeal to the Jews of the dispersion in Rome was refused and "they departed" (Acts 28:25, 29). Let us repeat that with the declaration as reported at Acts 28:25-28 Israel as a people, and all the purposes with which they as "the people of God" were linked, were suspended, and the various ministries *to* Israel and *to* such Gentiles as were associated with them in Abrahamic and new covenant blessing, also ceased to apply.

The gospel ministry of John and the second ministry of Paul linked

With the closing of the period covered by the Acts, and when, as betokened by the destruction of Jerusalem, the opportunities and privileges of Israel were suspended and the various ministries *to* them had ceased to be effective, in the "*riches* of His grace" (Ephesians 1:7) God thereupon opened wide the door of salvation to the Gentiles, to "whosoever" as intimated in Paul's final word to the Jews at Rome (Acts 28:28), and as seen in the Gospel of John, which, as we stated earlier, was written *after* the close of the Acts, and in view of Israel's final refusal of their Messiah as seen from the statement at John 1:11.

The grace, love and salvation of God are now *for all* irrespective of nationality or covenants, and all may receive and enjoy the wondrous blessings that flow out from the Lord Jesus Christ, Who, as the "one sacrifice" gave Himself for the sins of the whole world. Glorious blessings indeed, but we have not reached the apex yet, for when Israel "received Him not" (John 1:11) and "departed" – or were "divorced" (Acts 28:25, 29), and as a result the full and free good news was extended to all men everywhere, Paul then entered upon his second ministry, a ministry *to* "the saints and faithful in Christ" (Ephesians 1:1; Philippians 1:1; Colossians 1:2) a ministry *to* believers, to whom God desires to make known further wondrous blessing in the "*exceeding riches* of His grace" (Ephesians 2:7) and according to "the mystery of His will" (Ephesians 1:9).

It is in connection with this that Paul, as "the prisoner for you Gentiles" (Ephesians 3:1; 4:1) *alone* of all the ministers and ministries of the scripture, writes of an reveals "the mystery" (Ephesians 3:3) "the church which is His body" (Ephesians 1:21, 22) the members of which, he writes, were "chosen in Christ before the foundation of the world" (Ephesians 1:4).

Paul's second ministry

In writing of this supreme revelation of glorious and blessed truth Paul says that he was made a "minister of the mystery" (Ephesians 3:7-9) and claims "unto *me* ... was this grace given, that *I* should preach among the Gentiles the unsearchable riches of Christ" (Ephesians 3:8). Moreover he claims that this particular ministry and truth concerning "the church ... His body" (Ephesians 1:22, 23; Colossians 1:24) was given to him "to fulfil the word of God" (Colossians 1:25), that is, that this particular revelation 'fills full' or 'completes' the whole of the revelation of the redemptive purposes of God, as made known in and through the inspired scriptures.

Further, Paul says that this revelation was given to him "to make all men see ... the fellowship of the mystery, *which from the beginning of the world hath been hid in God"* (Ephesians 3:9) and "*which from the beginning of the world hath been hid in God"* (Ephesians 3:9) and "even *the mystery which hath been hid from ages and generations, but now is made manifest to his saints,* to whom God would make known the riches of the glory of this mystery among the Gentiles ... which is Christ in you, the hope of glory" (Colossians 1:26, 27). These statements surely reveal that this second ministry of Paul was the setting forth and making known of *the hitherto undeclared and unrevealed* apex or top-stone of the amazing edifice of the truth of God. Neither of the previously considered ministries or ministers, whether in the Old or New Testaments had anything to say about this, which had been *kept hidden* in God until revealed to and through Paul.

Paul's second ministry was by special revelation

As we have before stated this second ministry was given to Paul about the time of the closing of the Acts, when he was in prison in Rome (Acts 28:30) and from which prison he wrote the epistles to the Ephesians, the Philippians and the Colossians. It was not connected with his previous ministry, which was wholly founded upon "the prophets and Moses" – excepting in so far as all the truth of God, be it for any age or in connection with any part of the unfolding purposes of His grace and love, is founded on redemption by blood, and finds its true outworking and fulfilment in Christ, for "of Him" and "by Him" and "for Him" and "to Him" are all things (Colossians 1) – we repeat, it was not connected with, nor had its content been predicted by "the prophets and Moses" as his first ministry had been.

The revelation by which he received this hitherto unrevealed truth was the fulfilment of the promise given by the risen Lord to Paul at the time of his conversion, when he was told that there would be made known to him "those things in the which I will appear unto thee" (Acts 26:16). This supreme 'top-stone' revelation is made know *to* us believing Gentiles in and through the epistles written by Paul *after* the setting aside of the Jews as recorded at the end of the Acts (Acts 28:28) – these epistles being Ephesians, Philippians, Colossians, Philemon, 1st and 2nd Timothy and Titus – and these epistles *alone* bring to us the knowledge of the previously unthought-of-revelation of the grace of God and are the complement of the "whosoever" and world-wide ministry of the Gospel of John, which, as we have already more than once pointed out, was likewise written *after* the close of the period covered by the Acts.

The ministries that are *to* us Gentiles *now*

We can now state that *this second of Paul's two ministries* "To you Gentiles" "to make all men see", (as contained in the epistles Ephesians, Philippians, Colossians, Philemon, 1st and 2nd Timothy and Titus) *and the "whosoever" gospel ministry of John are the parts of the scripture to which we as Gentiles should pay primary, particular and obedient heed. If there is any part of scripture truth that we can claim as being to us, we fill find it here.* We can fit ourselves perfectly into this part of the revelation of God's will and ways without doing despite to the standing, blessing or privileges of others, for indeed we are of the "whosoever" and can be, by His grace, of the company of the "as many as receive Him"; we are Gentiles, "uncircumscision", who in the unregenerate state were "without Christ, aliens from the commonwealth of Israel and strangers from the covenants of promise, having no hope and without God in this world", but now as believers, "in Christ Jesus we who sometimes were far off have been made nigh by the blood of Christ" (Ephesians 2:11-13).

In the 'whosoever' ministry of John and in this ministry of Paul to the Gentile saints, both exercised *after* the close of the Acts, we find the truth which is *to* us, *about* us and *for* us, and we do well to study it closely.

An objection answered

But an objection might arise. Some might complain that, if John's Gospel and Paul's later seven epistles are really the only parts of the scripture that are in the strict sense *to* us Gentiles *now*, then the major part of the scriptures from which so much comfort and help can be gained, have been taken from them. This is really not so ... consider but a moment. To understand and rightly appreciate those parts of the sacred word that are definitely *to, about* and *for* you, it is absolutely essential to have the background and foundation of all the other inspired scriptures, in which the wonderful revelation of the love and grace of God, and the doctrines of redemption, justification, sanctification, etc., are progressively unfolded until they reach their climax in this part of scripture, where they are shown to be the strength and foundation for the special truths given through Paul and John for "Gentiles" in "the world" today. It is just for this purpose, as stated in 2 Timothy 3:16, 17 that "all scripture" has been "given by inspiration of God and is profitable *for*" us "that the man of God may be thoroughly furnished unto all good works".

The writer sincerely believes that to answer the question "Understandest thou what thou readest?", it is essential to have the key which will enable us to "rightly divide the word of truth" (2 Timothy 2:15) and in order to "rightly divide" we *must* apply the key, we *must* always ask, as we have done throughout this study, "*is this scripture really to me at this time?*" Only thus can we receive and truly enjoy such blessing and grace as God has for us Gentiles in these days.

Summary and Conclusion

Before concluding our study let us summarise our findings. We have found that the various parts and books of scripture are in connection with and are directed *to* different companies of people, at different times, viz:

A. The Old Testament books (in the man)

> *To Israel nationally.* The 'first' or 'old' covenant made and broken; the 'new covenant' promised and its effects foretold.

B. The Gospels of Matthew, Mark and Luke

> Record of the ministries of John the Baptist, the Lord Jesus Christ, and 'the twelve'. *To the lost sheep of the house of Israel.* The promise of, and the conditions for entry into, "The Kingdom of Heaven".

C. The Acts chapters 1-12 and the Epistles of Peter, John, James and Jude

> Record of the continued ministry of 'the twelve' collectively, and the individual ministries and epistles of Peter, John, James and Jude *to* "the circumcision" (or Israel).

D. The Acts chapters 13-28, Paul's Epistles to Galatians, 1st 2nd Thessalonians, Hebrews, 1st 2nd Corinthians and Romans

> Record of the ministry and epistles of Paul *to Jews and Gentiles,* who were called to be all in one in Christ Jesus" under Abrahamic and new covenant blessing. A time when Jews had 'advantage', and when the gospel was "to the Jew first".

E. The Gospel of John

> Record of the ministry of John the Baptist and of Christ, written *after* Israel as a people had been temporarily set aside, and in view of the need of all men for "life" in place of "condemnation" and "death". Written *to "the world" "whosoever"* embracing all men, *now.* [Editor's note: Ernest Streets was later to change his view on this: see the later chapter *Another Look at the Gospel of John.*]

F. The Epistles of Paul to Ephesians, Philippians, Colossians, Philemon, 1st and 2nd Timothy and Titus

> Written *after* Israel had been temporarily set aside. *To "the saints and faithful in Christ", to "you Gentiles" to believers now.*

G. The Revelation

> *To the seven names churches.* The prophetic record of things pertaining to "the day of the Lord" yet *future.*

For fear that the above division of the scriptures might be misunderstood and misapplied by some, *we feel it necessary to repeat and emphasise,* that whilst we have pointed out that the various books and parts of the scripture are definitely directed *to* different companies of people and believers at different times (in order that may accomplish the varying phases of the outworking of the eternal purpose) nevertheless *the great doctrines of salvation, viz. redemption, justification, sanctification etc.,* as set forth in the Old Testament by type, shadow etc., and explained and amplified in the unfolding revelation of the New Testament, *are basic to all ministries* with their varying callings and hopes, and are vital to the appreciation of the calling and hope revealed for those who by grace acknowledge the truth and enter into membership of "the church which is His body".

We conclude with prayer for ourselves and our readers, "That the God of our Lord Jesus Christ the Father of glory may give unto us the spirit of wisdom and revelation in the acknowledging of Him: the eyes of our understanding being enlightened; that we may know what is the hope of His calling, and what the riches of the glory of His inheritance in the saints, and what is the exceeding greatness of His power to us ward who believe. That Christ may dwell in our hearts by faith, that we may be able to comprehend ... and know the love of Christ which passeth being fruitful in every good work and increasing in the knowledge of God, Who hath delivered us from the power of darkness and translated us into the kingdom of His dear Son, in whom we have redemption even the forgiveness of sins" (Ephesians 1:17-19; 3:17-19; Colossians 1:10-14).

"These Signs ..."
Mark 16:17

Preface

Because this study is cast in the form of a testimony, the personal note is much to the fore and the recurring use of the personal pronoun has been unavoidable. In Ecclesiastes we read: "There is a time to keep silence, and a time to speak" (Ecclesiastes 3:7). Feeling that the "time to speak" of the subject of the "signs" and "miracles" had come, we could think of no better way to recount our own parade 'self' for we truly recognise the necessity as expressed by John the Baptist: "He must increase ... I must decrease" (John 3:30), but trust that the outcome may be to the glory of God, the exaltation of our Lord and Head, and the blessing of His believing people.

Ernest H. Streets

[For more on the 'signs' and 'miracles' see *The Miracles of the Apostles* by Michael Penny details in Further Reading towards the end of this book.]

****

To the honest onlooker – and we must admit that there are many such in the world of men outside our churches and other meeting places today – the many shades of thought and opinion, sometimes absolutely opposed the one to the other, and the cleavages in the varied methods of 'church' government and order, are a very real stumbling-block in the way of the acceptance of saving truth.

How sad it is that our many differences tend to keep souls in the darkness, and often prevent young believers from entering into their true heritage in Christ. In this connection, the implications of the words of the Savior as reported at Matthew chapter 18, and Luke chapter 17, need to be taken to heart.

> "Woe unto the world because of offences (lit: stumbling-blocks) ... woe to that man through whom the offence cometh ... It were better for him that a millstone were hanged about his neck, and he cast into the sea, than that he should offend (cause to stumble) one of the little ones which believe in me."

Are our divergent beliefs and differences of method keeping others in the dark, causing them to stumble? I am very much afraid that they are. Surely the God who created the great and wonderful universal systems, and whose wisdom and power keep the myriads of heavenly bodies in ordered motion; the God Who formed the infinitesimal feathers that, through the microscope, are to be observed on most butterflies wings; the One Who is God of love, of all race, perfect in goodness and truth, surely He is a God of *order*, and must be grieved by the confusion of Christendom today.

There *must* be some way which is the designed, and therefore that right way, of Christian doctrine and practice – the way that our God Himself intended His believing people to follow. We cannot *all* be right, can we? Is it possible for us to discover that right way!

I do not wish to "make confusion worse confounded", but from my own experience will try to point to a path which has led me, and many, many more, out of the prevailing confusion, and which I trust, when put on record, will be the means of helping others, and leading them to similar blessing.

In 1929, when in Bible School preparing for Christian service, the words of the closing verses of Mark chapter 16 caused me serious heart-searching. Here I read, (from verse 15 onwards), "And He said unto them,

> 'Go ye into all the world and preach the gospel to every creature. *He that believeth and is baptised shall be saved ... and these signs shall follow them that believe*; in my name they shall cast out devils; they shall speak with new tongues; they shall take up serpents; and if they drink any deadly thing it shall not hurt them; they shall lay hands on the sick and they shall recover'.

So then after the Lord had spoken to them ... they went forth and preached, the Lord working with them, and confirming the word with the signs following".

Well now! There it was, plain to read, but did I really believe this? I called myself a believer, I had been baptised – in fact I had been baptised twice, both times by total immersion, first when between 16 and 17, and the second time when 22 years of age – but that is another story. I sat regularly at the Lord's Table. I had received the 'laying on of hands' when set apart for the service of the Lord. And here was I at Bible School, diligently preparing myself because I felt called to obey the command, "Go ye – and preach" (verse 15). "But those signs are not following my testimony", I said to myself, "Yet I *am* a believer, and really do know salvation".

With all the sincerity of Christian young manhood, I sought an answer to the problem. Oh yes! I had heard these words explained away, spiritualised, and glossed over. There were those who said, "Ah! These things do happen sometimes, when one is really faithful, and there are occasions of faith-healings, and of the exorcising of demons, etc., on the mission fields abroad, in China, Africa, and other places, which have surely fulfilled this promise". There may have been, I was ready to believe that this was so. Furthermore there were various companies of believers who claim to speak with tongues, and to perform "faith-healings".

Then there were others who at once pointed to 1 Corinthians 13:8 and said Paul stated that "prophecies shall fail", "tongues shall cease", and that miraculous "knowledge shall vanish away", and no doubt the other miraculous signs would gradually become unnecessary, and so they have all finally stopped. What a muddle it all was! What was the truth of the matter?

I simply had to face up to this *for myself*, for Mark 16:15-18 was the record of the words of my Lord, and on the fact of them clearly indicated that the signs He enumerated were to be the accompaniments of *all* who believed and were baptised. They were backed up by many other passages, and the experiences of the believers all through the record of the Acts attested their reliability. Then just what had happened?

I looked around me. Not one of the earnest students at Bible School had any "signs" following them. Neither were "these signs" following our highly respected teachers, lecturers and professors!

Pause awhile, reader. Are "these signs" giving confirmation to your faith and testimony? If not, have you ever *seriously* considered why not! Have you *conscientiously* faced up to this, and really sought to find an answer or reason? Have you, for yourself, tested out this statement and promise spoken by the Lord?

To return to my own problem of those years ago. I resolved that I would not rest until I had for myself really found a satisfactory explanation to account for the seeming inability, powerlessness and faithlessness of the multitudes of Christian believers all down the years.

I searched back into church history. I sought out, and read all I could of the documented accounts of those movements which claimed the perpetuation of "Pentecostal" signs. Except for a few, more or less isolated, cases of the "miraculous" which are claimed by the Roman Catholic church: a few, unrelated, occasions of supposed "speaking with tongues", scattered down the centuries;[6] a variety of "manifestations" during the early years of the Moravian church, (early 18th century); scenes of religious ecstasy, prostrations with violent agony, occasions of sudden loss of motion and speech, loud declamations in "tongues", and other curious results and manifestations at intervals during the ministry of John Wesley, from the year 1739 until about 1780, - except for these the only movement of any consequence seemed to be that which arose from the ministry of one Edward Irving in the first half of the nineteenth century. So far as I could trace, the "Irvingites" were the forerunners of the present-day "Pentecostal', 'Tongues' and 'Faith-healing' movements. But in all this, I found no records of the miraculous which were in any way comparable with the promise of Mark 16:16-17, or with the experiences of the believers of the period of history covered by the book of Acts, and I was rather disappointed.

After much meditation and prayer over the whole problem, I asked the Lord to give me grace and courage to make myself, if need be, a fool for His sake, if that was to be the way in which "these signs" would follow in my life. I earnestly sought a fresh infilling and empowerment of the Holy Spirit. I prayed and prayed. I surrendered myself to the Lord and His Spirit, in every way I knew. Nothing happened! Never a word of "new tongues" crossed my lips: no opportunities for proving or disproving the other stated "signs" presented themselves.

I attended a meeting of a 'healing campaign' then being conducted in Glasgow. There was fervor, there was expectation. The singing was hearty, the gospel message and appeal which followed were clear, and I am sure that many were brought to salvation. Then, to the accompaniment of non-stop chorus singing and exclamations of praise, various sick folk walked, were helped and were carried to the platform, where the evangelist – a then well-known leader of the 'Pentecostal' movement – prayed with them. The prayer could not be heard because of the singing and exclaiming which continued with increasing fervor. It was stated that many were healed that evening, but an on-looker like myself could not really be sure. Frankly, I was not impressed, and the thought arose in my mind that if it had been intended that the promise of Mark 16 was to continue in force all through this present period, and until the return of the Lord, then surely, with the spread of Christianity, there should be no need for such 'healing' meetings and campaigns, when just one or two men exercise the so-called 'gift of healing', for according to the Scriptures, *each* believer would be partaker of some miraculous gift, as is recorded of the members of the assembly at Corinth (see 1 Corinthians 12:7, 11; 14:26 "every man", "every one of you"), and that if this were the case, there should be no need for doctors or hospitals. I really did not know just what to think.

Yet this great good came of it. I searched and searched my Bible, how I thank God that He led me that way, for the Lord has said "Thy word is truth" (John 17:17). We cannot know what to believe or practise, or not to practise, until by a thorough reading of the word of God we find *for ourselves* just what God would have us do. How apt are the words of the Lord to the Sadducees, "Ye do err, *not knowing the scriptures*" (Matthew 22:29). This lack of knowledge of God's written word, which is truth, is the root whence spring all the differences, difficulties and divisions of Christendom today. Reader, what do you believe and practise? Do you believe and do just what is suggested or dictated by others – just what is *said about* the Word of God, or do you take the trouble to read and study for yourself, and then believe and do what the Word itself teaches? There is most often a vast difference between these two. I do indeed thank God that He led me to search my Bible until I had for myself found the solution to my problem.

Let me record a little of what I found, and give witness to the conclusions I arrived at, after more than five years before I could honestly say I had discovered, from the Word of God itself, a satisfactory answer to the questions which arose from the Lord's statement "These signs shall follow them that believe". I found it very difficult to break away from previous teaching and preconceived notions, but I thank God that He so overruled and ordered my circumstances that I had time for such protracted searching, study, and necessary readjustment. And let me also place it on record that I stuck to the Word of God *alone*. There were undoubtedly books which could have helped me, but I was determined not to accept or trust in what others might have written or said. In my heart I was convinced that God's Word, which I then believed and still do without any reservation believe to be fully "God-breathed" (2 Timothy 3:16, 17) would most surely carry within it all the needed instruction, and if allowed, would itself make all matters quite plain. Further, my circumstances confined me to this course, for I was but a poor student (in more ways than one!) and did not have the means to purchase books, had I desired them.

The only outside help I received during my period of searching, was through conversations with an older, much respected Christian friend and faithful helper, who had himself faced somewhat similar problems. Remarks passed by him proved to be pointers to paths through the

Scriptures which I had not traversed or studied before. It is fitting that I should here acknowledge the tremendous help thus afforded me. I am deeply indebted to that friend, Mr. Robert Ritchie, of Gourock. Scotland (who died in 1960), for it was through his words that I was thrown back, again and again, upon the Scriptures, to search, test, and check each particular, until a solid and really satisfactory explanation of my problem had been found.

What did I find? The results could not be condensed into a few pages, for the field of study ever widened, and actually to this very day continues to widen and reveal the richness of the marvels of God's incomparable revelation. Only the narrower issue, the answer to the original problem, can here be stated.

I found that "signs" or miraculous happenings such as are mentioned by the Lord at Mark 16:17, 18, first appear on the page of the New Testament as recorded at Matthew 4:23. "And Jesus went about all Galilee, teaching in their synagogues, and preaching the gospel of the kingdom, and healing all manner of sickness and all manner of disease among the people ... and they brought unto Him all sick people that were taken with divers diseases and torments, and those that were lunatic, and those that had the palsy, and He healed them." It was evident that the miraculous element was a confirmation of the teaching and preaching of "*the gospel of the kingdom*". At Matthew 9:35 we have almost a repetition of 4:23, and when the Lord sent "the twelve" on their preaching mission as we read at Matthew 10:1, "He gave them power against unclean spirits, to cast them out, and to heal all manner of sickness and all manner of disease", and He specifically instructed them, verses 5-8, "*Go not* into the way of the Gentiles and into any city of the Samaritans enter ye not: but go rather to the lost sheep of the house of Israel. And as ye go, preach, saying 'the kingdom of heaven is at hand'. Heal the sick, cleanse the leper, raise the dead, cast out devils".

Again, as recorded at Luke 10, when the Lord sent out "the seventy", He must have given them similar instructions, for we read at verse 17, how "they returned again with joy, saying 'Lord, even the devils are subject unto us through thy name'".

Thus I found that "signs" or "miracles" were the outward confirmations of the teaching and preaching of "the gospel of the kingdom", which, during the Lord's earthly ministry, was confined to "the lost sheep of the house of Israel" (Matthew 10:5, 6; 15:24). Further, I found that these "signs" and "miracles" were performed by such as had been baptised by John the Baptist, with "the baptism of repentance for the remission of sins" (Mark

1:4; Luke 3:3). Christ Himself was baptised with John's water baptism, and thereupon immediately a dove, symbol of the Spirit, was seen to descend and rest upon Him. "The twelve" were evidently also thus baptised (John 1:19-51; Acts 1:21, 22). A similar baptism was preached by Christ and administered by His disciples (John 3:22-26; 4:1, 2).

At and after Pentecost, I found both John's baptism and the baptism administered by Christ's disciples were superseded by another water baptism "in the name of the Lord Jesus", i.e. in the name of the risen Christ.
7

It can be demonstrated that until the end of the Acts, "signs" followed all those who believed and were baptised "in the name of the Lord Jesus for the remission of sins" (Acts 2:38-41; 8:12, 13; 19:5, 6). Paul received this baptism for the "washing away" of sins, immediately upon acknowledgement of the risen Christ (Acts 22:16; 9:18), and preached and administered it himself (Acts 16:14, 15, 31-33; 18:7, 8; 19:1-7; 1 Corinthians 1:13-17). *In those days, such baptism was essential to the realization of salvation* (Mark 16:16, where note the order 1. "believeth, ... 2. baptised ... 3. saved"), for baptism was the outward sign of the "washing away" of sins, prior to, or immediately upon the reception of the gift of the Holy Ghost (Acts 2:38; 9:17, 18; 19:5-7) which was then manifested by the "signs" which followed.

Thus the Pentecostal gift of the Spirit and the consequent "signs", are connected with the rite of water baptism. 'Believers' baptism, as practised by many today, is by them said to be a baptism *giving testimony to salvation, and the Spirit as having previously been received,* but the miraculous confirming signs are conspicuous by their absence!! 'Believers' 'baptism is also set forth as being *a following of Christ's example.*

If this is to be expected of believers today, then why not follow Him in circumcision, in synagogue attendance, the observance of the Jewish feasts, etc.? In the New Testament records, water baptism was usually administered *immediately* upon the reception of the particular message whether preached by John the Baptist (Matthew 3:6, 7; Mark 1:4, 8 etc.), by Christ and His disciples, (John 3:22-26), or by the apostles after the resurrection, (Acts 2:38-41; 8:35-39; 10:44-48; 16:14-15; 16:30-33; 18:8), and was the *immediate outward testimony of repentance,* administered for "the washing away of sins" (Acts 22:16; 1 Corinthians 6:11; Hebrews 10:22; 1 Peter 3:20-21). Thus water baptism was *then* necessary *before* salvation could be enjoyed, and *before* the miraculous "signs" of the gift of the Spirit could be displayed.

As a Baptist I specially noted that there was no reference to water in the passages that use the work *baptism* in Ephesians 4:3-6 or Colossians 2:11-12. I asked myself, "Just what is this *one baptism, made without hands?*" Study of the Scriptural occasions where baptism is referred to, soon supplied the answer. Luke 12:50 is the key statement, where the Lord declared, "I have a baptism to be baptised with; and how am I straightened until it is accomplished". At the beginning of His earthly ministry, after protest – see Matthew 3:13-17 – the Lord was baptised in the waters of the Jordan, but He pressed forward to *another baptism*. The washings, baptisms, sacrifices etc. of the Old Testament and of the New Testament until the important declaration of the Spirit through Paul at Acts 28:28, when the Jews "departed" (the word used is also rendered "put away" and "divorced") – were all "figures for the time then present" and named as "carnal – or fleshly – ordinances" at Hebrews 9:8-10, either pointing forward to, or for the time, back to the *baptism into death* which Christ endured and accomplished for us all by that death upon the Cross. *That death* was the essential *one baptism;* it is into *His death* that believers are now baptised by the Spirit, when those who trust, receive Salvation that His death alone could procure.

I have digressed a little from the main theme, and must again pick up the thread by continuing the study of Christ's ministry and miracles. I have previously stated that "signs" and "miracles" were the outward confirmations of the preaching of the "gospel of the kingdom", as can be seen in the earlier chapters of the Gospel records. As the record of the Gospels advances, we have brought before us an ever-growing list of these "signs" and "miracles", "wonders", "mighty works" and "powers", which confirmed Christ's ministry. So many there were, that John writes, "There are also many other things which Jesus did – (not said, but '*did*') – the which, if they should be written every one I suppose that even the world itself could not contain the books that should be written" (John 21:25).

During the Lord's last words to His own in the upper room, He made to them the definite promise, "Verily, verily, I say unto you, he that believeth on me, the *works* that I do he shall do also, and *greater works* than these shall he do, because I go unto my Father" (John 14:12). Coupled with this is the promise of "another Comforter ... the spirit of truth" (verses 16, 17), in whose power the "greater works" were to be accomplished.

After the resurrection, the statement that the "signs" should continue, with the addition of "new tongues", the taking up of serpents, and being unhurt by drinking any deadly thing, was renewed to the disciples, (Mark 16:16,17), with the amplification that *all* who believed and were baptised, would share in the great demonstration of these "powers of the age to come", as Paul writes of them in his epistle to the Hebrews (Hebrews 6:5). The record of Mark concludes with the comment that the preaching "everywhere" was "confirmed" by "signs following", and again we turn to the epistle to the Hebrews where Paul adds his inspired commentary upon the events of the Acts period, by writing that the "great salvation ... at first spoken by the Lord ... was confirmed ... God bearing witness, with both signs and wonders and with divers miracles, and gifts of the Holy Ghost" (Hebrews 2:3, 4).

Continuing the study of the historical facts as recorded, I found that God did indeed keep the promise as given through His Son, and that in the power of the Spirit, poured out at Pentecost time in Jerusalem, the signs and miracles, all of them, continued in full force, year after year, *right to the end of the historical period covered by the record of the book of the Acts,* which we might call the 'Pentecostal period'.

From Acts 1:6, I saw the Apostles' great concern, even after receiving the teaching from the Lord during the "forty days" (Acts 1:3), was the restoration of "the kingdom to Israel". As I thought about this, and studied more closely, I was somewhat startled to realise that during the "forty days" instruction, the Lord had *not* told them, nor did he, in answer to their question of verse 6, even *then* tell them, that they were in any way mistaken in their expectation of the setting up of Israel's kingdom, as promised and predicted from earlier times, and as preached by John Baptist, Christ and themselves at that very time. The Lord had certainly *not previously* told them, nor did he *subsequently* tell them, that instead of the expected "kingdom", He would, by the giving of His Spirit at Pentecost time, inaugurate and commence a new purpose and movement, "the church ... his body", in which believers whether Jew or Gentile would all be on the one spiritual plane, and be partakers of equal blessings. No! He says absolutely nothing about any such development, so they rightly continued to operate under His previous instructions, and went on preaching "this gospel of the kingdom" (Matthew 24:14 etc.), and exercising the promised miraculous signs.

When eventually some Gentiles were brought into the sphere of Israel's blessing – (being made partakers of Israel's spiritual things (Romans 15:27) as promised and covenanted originally to Abraham "In thee shall all families of the earth be blessed" (Genesis 12:3)) – these Gentiles were treated as inferiors, and the division between them and the Jewish believers continued right to the end of the Acts, for the Jewish believers continued to be "zealous of the Law", i.e. the Mosaic Law (Acts 21:20), while the Gentile believers did not observe any Jewish laws or customs (Acts 21:25) and were only restricted by the "decrees" of Acts 15:28, 29; 16:4. *This distinction between "circumcision" and "uncircumcision" remained to the end of the Acts. A church in which all believers shared equal status and blessings was not known during the Acts or Pentecostal period.*

As a young believer I had been taught that the giving of the Spirit on the day of Pentecost was the signal mark of the 'birthday' of the church which, it was stated continued, and still continues, to this day. I was indeed startled when I could find absolutely nothing to support that teaching. Most certainly a church, or assembly, was commenced at that time, but I found that *it* was the assembly with which Peter was intimately associated. (Matthew 16:18) and that *it* was connected with "the kingdom of heaven" (Matthew 16:19), i.e. Israel's earthly kingdom, which was to be "of" i.e. 'out from' or 'proceeding from' heaven, in that it would be heaven's rule exercised on earth, as predicted by Moses, (Deuteronomy 11:21).

Now Peter used the "keys" of *that kingdom* (Matthew 16:19) on the day of Pentecost, when in the power of the outpoured Spirit, and with the aid of the miraculous gift of tongues, (one of the signs given for "this people", i.e. Israel, see Isaiah 28:11; 1 Corinthians 14:21, 22), he was instrumental in commencing a "church", *or assembly of Israel in relation to their kingdom.*
That this is so, is made clear in that Peter promised the assembled people, if they would repent and receive the message, that Christ would return "to sit on his throne" (Acts 2:30), so that the everlasting kingdom promised to David and his seed and set forth by all the prophets, could be established (Acts 3:19-21). Peter said nothing about a universal or world-wide church; absolutely nothing about "the church, the body of Christ". Thus Peter was fulfilling the ministry to which he was appointed, and in which he continued, as can be seen from reference to Galatians 2:7-9, and to his epistles, both of which were written to the dispersed of Israel, "strangers" in the lands to which providence and persecution had scattered them (1 Peter 1:1; 2 Peter 3:1; Acts 8:1; 11:19. See also Galatians 2:11-15, and 2 Peter 3:15, 16, where we note that Peter never fully understood Paul's ministry to the Gentiles).

As I further studied I was more and more convinced that Pentecost was certainly not the birthday of the church which, supposedly, has continued to this present day, but that as Pentecost was purely a Jewish festal occasion, so the outpouring of the Spirit on that occasion was for Jewish or Israelitish purposes, to make possible the fulfilling of the Old Testament promises. Thus the Spirit was given: -

1. To enable Israel, as prophesied by Ezekiel (chapter 36:21-28, particularly verses 25-27) to keep and fulfil the requirements, injunctions and laws, necessary to the outworking of the covenants made with Abraham, Moses, and David, - covenants which, because of Israel's former disobediences, could only be brought to fruition under the prophetically promised New Covenant (Jeremiah 31:31-34), which was made possible for Israel by the obedience of Christ who, as the "Redeemer" of Israel (Isaiah 41:14 etc.) and as the "messenger of the covenant", (Malachi 3:1), gave Himself in sacrifice, and thus shed "the blood of the covenant", (Hebrews 10:29; 13:20; Matthew 26:28; Mark 14:24; Luke 22:20. The word 'testament' in the gospel references should be rendered 'covenant'), which sealed and ratified the stated terms under which God would use and bless the former stiff-necked and disobedient people.

2. The Spirit was given in order that Israel might be resettled in the land, the Promised Land, the Holy land. See Isaiah 32:13-20, noting particularly verse 15, which teaches that the land should be desolate "until the spirit be poured upon us from on high". See also Joel 2:18-32, where the pouring out of the spirit is linked with the restoration of 'the land'.

3. The Spirit was given in order that the confirmatory signs (Joel 2:28, repeated by Peter on the day of Pentecost) should be made possible for those who believed and were baptised.

4. The Spirit was given in order to lead the disciples into all truth" (John 16:13). It must be remembered that in the day this was spoken there was no New Testament. The "truth" into which the disciples were to be guided, was what we now know as the Old Testament truth, the truth to which Christ referred when He said "Thy word is truth" (John 17:17).

Thus the giving of the Spirit on the day of Pentecost was not the sign of the birthday of the "church" of this present day, i.e., the "church which is His body" (Ephesians 1:22, 23; Colossians 1:24) but was wholly connected with Israel, with its land, its promised earthly kingdom and with the implementing of the new covenant promised for Israel and Judah.

When this is recognised it explains why Peter's words are addressed to "Ye men of Judea and all that dwell at Jerusalem" (Acts 2:14); "Ye men of Israel" (2:22; 3:12); "Ye children of the prophets and of the covenant"

(3:25) etc. Peter calls upon them to repent and be baptised (2:38) that they might receive the gift of the Holy Ghost which had been promised to them (1:4, 5; 2:38, 39). Those who believed and were baptised, received the Spirit, and exercised the confirming "signs", including the gift of "other tongues", about which we read at Isaiah 28:11, "for with stammering lips and another tongue will He speak to this people", a statement which Paul later quotes in support of his teaching that "tongues" were a "sign" for "this people", i.e. Israel (1 Corinthians 14:21, 22).

From this point at Pentecost, I found that miraculous gifts are traceable all through the Acts with no diminution (see again Hebrews 2:2-4); also Romans 12:6-8; 1 Corinthians 12:1-13). Miraculous gifts accompanied *all* who received the various messages or ministries given or written in connection with the Acts, or Pentecostal period, and who were baptised in the name of the Lord Jesus, (see Acts 2:38; 19:1-7). References to this miraculous element are to be found in Romans 1:11; 11:29; 12:6; 1 Corinthians 1:5-7; 12:3-11 (see particularly verses 7 and 11 "every man" a partaker of the manifestation of the Spirit), 14:26, ("every one of you"); Galatians 3:5; 1 Thessalonians 1:5; Hebrews 6:5; in James, where the insistence on "works", links up with the promise of "greater works than these shall ye do" (John 14:12), this promise referring to miraculous "works"; in 1 Peter 4:10, "every man hath received the gift"; in 1 John 2:20, 27, miraculous knowledge, and in 1 John 3:22; 5:14, 15, where immediate miraculous answers to prayer are indicated.

One very valuable lesson which I learned as a result of my searching and study was that to understand and truly appreciate the Epistles of the New Testament, it is imperative to take into consideration both the *people* to whom they were written, and the *time* at which they were written. With my little knowledge, I had previously treated and thought of all the epistles as being for all believers as from the time of their being written, and as all of them coming chronologically *after* the end of the Acts, just because they were printed and placed after the Acts in our New Testament! But as I studied, I learned that the greater number of the epistles, *were written in connection with the messages and ministries given and exercised during the Acts.* It was with real joy that I found and learned that only the epistles of Paul in which there is any reference to "the church which is His body" are devoid of any mention of signs or miraculous gifts. The gift of grace by faith salvation (Ephesians 2:5, 8-9); grace according to the measure of the gift of Christ (Ephesians 4:7), and gifts of ministry for edifying the body of Christ (Ephesians 4:8-13), are the only gifts mentioned. When I had a good grip of this fact, a flood of light was let in upon my studies, and I soon saw that all the references in the epistles to "signs", "miracles", "healings", "tongues", "the interpretation of tongues", miraculous "wisdom and knowledge", "discerning of spirits" and other 'Pentecostal' manifestations were confined to the Acts or Pentecostal period, and most certainly did not extend beyond it.

Proof of this statement can readily be seen in what happened in this very connection in the experience of the apostle Paul. At Acts 19:12 we read that "handkerchiefs and aprons" sent from him, were effective in the overcoming of disease and evil spirits. At Acts 20:9-12, we read of the miraculous restoration of Eutychus. At Acts 28:3-6 is the incident of Paul's miraculous deliverance from the death-dealing viper, and in the same chapter at verses 8, 9 the healing of the father of Publius of Melita and many others. From this it is clear that Paul had "these signs" following him throughout all his ministry to the end of the Acts or "Pentecostal" period. But, having seen through my study, that the miraculous element continued, without diminution right to the end of the Acts, but was completely absent from the epistles written *after* the end of the Acts, and from the experiences of Paul and the others who are brought before us in those epistles, I naturally asked myself "Why!". Why did "these signs" cease when they did[2]? Surely some change must have taken place. Were there any clues to help and guide me? Yes! Not long after the end of the Acts an action took place which was the historical event underlining the change. In A.D. 70, after a terrible siege – if you desire you can read all about it in Book 5 of *The Wars of the Jews* by Josephus, - the invading armies of Titus completely destroyed the city of Jerusalem. The Lord had spoken and prophesied concerning this event (Matthew 23:34-38; Luke 13:34, 35; Matthew 24:1, 2; Luke 19:41-44; 21:20-24).

Now Jerusalem was the Jewish national centre from which the civil and religious life of the whole Jewish people was controlled. When the city and temple were destroyed, and the survivors of the siege were "led away captive unto all nations", all the Jewish national and religious privileges came to an end, and unto this very day, sometimes in a truly frightening measure, the Jewish people are suffering the fulfilment of their forefather's dread request "His blood be on us and our children" (Matthew 27:25). Thus Israel was "cut down" (Luke 13:6-9), or is "withered away" (Matthew 21:17-22), and has ceased to stand as a people before God, and "these signs" which had been specially given for Israel, also ceased.

---

[2] For more on this subject see *The Miracles of the Apostle* by Michael Penny – for more details see under *Further Reading* at the end of this eBook.

Running parallel with this outward historical event, was another which occurred a few years earlier and is reported in the closing verses of Acts 28. This event furnishes the true inner reason for the temporary casting away of this people. To enable you to understand and appreciate just what really happened, I must briefly repeat some of my former findings and so set the scene.

1st "Signs" and "miracles" were the confirmations of the preaching and teaching of the "gospel of the kingdom".

2nd After the resurrection, the apostles still expected the restoration of "the kingdom to Israel", and, not being otherwise instructed or commanded, continued the preaching and teaching of "the gospel of the kingdom" both at and after Pentecost.

3rd The Spirit was poured out at Pentecost, in order to fulfil Old Testament promises and prophecies, and in accordance with the promise of Christ as reported at Mark 16:15-18, to make the confirming "signs" possible to all who believed and were baptised.

Now it became quite clear to me, that so long as Israel were reckoned as "the people of God" (1 Peter 2:10; Romans 11:1, 2); so long as the gospel was "to the Jew first" (Romans 1:16; 2:9-10; Acts 3:25-26 and[8]); so long as appeals for repentance were directed to the chosen people; so long as the expectation of the return of Christ as King "to sit on David's throne" was a lively expectation (Acts 2:30 and[9]), so long as the "restoration of the kingdom to Israel" – (the "hope of Israel", Acts 28:20) – was a possibility, then "signs" and "miracles" continued.

Despite the awful fact that this very people had encompassed the murder of their promised King, despite their persecution of His messengers and their persistent hindrance of His message (1 Thessalonians 2:15-16), the offers of mercy and appeals for repentance continued for about 35 years after the crucifixion. This period of the re-offer of the King and the kingdom under the new covenant, was an answer to the prayer from the cross, "Father, forgive them, for they know not what they do" (Luke 23:34).

Throughout this period it can be seen that the leaders of the Jewish people in Jerusalem (Acts 4:1-2, 5-21; 5:17-40; 6:9-7:60; 12:1-3 etc.), and the leaders of the Jewish people in the various centres to which many, by providence and persecution, had been dispersed, (Acts 13:42-48; 14:2, 5, 19; 17:5-9, 13; 18:6, 12, 13; 20:2, 3; 21:27-31; 23:12-14; 28:23-29), refused their offered King and kingdom, and persecuted the various messengers. But the day came when the privileges, expectations, appeals and possibilities came to an end. This people "filled up their sins", and the threatened wrath of God fell upon them (1 Thessalonians 2:16). But the infliction of that wrath was, to begin with, almost unnoticed. Paul, having been taken a prisoner at Jerusalem (Acts 21:30), appealed unto Caesar (Acts 25:10, 11) and was eventually sent to Rome. On arrival there, he called the chief of the Jews to his place of detention (Acts 28:16, 17), and placed before them what proved to be the final opportunity of receiving what God had for so long offered this stiff-necked and rebellious people.

But alas, only "some believed" (verse 24) "and they agreed not among themselves" (verse 25). As a consequence Paul uttered the significant words which were first spoken by the Old Testament prophet (Acts 28:25-27; see Isaiah 6:9-10); and then announced the change, "Be it known therefore unto you, that *the salvation of God is sent unto the Gentiles* and that they will hear it" (Acts 28:28). "Salvation *sent* unto Gentiles"! Yes, this is the far-reaching change. Until this time Israel had been the "key" nation in all the purpose of God, the message of "salvation" had been "*sent*" to them (Acts 3:26; 10:36; 13:26), and other nations (Gentiles) could be blessed only on the basis of God's covenant with Abram, which appointed the chosen people as the channel (Genesis 12:3; 18:18; 22:18; 26:4; 28:14).

Until this time Gentile believers who were "blessed with faithful Abraham" (Galatians 3:9; read all Galatians 3), were but "wild olive branches grafted into Israel's good olive tree" (Romans 11:17-24), and so were made partakers of "Israel's spiritual things" (Romans 15:27). Until this time the statement of Christ to the woman at Sychar's well held, "Salvation is of the Jews" (John 4:22). But now! The chosen, key people, having refused to repent, and to co-operate in the purpose of God, are cast aside, and the purposes that hinged on them all fell into abeyance, and cannot be brought to fruition or completion until they, as a nation and people, are re-instated as "the people of God".

Some may say "Israel was surely cast away before Acts 28, for what about Paul's words to the Jews at Antioch (Acts 13:44-48), and at Corinth (Acts 18:4-6)". No! They could not have been cast away as a nation on either of those occasions, for Paul, writing his epistle to the Romans from Corinth *after* the events recorded at Acts 18:4-6 states plainly that then, *at the time he was writing* "God had *not* cast away His people" (Romans 11:1, 2), What happened at Antioch, at Corinth, and at other places during Paul's missionary journeys, where the Jews stirred up trouble and refused the message brought to them, was that those local "branches" of the nation "were broken off" (Romans 11:17), while the "olive tree" itself still stood, for Gentiles were being grafted into those very places where previously grew the "natural branches", which, because of the impenitence and unbelief, had been broken off (see Romans 11:17-24).

With this statement through Paul at Rome, the great change took place, and we read "the Jews departed" (Acts 28:29). In actual fact, that they "departed" is an understatement, for as the original word used indicates, they were "dismissed" or "divorced" – they became, as prophetically stated by Hosea, "Lo-ammi – not my people" (Hosea 1:9). The whole tree was now cut down, as Christ by parable foretold (Luke 13:6-9). So it is here, at Acts 28:28, that the great change takes place and a fresh administration (dispensation) of God begins.

From this point no more appeals were made to this people who for long had held the prior place amongst the nations; opportunities and appeals for their repentance were withdrawn, and amongst the outward changes that then took place – the greatest outward change being the destruction of Jerusalem that we have mentioned on earlier, I found that "these signs" ceased. No more "speaking with tongues", no more "miracles", no more "healings" etc.

As we have already pointed out, miraculous powers evidently left those who had formerly enjoyed and employed them, for they plainly departed from Paul, and to him, who was designated "the prisoner for you Gentiles" (Ephesians 3:1), was given a message not before made known. As "the Apostle and teacher of the Gentiles" (1 Timothy 2:7; 2 Timothy 1:11) Paul now becomes the vehicle of a special message which reveals truths that until then had been "hid in God" (Ephesians 3:5, 9; Colossians 1:26), concerning "the mystery", "the church which is His body", which was connected with a choice made "before the foundation of the world" and was not in any way related to, or dependent upon Israel (Ephesians 1:4). But that wondrous truth is not just now my topic.

In closing this testimony and study, let me state again that I found "signs" and "miracles" were connected with Israel, and were given to confirm the messages *to them* concerning their kingdom in all its phases, but when, because of their refusal to repent and believe these messages, "the salvation of God" was taken from them, as we see by the statement of Paul at Acts 28:28, then all the outward miraculous confirmations also ceased, and *there are none at all connected with the present ministry to the Gentiles.*

I looked back again at Mark 16, and say that the Lord's words were spoken to the eleven, (Matthias had not then been chosen to fill the place vacated by the suicide of Judas), and these men, who had companied with the Lord from the baptism of John until that day of His ascension, were representative of the nation of Israel, and as such had received all the teaching and training from the Lord in connection with the "kingdom of heaven", i.e. Israel's kingdom, and also had the definite promise of places of authority in that kingdom. *It was to these men, as representing Israel, that the promise of the outward signs was originally given.*

When this became really clear to me, my search for the reason for the lack of the miraculous in my own experience was at an end. I could plainly see that the particular message given through Paul *after* Acts 28:28, that is, *after* "the salvation of God" had been taken from Israel and had been "sent to the Gentiles", was a message specially for Gentiles, therefore it was for me, for I am a Gentile. I saw that this message to Gentiles, *as given through Paul's epistles written after the end of the Acts*, has no word in it for Israel as a people, or anything to say about Israel's kingdom or covenants, or confirming "signs" and "miracles", but points right away from such a line of teaching and practice, to "spiritual blessings" "at God's right hand", "far above all" spheres or places of blessing previously revealed or spoken about in the scriptures.

But I can hear some asking, "what about the 'healings' that have been authenticated from time to time, and that are being claimed by 'Pentecostal', 'Apostolic', and other such faith-healing groups and individuals in these present days? What about the 'speaking with tongues' that apparently does take place?"

To answer the second question first. Please consider it further discussed in the endnote number 6. Any glossolalia exercised by Gentiles today, is not a repetition or continuation of the true scriptural speaking with tongues, for that was in languages which could be identified and understood (Acts 2:7-11), and not in unintelligible gibberish such as is voiced in the modern supposed counterpart. Furthermore, we have yet to hear of any cases of unbelieving Jews being brought to blessing as a result, as should be the case if these occasions were the true speaking with tongues, as "tongues are for a sign", a sign-witness for "this people", i.e. Israel (1 Corinthians 14:21, 22; Isaiah 28:11).

As to healings. Medically inexplicable cases of sudden recovery from illnesses of all kinds, sometimes severe and deadly, are to be found throughout all history.[10] The power of mind over matter is often mistaken for the miraculous. One has only to study some of the mystic Eastern cults, or some of the practices of primitive peoples under the sway of witch doctors, or Spiritism (mistakenly called 'spiritualism' by many), or the modern application of hypnotism and mesmerism which is being increasingly employed in these days, often by members of the medical and dental professions, to be convinced that we as yet know but little about the powers resident within our own bodies. 'Healers' are operating who disclaim all connection with religious matters, and apparently they use their powers successfully.

That medically inexplicable 'healing' can and do sometimes take place under the emotional stresses of religious fervor and ecstasy, are no proof that such are a repetition or continuation of the scriptural "signs" "miracles" or "wonders", and I am sure that those who make such claims are mistaken – that they are genuinely sincere makes no difference.

A word of warning might not be out of place here. The credulity of those whose emotions are unduly stirred by religious fervor amounting to ecstasy, may easily fall prey to the operations of Satan, who, through his emissaries, during the approaching "last days" (2 Timothy 3:1-7; 1 Timothy 4:1-3) will manifest "power and signs and lying wonders" (2 Thessalonians 2:9), even as foretold by Christ (Matthew 24:24).

The scriptural "signs" and "miracles" were given as confirmations to accompany the preaching of "the gospel of the kingdom" – i.e. Israel's kingdom – and to accompany those who were blessed by that gospel or by the ministries of "the circumcision" Galatians 2:7-9), "the uncircumcision" (Galatians 2:7-9), "the reconciliation" (2 Corinthians 5:18), and "the new covenant" (2 Corinthians 3:6), which ministries ran parallel to the message and offer of the kingdom. As the offer of the kingdom to Israel, and the associated ministries of 'circumcision', 'uncircumcision', 'reconciliation' and 'new covenant' all ceased with the destruction of Jerusalem in A.D. 70 it logically follows that the 'signs' given to confirm and accompany those messages and ministries – (signs given initially and primarily for Israel) – also ceased.

My Gentile friend, what do you believe? That Israel's kingdom is still being offered? That you have a place and part in that kingdom? If this were really so, then scripturally, miraculous signs should follow and be confirming your faith and witness for the Lord. Are "these signs" following in your experience? You say they are not? Then do not any longer continue in a state of muddled uncertainty as to the meaning and outworking of this promise concerning "these signs", and also as to the place of many other parts of the Scripture which do not appear to be working out in these days. Simply apply this test. Was this Scripture command, injunction, exhortation or promise made or given *before* Acts 28:28, or *after*? Was it to Israel, and to people related to Israel and its kingdom, or was it *after* "the salvation of God" had been taken from Israel?

Acts 28:28 is the boundary at which the great change took place. It was then that the kingdom and covenant purposes, which had all been centred in and dependent upon Israel, gave way to the revelation and purpose of salvation for all, irrespective of nationality or covenants, and to the "mystery" concerning "the church which is His body", in which Israel as a nation does not play any part.

My friend, apply the test, "rightly divide the word of truth" (2 Timothy 2:15), and I can assure you, from my own experience and the testings of the Scripture over the 48 years since I found the satisfactory answer to my problem, that its application will solve your scriptural difficulties, and your experimental difficulties too. I sincerely pray that my testimony in this matter may prove to be a source of enlightenment and blessing to all who may read it.

Appendix 1 – To the Jew first

See Luke 24:47; Acts 1:8; 2:14; 2:22; 2:36; 3:12 (Jerusalem, Judea, Israel) Acts 3:25, 26 "unto you (Jews) first"; Acts 11:19 "unto Jews only"; Acts 13:45, 46 "The Jews saw ... filled with envy ... contradicted". Then Paul said, "It was necessary that the word of God should *first* have been spoken to *you*". Until well through the 3rd missionary journey Paul always used the synagogue, (if there was one in the place being visited) as his preaching centre, - see Acts 13:14; 14:1; 17:1; 17:17; 18:4; 18:19; 19:8 – and gave his gospel to "the Jew first". He acted upon this principle to the end of the Acts, as we see when he called the Jews together to his place of detention in Rome (Acts 28:17), to place before them what proved to be the last opportunity of repentance and acceptance of such blessing and grace as God, even then, was still waiting to bestow upon them.

Appendix 2 – Scriptural proof of the "lively hope"

We have stated the "hope of Israel", or expectation of the return of the Lord as "King to sit on his (David's) throne", was *at that time* a lively hope, and in support of this please see the following (along with the references already quoted). Matthew 24:36, 42, 44; John 21:22, - words of Christ hinting possible speedy return. Acts 3:19, 20 "He shall send Jesus".

Romans 13:11, 12 "Salvation near ... day at hand". 1 Corinthians 7:29 "Time is short", therefore unless absolutely necessary, do not marry. 1 Thessalonians 4:15 "we"; Paul *at that time* expected to be "alive unto the coming". 1 Corinthians 10:11 "The ends of the age are come" upon us, says Paul. 2 Thessalonians 2:1-7; 3:10-13; some evidently ceased working, thinking Christ's return imminent. Hebrews 1:2 "These last days"; 10:25 "the day approaching"; 10:37 "a little while ... He shall come". James 5:1-3 "Rich ... heaped treasure for last days"; 5:8 "nigh". 1 Peter 4:7 "end at hand". 2 Peter 3:3-14; 1 John 2:18 "It is the last time". Jude 18 "mockers" a sign of "the last time".

Lack of space prevents comment on these passages, but it is evident even from a cursory reading of them, that those who wrote and spoke thus, and those to whom this truth was ministered or written, expected that the Lord would return quickly to "restore the kingdom to Israel" (Acts 1:6), and so to bring in a new covenant blessing and grace. Thus the believing Christian Jews were directed to observe the Passover with the added significances attached to "This bread" and "This cup", "until" the soon expected coming of the King should be a fact. Thereupon, the annual feast would change character a little, it being partaken again in the presence of the King as He stated (Matthew 26:29; Mark 14:25; Luke 22:16, 18, 29-30; and see Ezekiel 45:21).

The "coming" deferred

But that soon expected 'coming' was not realised, the King did not return, - has not yet returned, though more than nineteen hundred years have passed! Why? Simply *because Israel as a people would not respond or repent.* "His own received Him not" (John 1:11), so that after many opportunities had been given them, the offer of the kingdom and the implementation of the new covenant was temporarily withdrawn, as seen from a reading of Acts 28:23-29, where, after Paul had "expounded and testified the kingdom of God ... out of the law of Moses and the prophets", only *some* believed.

Thereupon Paul utters the words which temporarily closed the door to this people Israel: "The salvation of God" ... is taken from you "and sent unto the Gentiles". Then "the Jews departed", - they were "sent away", "dismissed", or "divorced", and all the kingdom and new covenant purposes and hopes were suspended. The historical evidence of this was the destruction of Jerusalem in 70 A.D. (as prophesied by the Lord, Matthew 23:34-39; Luke 19:41-44; 21:20-24) which is a sure indication that Israel's national privileges and spiritual advantages were brought to an end, and the Jews were further dispersed "until the times of the Gentiles be fulfilled".

A new hope revealed through Paul

At the time of this temporary withdrawal of Israel's opportunities, Paul was given the revelation concerning "the church which is His body" – truth not before revealed in any way – making known purposes of grace completely unrelated to either Israel's kingdom or covenants. This truth of the "mystery" pertains to this present time, and in relation to *it* a new hope is given.

Appendix 3 – The last twelve verses of Mark's Gospel

Readers of this chapter will probably be aware that there is some controversy over the authenticity of the last verses of Mark's Gospel. The publishers feel that Appendix 168 of *The Companion* Bible is worthy of consideration.

Most modern critics are agreed that the last twelve verses of Mark 16 are not an integral part of his Gospel. They are omitted by T[A]; not by the Syr. Ap. 94 V.ii.

The question is entirely one of evidence.

From Ap. 94 V. we have seen that this evidence comes from three sources: (1) manuscripts, (2) versions, and (3) the early Christian writers, known as "the Fathers". This evidence has been exhaustively analysed by the late Dean Burgon, whose work is epitomized in Nos. I-III, below.

I. As to MANUSCRIPTS, there are none older than the fourth century, and the oldest two uncial MSS. (B and N, see Ap.94.V.) are without those twelve verses. Of all the others (consisting of some eighteen unicals and some six hundred cursive MSS. which contain the Gospel of Mark) there is not one which leaves out these twelve verses.

II. As to the Versions: -

    1.   The SYRIAC. The oldest is the Syriac in its various forms: the "Peshitto" (cent. 2), and the "Curetonian Syriac" (cent. 3). Both are older than any Greek MS. in existence, and both contain these twelve verses. So with the "Philoxenian" (cent.

5) and the "Jerusalem" (cent. 5). See note on page 136 of *The Companion Bible*.

2. The LATIN Versions. JEROME (A.D. 382), who had access to Greek MSS. older than any now extant, includes these twelve verses; but this Version (known as the *Vulgate*) was only a revision of the VETUS ITALA, which is believed to belong to cent. 2, and contains these verses.

3. The GOTHIC Version (A.D. 350) contains them.

4. The EGYPTIAN Versions: The Memphitic (or Lower Egyptian, less properly called "COPTIC"), belong to cent. 4 or 5, contains them; as does the "THEBAIC" (or Upper Egyptian, less properly called the "SAHIDIC"), belonging to cent. 3.

5. The ARMENIAN (cent. 5), the ETHIOPIC (cent. 4-7), and the GEORGIAN (cent. 6) also bear witness to the genuineness of these verses.

III. The FATHERS. Whatever may be their value (or otherwise) as to doctrine and interpretation yet, in determining actual *words*, or their *form*, or *sequence*, their evidence, even by an allusion, as to whether a verse or verses existed or not in their day, is more valuable than even manuscripts or Versions.

There are nearly a hundred ecclesiastical writers older than the oldest of our Greek codices; while between A.D. 300 and A.D. 600 there are about two hundred more, and they all refer to these twelve verses.

PAPIAS (about A.D. 100) refers to verse 18 (as stated by Eusebius, *Hist. Ecc.* iii.39).
JUSTIN MARTYR (A.D. 151) quotes verse 20 (*Apol.* 1. c.45).
IRENAEUS (A.D. 180) quotes and remarks on verse 19 (*Adv. Haer.* lib.iii.c.x.).
HIPPOLYTUS (A.D. 190-227) quotes verses 17-19 (Lagarde's ed., 1858, p. 74).
VICENTIUS (A.D. 256) quoted two verses at the seventh council of Carthage, held under CYPRIAN.

The ACTA PILATE (cent. 2) quotes verses 15, 16, 17, 18 (Tischendorf's ed., 1853, pp. 243, 351).
The APOSTOLICAL CONSTITUTIONS (cent. 3 or 4) quotes verses 16, 17, 18.
EUSEBIUS (A.D. 325) discusses these verses, as quoted by MARINUS from a lost part of his History.
APHRAARTES (A.D. 337), a Syrian bishop, quoted verses 16-18 in his first Homily (Dr. Wright's ed, 1869, i., p. 21).
AMBROSE (A.D. 374-97), Archbishop of Milan, freely quotes verses 15 (four times), 16, 17, 18 (three times), and verse 20 (once).
CHRYSOSTOM (A.D. 400) refers to verse 9; and states that verses 19, 20 are "the end of the Gospel".
JEROME (b. 331, d. 420) includes these twelve verses in his Latin translation, besides quoting verses 9 and 14 in his other writings.
AUGUSTINE (fl. A.D. 395-430) more than quotes them. He discusses them as being the work of the Evangelist MARK, and says that they were publicly read in the churches.
NESTORIUS (cent. 5) quotes verse 20, and
CYRIL OF ALEXANDRIA (A.D. 430) accepts the quotation.
VICTOR OF ANTIOCH (A.D. 425) confutes the opinion of Eusebius, by referring to very many MSS. which he had seen, and so had satisfied himself that the last twelve verses were recorded in them.

IV. We Should like to add our own judgment as to the root cause of the doubts which have gathered round these verses.

They contain the promise of the Lord, of which we read the fulfilment in Hebrews 2:4. The testimony of "them that heard Him" was to be the *confirmation* of His own teaching when on earth: "God also bearing them witness, both with signs and wonders, and divers miracles, and gifts of *pneuma hagion* (i.e. spiritual gifts. See Ap. 101. II. 14 of *The Companion Bible*) according to His own will".

The Acts of the Apostles records the fulfilment of the Lord's promise in Mark 16:17, 18; and in the last chapter we find a culminating exhibition of "the Lord's working with them" (verses 3, 5, 8, 9). But already, in 1 Corinthians 13:8-13, it was revealed that a time was then approaching when all these spiritual gifts should be "done away". That time coincided with the close of that dispensation, by the destruction of Jerusalem; when they that heard the Lord could no longer add their confirmation to the Lord's teaching, and there was nothing for God to bear witness to. For nearly a hundred years (see above) after the destruction of Jerusalem there is a complete blank in ecclesiastical history, and a complete silence of Christian speakers and writers.[11] So far from the Churches of the present day being the continuation of Apostolic times, "organised religion", as we see it today, was the work of a subsequent and quite an independent generation.

When later transcribers of the Greek manuscripts came to the last twelve verses of Mark, and saw no trace of such spiritual gifts in existence. they concluded that there must be something doubtful about the genuineness of these verses. Hence, some may have marked them as doubtful, some as spurious, while others omitted them altogether.

A phenomenon of quite an opposite kind is witnessed in the present day.

Some (believers in these twelve verses), earnest in their desire to serve the Lord, but not "rightly dividing the word of truth" as to the dispensations, look around, and, not seeing these spiritual gifts in operation, determine to have them (!) and are led into all sorts of more than doubtful means in their desire to obtain them. The resulting "confusion" shows that God is "not the author" of such a movement (see 1 Corinthians 14:31-33).

The Covenants

Introduction

Bible themes and doctrines are the "bones" of revelation and the attentive reader and student cannot fail to be impressed by the New Testament emphasis on "sound doctrine" (see Matthew 7:28; John 7:16, 17; Acts 2:42; Romans 6:17; Ephesians 4:14; 1 Timothy 1:3, 4; 4:6, 16; 6:1; 2 Timothy 1:13; 3:10; 3:14-17; 4:2-4; 2 John verses 9, 10). Not knowing the doctrines of the Scripture, the child of God will be, even when absolutely sincere, in danger of being "tossed to and fro, and carried about with every wind of doctrine, by the sleight of men and cunning craftiness" (Ephesians 4:14), the many well-intentioned believers who are drawn into modern cults, sects and heresies, and taken up with excessive emotional exercises, being sufficient proof.

On the other hand the divine purpose is that the believer and servant of the Lord shall have full equipment through an enlightened understanding gained by the study of the divinely inspired Holy Scriptures (2 Timothy 3:14-17), and thus be able to "give a reason for the hope that is in him" (1 Peter 3:15); "to speak the things which become sound doctrine" (Titus 2:1); to "preach the word, being instant in season, out of season", able to "reprove, rebuke and exhort with all long-suffering and doctrine" (2 Timothy 4:2).

It is not the prerogative of the writer to dictate what another shall believe, but rather to seek to set forth and point out what the Bible teaches. To be effective, faith must always rest upon a *personal* understanding of the Scriptures rather than on the teaching of men; a personal understanding of the Scriptures will eventuate in a humble acknowledgment of the One around whom all Scripture revolves, and about whom all the prophets testify.

Almost everyone knows that our Bible is divided into two major parts, viz: - The Old Testament and the New Testament. But why are these two sections of the Scriptures so named? We will seek to answer this question as clearly and briefly as possible.

As early as the middle of the first century, when writing to the believers at Corinth, Paul referred to the books of Moses as the "old covenant" (2 Corinthians 3:14 *R. V.* – the word for 'covenant' being wrongly rendered 'testament' in the *A. V.*), and when the Gospels and other apostolic writings gradually took their place as Scripture, they were distinguished by the usage of the phrase employed by the Lord at His last Passover feast, when, referring to His own impending sacrifice, and linking it with the prediction and promise made by God through the prophet Jeremiah (Jeremiah 31:31-34), He spoke of "my blood of the New Covenant" Matthew 26:28; Luke 22:20 – the word 'covenant' again being wrongly rendered in the *A.V.*). This usage appears to have been fairly well established by the beginning of the third century, when Origen spoke and wrote of "the Divine Scriptures, the so-called Old and New Covenants".

Towards the end of the third century, Jerome was responsible for the production of a Latin version of the Scriptures, translated direct from the Hebrew, etc., and in this translation (called the *Vulgate* i.e. the 'current' version) the Hebrew word for 'covenant' is rendered by the Latin word 'testamentum', hence our word for 'testament'. Briefly, all this means that the names of the two major parts of our Bible give the hint of an important truth and theme that runs through nearly all the sacred writings, for it is a fact that woven into the very texture of both Old and New Testaments is the idea and teaching of the covenants made between God and man. The doctrine concerning the covenants is indeed one of the major themes of the Scriptures. Unfortunately but scant attention is paid to it, so that it is relatively unknown by the majority of believers. In this chapter we will endeavour to set out the Scripture teaching of this rather sadly neglected truth.

The Old Testament Covenants generally

As we approach this subject we must be quite clear in our minds as to what it is we are studying. We must first of all lay a good foundation by asking "What is a covenant?".

A. In the English usage, 'covenant' indicates:
    1. A mutual agreement between two or more parties.
    2. Sometimes the document containing the details of such an agreement.

B. In the Hebrew usage, the word rendered 'covenant' indicates:
    1. An arrangement, league, bond or alliance entered into for mutual interest.
    2. The means by which such arrangement between the parties was attested by a sacrificial 'cutting' (see Genesis 15:8-18; Psalm 50:5; Jeremiah 34:17-20 and *An Alphabetical Analysis* C. H. Welch, Vol. 1, page 172).

3. Sometimes the written details of the arrangement or agreement. (Exodus 24:4, 7).

The etymology of the Hebrew word for 'covenant' indicates something that has been "cut". In most cases where "made a covenant" occurs, the literal rendering could read "to cut a cutting". The sacrifice used in confirmation of a stated covenant was cut, divided and set out in a particular manner, and the parties to the agreement then being entered into observed a special ritual of passing or walking through or between the pieces or parts so cut, divided and set out before them. (Genesis 15:17; Jeremiah 34:18, 19). In this way, most often before witnesses, they bound themselves to keep and observe the conditions of the agreement then made, by putting themselves, as it were, into the sacrifice and becoming part of it, and, as they walked between the cut pieces, saying, in effect, on the one hand, "For my part I guarantee to complete, fulfil or fill up the terms imposed upon me, and agreed to, even though it should mean the sacrifice of myself", and on the other hand, "May I be thus cut, divided and destroyed if I fail to keep the promise now made". Thus "to cut a cutting" imposed a most solemn obligation.

We are therefore upon quite stable ground here, and can say that in the Scriptures a covenant is a singularly solemn and binding contract or agreement between man and man, or between God and man, the terms of which were attested and ratified by sacrifice. In this study we have no particular concern with covenants made between men, but the interested reader will find instances of such in Genesis 21:22-23; 31:43-55; Joshua 9:3-15, etc.. (In Joshua 9, and on 15 other occasions, the Hebrew word for 'covenant' is rendered 'league' in the *A.V.*)

The Bible reveals the fact that it has pleased God to enter into arrangements, agreements or covenants with men. The declarations of these covenants or agreements contain the statement of a divine *purpose,* and most of them include an absolute *prediction* as well as an unbreakable *promise* as to the implementing of whatever God has designed. Reckoning from the time such agreement or covenant is stated or entered into, it looks forward to, and in measure anticipates, the future, and thus constitutes a message of hope, encouragement and assurance for those to whom it is addressed or with whom it is made.

There are eight matters of major importance concerning which it is recorded that God entered into agreement with man or men, and these eight occasions include the most vital facts of man's relationship to God throughout the history of the human race, as well as the most vital facts concerning Israel's relationship to God, and to the outworking of His purpose to make them the centre of the world-wide blessing. The eight occasions to which we refer are as follows:

1. God's declaration to man at the beginning. (Genesis 1:26-31; 2:16, 17).

2. God's declaration immediately after the fall. (Genesis 3:11-19).

3. God's covenant with Noah and his sons. (Genesis 8:20-9:17).

4. God's covenant with Abram concerning "the land", the "great nation", the world-wide blessing, and "The seed". (Genesis chapters 12-22).

5. God's covenant (through Moses) with Israel. (Exodus 20:1-31:18).

6. God's declaration to Israel concerning their return to "the land". (Deuteronomy 30:1-10).

7. God's covenant and oath to David concerning the establishment of "the kingdom". (2 Samuel 7:4-17; 23:1-5; Psalm 89:2-4; 20-37; Acts 2:30).

8. God's prediction, promise and purpose concerning the "new covenant". (Jeremiah 31:31-37).

It will at once be noticed that on three of the occasions we have cited, the actual word 'covenant' does not appear on the page of Scripture, but we mention these occasions because of the far-reaching consequences attaching to them, and because of their connection with the five major occasions upon which a definite 'covenant' was entered into. We propose a brief study of each of the instances of declaration and covenant listed.

Study of the eight major declarations and Covenants in the Old Testament.

1. God's declaration to man at the beginning (Genesis 1:26-31; 2:16, 17).

According to this record, God announced the conditions under which man was to live. This declaration and announcement was not a covenant in the true Scriptural sense, for it is not recorded that any sacrificial element was involved; there was no "cutting" to attest the terms stated. Nevertheless, there is here a sense in which definite agreement was entered into, for man was created to exercise "dominion", i.e. 'to tread down an enemy' (Genesis 1:26), and to "subdue", i.e. 'to have authority over' (Genesis 1:28) – to be, as it were, God's vice-regent "over" – all the earth and what we know as the lower forms of life, in order that the enemy who makes his presence known (Genesis 3), might not gain an advantage.

It would appear that Adam was placed in the garden of Eden and there acquainted with the conditions which were to form his side of the agreement. He was told (Genesis 2:15) to "dress", i.e. to 'serve' or 'care for', the garden, and to "keep" it, i.e. to 'take heed' concerning it. Surely here is the hint that man would be in danger or losing his "dominion" if he were not careful and watchful, and undoubtedly in this way God was warning him against the possible incursion of "that old serpent, called the devil, and Satan" (Revelation 12:9).

Added to this was the direct requirement of obedience (Genesis 2:17), with the judgment of "thou shalt surely die" as punishment for the failure to comply. So long as man could keep and observe these terms, which were in effect his part of the agreement, he was ensured of enjoying "dominion over" the earth, of a sufficiency of food (Genesis 1:29; 2:16), and had he partaken of "the tree of life" (Genesis 2:9), of life "for ever" (Genesis 3:22) under truly ideal conditions[12]. But this was not to be!

The sad story of human failure follows and "the serpent" seemingly triumphs, deceiving Eve (2 Corinthians 11:3; 1 Timothy 2:14), and through her causing Adam to act in direct disobedience (1 Timothy 2:14; Romans 5:19). In the hour of his apparent triumph "the serpent" is judged (Genesis 3:14, 15), this being the early pre-figurement of his seeming victory over the Son of God at Calvary, which was, in reality, his crushing defeat (Hebrews 2:14, 15).

This brings us to the second of the eight occasions when God entered into agreement with man.

2. God's declaration immediately after the fall (Genesis 3:11-19).

Rightly interpreted and understood, this record is the most wonderful proof that our God is "the God of all grace" (1 Peter 5:10). Read again, slowly and prayerfully, the whole passage from Genesis 2:15 to Genesis 3:24. So much that is completely unscriptural is foisted on to this passage, that we are convinced that the "old serpent" does indeed still operate, and most skilfully sees to it that the imaginings and errors of men are perpetuated, in order that deception and delusion might prevail (John 8:44; 2 Corinthians 4:3, 4).

First, notice that the dread penalty of immediate physical death, "Thou shalt surely die" (Genesis 2:17), was *not* executed. For the Scriptural meaning of "surely die" we need to examine the other occasions where the same phrase occurs, and note in what contexts it is used. When we do this, we find that it does not imply, and cannot be made to imply, 'physical, moral, spiritual and eternal death', such as so many declare it to mean, but that it can only mean the definite, immediate cessation of physical life.

The word "surely" is a word of emphasis, used to express and underline the inevitability of the act of occurrence being spoken of or written about. It occurs in connection with "die" or "be put to death" about 50 times in the Old Testament. Look at just a few of these occurrences. In Genesis 20:7 it is used in contrast with "thou shalt live", whilst at vs 3 and 4 the idea of "surely die" is expressed by "thou art a dead man", and "slay". Thus the words in verse 7 just mean that Abimelech would "surely die" physically. If "surely die" is to be understood as many insist it should be interpreted at Genesis 2:17, then the contrasting "thou shalt live" should be interpreted to mean that Abimelech should have physical, moral, spiritual and eternal life if he restored Sarah unharmed. Only to state this proves the absurdity of the argument. See a similar case at Judges 13:22, 23, where the phrase "surely die" is rightly understood by Manoah's wife as meaning "kill us", which can only be interpreted by "put to death physically". The reader should be convinced after comparing Numbers 26:65, with Numbers 14:29, where "surely die" is explained by "your carcasses shall fall in this wilderness", i.e. they would surely die and their dead bodies would rot in the wilderness. See also 1 Samuel 22:16; 1 Kings 2:37, 42, 46, etc.. All the references point clearly to the same conclusion, that "surely die" means just what the proverbial 'man in the street' would reckon it to mean: the definite immediate cessation of physical life and nothing more.

Now let us get back to the Genesis account. The guilty pair, Adam and Eve did *not* "surely die", forfeiting physical life "in the day" of their disobedience, for we are told that Adam lived until he was 930 years old (Genesis 5:5); Eve lived at least until she had borne Seth (Genesis 4:25), when she was 130, and undoubtedly she lived for many years after that, for Genesis 5:4 tells us that "after" the birth of Seth, Adam "begat sons and daughters" and there is no mention of Adam taking a second wife.

From Genesis 3:7 it is clear that some startling change took place in the outward appearance of both Adam and Eve as a result of the reception of the knowledge of good and evil. Just what this change was it is impossible to conjecture, but "the eyes of them both were opened" (Genesis 3:7), and so far as the reaction of both of them was concerned, shame, previously unknown, took hold upon them and they endeavoured to cover such evidence of their guilt as was then plain to see. True innocence fled, and the voice of the Lord, previously sweet to them, now struck terror into their minds (Genesis 3:8) – but let us repeat, they did not "in that day surely die". Why not? What happened?

Perhaps it can best be expressed by the New Testament statement, "Where sin abounded grace did much more abound" (Romans 5:20), for the guilty pair were reprieved. They were given hope. God entered into fresh agreement with them. Oh! What wonderful grace! The slaying of an innocent animal (Genesis 3:21), which pointed forward to the "One Sacrifice for sins" (Hebrews 10:12), provided the coverings which were the symbols of their deliverance from the immediate execution of the sentence of death which had earlier been imposed, and, as they listened to the terms of the fresh agreement, hope of a complete deliverance – the lifting away of the terrible shame, and the removal of the fearful dread and terror which had caused them to seek to cover themselves and hide from God (Genesis 3:7, 8) – rose high in their hearts.

They heard that the serpent who had beguiled Eve was to be debased under the curse of God, and that through Eve's "seed" the debased one was to be "bruised" i.e. crushed and conquered (Genesis 3:14, 15). This would not be accomplished without travail and sorrow, and the woman would be in subjection to the man (Genesis 3:16). And Adam? No more the comparatively easy task of carefulness and watchfulness in a specially prepared garden (Genesis 2:8) which provided its fruit for food without the labour and toil of its inhabitants (Genesis 1:29; 2:16). No! Adam, your part of this agreement will be, like the part of Eve, shot through with sorrow and hardship. Yes! You will live, if you labour on the ground which now shall bear a curse, and finally, when through the passage of the years the returning to the dust out of which you were formed and upon which, by labour and sorrow, you must live (Genesis 3:17-19).

Perhaps this declaration was indeed the first covenant, although not specifically so named. Genesis 3:21 tells us that an animal must have been slain, and perchance it was not only to provide the necessary coverings for the guilty pair, and thus to teach the way of sacrifice pointing forward to the "Lamb of God" – but possibly the agreement was attested by the "cutting" of that same animal. At least the two sides of the agreement are made plain. God says, as recorded in verses 15 and 16 "I will ...", whilst both Eve and Adam are instructed in verses 16, 17, 18, and 19 "thou shalt ...". This agreement in which God declares to man what his lot in life will be because of his sin, is in force to this present day, and will continue in force, until the outcome of the "bruising" of the Devil at Calvary is finally seen in the overthrow of the "seed" of the serpent (who is "the beast" of Revelation 13:17; 17:18, and 19:19-20), and the ultimate destruction of "that old serpent, called the Devil and Satan", as stated at Revelation 20:10.

3. God's covenant with Noah and his sons (Genesis 8:20-9:17)

Lack of space imposes upon us the utmost brevity, and we must of necessity pass over much that really calls for comment. Let us set the stage for the brief consideration of this, the first stated covenant of the scriptures, by pointing out that in Genesis chapters 4 to 9 is revealed the progress of the promised deliverance through the "seed" of the woman, and the increasing antagonism of the evil one against it, which is focused, "in the days of Noah" (1 Peter 3:19, 20; 2 Peter 2:4, 5), in an eruption of fallen angels (Genesis 6:1-4a), which so corrupt all the human race that finally only of Noah could it be said that he "found grace in the eyes of the Lord", for he alone was "a just man and perfect" (plain, whole, uncontaminated – "in his generations" – i.e. among the circle of his contemporaries (Genesis 6:8,9)). This wholesale contamination calls forth the judgment of God (Genesis 6:11-13), out of which only "eight souls were saved" (1 Peter 3:20), to become the progenitors of the human race now peopling the earth. Most surely, Noah is a type of "the second man" (1 Corinthians 15:45-47), in whom a fresh start – through resurrection, "a new creation" (2 Corinthians 5:17) – is inaugurated.

In dealing with the far-reaching details concerning the course and destiny of the human family as represented in the sons of Noah, God entered into a specific covenant with man, in it faithfully promising that there would be no additional curse upon the ground (the original curse in this respect, Genesis 3:17, was not withdrawn), nor would there ever again be a wholesale smiting of every living thing (Genesis 8:21; 9:11). There was the prediction and promise of an unbroken continuance of necessary light and darkness, providential temperatures and seasonal fruitfulness for the ordered regulating and sustaining of life (Genesis 8:22).

The "dominion" forfeited by Adam was partially restored (Genesis 9:2), and with it the establishing of the authority of human government on the earth. The flesh of animals was added to the fruitfulness of the vegetable creation to provide a sufficiency of food, with a restriction in respect of blood, which leads to the statement concerning the sanctity of life, and the responsibility for the taking of any life, be it animal or human (Genesis 9:3-6). Thus this covenant comprehends not only Noah and his seed, but every living creature (Genesis 9:9, 10). Through it the blessings and benefits of God were to be extended as widely over the earth as they possibly could be[13]. Thus was commenced a fresh era of human history.

The effects of this covenant obtain to this day, as also does the spectacular token of the "bow in the cloud" (Genesis 9:13), a perpetual reminder to God of the "everlasting covenant"[14] then entered into. In *Lesson Studies in Genesis*, Mr. Eugene Stock says, "There is never rain without a rainbow being visible if we could only get to the right spot to see it, but as God is always above the clouds, He always sees it". This is exactly what is stated in the Scripture, "The bow shall be in the cloud, and I will look upon it" (Genesis 9:16). It is not our sight of the token, but God's, that guarantees the permanence of this covenant, just as it was His sight of the blood token in Exodus 12:7 and 13, that guaranteed the safety and consequent deliverance of the Israelites at the time of the slaying of the firstborn, and the exodus.

The next covenant to claim our attention is that made by God with His "Friend" Abram (James 2:23).

4. God's covenant with Abram. (Details Genesis chapters 12-22).

A careful reading of Genesis chapters 12 to 22, reveals that there were eight separate occasions upon which God made specific promises to Abram. They are as follows:

> A. Genesis 12:1-3: - Commandment to Abram and promise of blessing in respect of "land", verse 1, "a great nation", verse 2, "a great name", verse 2, and "all families of the earth", verse 3.

> B. Genesis 12:7: - The land specified as "this land", i.e. Canaan, verse 7. An altar built.

> C. Genesis 13:14-17: - Promise of land renewed, verses 15, 17. Extent of land specified, verses 14, 15 and 17. Promise and prophecy concerning seed verse 16.

D. Genesis 15: - The making of the covenant. Promise of a son, "thine heir" verse 4. The seed, verse 5. Reiteration of promise of land, verse 7. The actual attesting of the covenant, verses 9-12, 17. Prophecy concerning "the seed" 400 years. 4th generation, verses 13-16. The land and its boundaries verses 18-21.

E. Genesis 17:1-22: - Renewal of promises and terms of covenant, verses 1-4, 6-9. Change of name from Abram to Abraham, verse 5. The sign of the covenant, circumcision, verses 10-14. Change of name Sarai to Sarah and blessing of Sarah, verses 15, 16. Renewal of promise of a son, verses 17-19a. Isaac named by God before birth, verse 19b. The covenant to be established with Isaac. Ishmael blessed, verses 19c-22.

F. Genesis 18:9-15: - Reiteration of promise of a son.

G. Genesis 21:12, 13: - The 'election' of Isaac (see Romans 9:6-18).

H. Genesis 22:15-18: - After the 'figurative' sacrifice and resurrection of Isaac (Hebrews 11:17-19), a renewal of original blessing and promise, and renewal of prophecies concerning "the seed".

There is a veritable goldmine of truth and teaching here, but we leave interested readers to dig into the most of this for themselves. We must restrict our comments to two central occasions upon which God made promise to Abram (i.e. D and E), where in the Scripture the actual word "covenant" is employed.

The covenant at Genesis 15.

Here we read for the first time on the page of Scripture that "the word of the Lord came" to Abram (Genesis 15:1). The phrase occurs frequently thereafter throughout the Old Testament, and is linked with "the Word" of John 1:1, 14; 1 John 1:1; and Revelation 19:13. The divine communications came to Abram "after these things" (Genesis 15:1), i.e. after the battle of the kings (Genesis 14:1-11) which had as one of its results the capture of Lot who had been dwelling at Sodom (13:12, 14:12); Lot's consequent release by Abram and his armed servants; Abram's meeting with Melchizedec, who was so blessed and strengthened him that he refused reward from the king of Sodom in any shape or form (14:23). It was after this refusal of earthly reward, which was to Abram the test of his faith in all that God had already promised to do for him and give to him, that the Lord shewed Abram that his attitude was 'right', for God Himself was to be his "shield and exceeding great reward" (15:1). Abram's reply calls forth the promise that he, Abram, himself would literally have a son (15:4), through whom there would eventuate an innumerable progeny (verse 5).[15]

It must be remembered that Abram was "seventy and five years old when he departed out of Haran" (Genesis 12:4), and that it was before his departure from Haran (Acts 7:2-4) that God had originally promised to make of him "a great nation" (12:1, 2). Just how old he was when God impressed upon him that the promise was to be taken in its actual and literal sense, we cannot say. That he had believed the greater part of the promises given previously (Genesis 12:1-3; 12:7-13:14-17) is evidenced by his attitude as seen in Genesis 14:23, noted above, but apparently he had not entertained the thought of a literal son of his own, for as he now states, he was "childless", i.e. barren (Genesis 15:2), and also "Sarai was barren" (Genesis 11:30; 16:1). But in face of, and despite the truth of this barrenness, "he believed the Lord, and He counted it to him for righteousness" (Genesis 15:6, and see Romans 4:13-25).

It was not until Abram had been brought to this place of unquestioning belief[16] that God entered into specific covenant, gathering up the previous promises as to "seed" and "land", making prediction concerning the 400 year sojourn in Egypt, and giving the reason for such seeming delay by the statement, "the iniquity of the Amorites is not yet full" (verse 16).

Note particularly that Abram was in "a deep sleep" (verse 12) when the covenant was made. He did not, by way of ratification, "pass between the pieces" of the sacrifice, but "a smoking furnace and a burning lamp" was seen to do so (verse 17), these symbolising and expressing the Divine presence. It was God alone who "passed between those pieces", thus taking and declaring the full responsibility for implementing the terms and promises of this covenant.

Between Genesis chapters 15 and 17 is the revelation of a fresh endeavour of the evil one to frustrate the production of the true "seed". From the human angle it is a sad story of the energy of the flesh seeking to bring about the promise of God, with the immediate consequences of strife and trouble – strife and trouble that find their echo down to this present day in the animosity and antagonism between Arab and Jew. But when Abram was "ninety years old and nine" (17:1) God renewed the covenant so let us see: -

The covenant at Genesis 17:1-22

Whether the statements of this chapter imply the making of an entirely fresh covenant, it is not clear. There is no hint of an animal sacrifice, yet there was a definite cutting of flesh. It would seem to be that after the lapse of 13 years from the birth of Ishmael (Genesis 16:16), during which nothing of particular note had transpired, God comes to Abram and reminds him that despite the fleshly folly recorded in chapter 16, despite the passing of the years and perhaps the forgetfulness of His servant, He, "the Almighty God", had not been unmindful of His solemn covenanted promises.

The Lord is thus revealed to his servant under a name not hitherto used – "God all sufficient" (Genesis 17:1). The root idea seems to be that of power and ability, and this was surely the message that Abram needed, for he was now ninety nine years old, and as Sarai his wife was ninety, the actual fulfilment of the promise concerning a son would appear to be absolutely impossible. Abram is at once given the charge to "walk before" this powerful and ever able God, and is encouraged to be "perfect", or uncontaminated (verse 1). Turn back to see what was said concerning events in the days of Noah about whom the same word is employed (Genesis 6:9). Oh yes! The evil one was still seeking to contaminate the line whence "the seed" – i.e. Christ should come, and at this crucial time it was well that Abram should be warned.

Now follows the repetition and reiteration of all the previous promises, with amplification. Both Abram's and Sarai's names are changed (verses 5, 15) and what we might call 'a covenant within a covenant', concerning circumcision, is added (verses 9-14). In obedience, the rite was performed "the selfsame day" (verse 23), and as circumcision is a cutting of flesh, it might well be that this act was employed in definite covenant attestation, as we earlier hinted.

In respect of the terms of the repeated promises and covenant we see, as at the call of Abram (Genesis 12:1-3), so this declaration also contains seven features under the same encouraging "I will". Examine these details more closely (Genesis 17:2, 6-8):

     1. verse 2 "I will make my covenant between me and thee".

     2. verse 2 "I will multiply thee exceedingly".

     3. verse 6 "I will make thee exceeding fruitful".

4. verse 6 "I will make nations of thee, and kings shall come out of thee".

5. verse 7 "I will establish my covenant between me and thee and thy seed after thee for an everlasting covenant".

6. verse 8 "I will give unto thee and to thy seed after thee, the land ... all the land of Canaan for an everlasting possession".

7. verse 8 "I will be their God".

Before passing from this fruitful field of study it would be as well to take a glimpse at Genesis 28:1-4, where the covenant promises are passed on through Isaac to Jacob. Here (chapter 28:1) is the warning again given concerning such action as would contaminate "the seed", then in verses 3, 4 we read the following:

1. "God all-sufficient (Genesis 17:1) bless thee, and

2. make thee fruitful, and

3. multiply thee,

4. that thou mayest be a multitude of people, and

5. give the blessing of Abraham to thee, and

6. to thy seed after thee.

7. that thou mayest inherit the land ... which God gave unto Abraham".

The terms of this "everlasting covenant" are thus passed on; we have "the seed", pointing back to the primeval promise (Genesis 3:15) and forward to the Redeemer (Galatians 3:16; Romans 9:5); we have "the land", "this land"; we have the "multitude of people" who were to be the "great nation" (Genesis 12:2), and it is not without significance that Genesis 46:3-4 reveals that it would be in Egypt, through the furnace of affliction, that the people would be welded together to be that which God had promised.

There are those who have doubted the historicity of the characters and events of these early chapters of Genesis: there are those who 'spiritualise' all the promises concerning Israel and its land, or are inclined to treat them as figurative and somehow link their fulfilment to the 'church', saying that the believers to today are "spiritual Israel", and that "the land", i.e. Canaan, finds its antitype in 'heaven'. All this in spite of the indisputable fact that some of the terms of these promises have been partially fulfilled during the past history of the chosen people. Over the past 50 years archaeology has furnished proofs of the literalness of the early characters and events as recorded in the scriptures. (See for instance *The Bible Comes Alive* and *The Bible is True* both by Sir Charles Marston, and *The Bible as History* by Werner Keller). Just as truly as there was a man who became the "Friend of God", so also will all the items of the everlasting covenant be completely and absolutely brought to pass. Not one jot or tittle of His word shall fail (Hebrews 6:13-20). Now we must briefly consider: -

5. God's covenant (through Moses) with Israel (Exodus 20:1-31:18).

In transmitting the three fold law (the commandments, Exodus 20:1-17; the judgments, Exodus 21:1-23:33; and the ordinances, Exodus 25:1-31:18) to Israel, God entered into a covenant with that nation. Although a detailed account is not recorded, no doubt the rituals of covenant-making would be observed by Moses on behalf of all the people, and in Exodus 24 we read how the people were identified with him as a party to the responsibilities that devolved upon them, in a ceremony where the blood of the sacrifice was "sprinkled on the altar, and on the people" when "the book of the covenant was read in the audience of the people", while they responded with promises of obedience to the requirements thus imposed upon them (Exodus 19:3-8; 24:3-8). The inspired commentary in the epistle to the Hebrews adds that the blood was sprinkled on "the book" as well as "all the people" (Hebrews 9:19). The great covenant promise is stated at Exodus 19:5, 6, that "if ye will obey ... and keep my covenant then ye shall be a peculiar treasure ... and ye shall be a kingdom of priest and an holy nation".

In the books of Leviticus, Numbers and Deuteronomy the stipulations which conditioned the covenant are expanded in greater detail as to their application.

It must be clearly understood and recognised that this covenant of the law did not replace or repeal the covenant made with Abraham; see Galatians 3:15-18. No! This covenant of the law, though in many of its aspects but passing and preparatory (2 Corinthians 3:7-11; Hebrews 7:19; 8:6-13), nevertheless had a major place in the unfolding purpose of God for Israel. Why was it given? Galatians 3:19 supplies the underlying reason: "It was added because of the transgressions" of the chosen people; because of their inherent proneness to murmuring, disobedience and rebellion. The law was disciplinary (Galatians 3:10), and educative (Galatians 3:23, 24), whilst its "blessings" (Deuteronomy 28:1-14) supplied the incentive to a people who were at best faithless and failing.

It is impossible, within the limits of this chapter, to set forth the teaching of this covenant of the law at any length. It was a moral code, teaching duty to both God and man; it included ritual requirements; it was a civil institute, and it was a revelation of underlying truth. Regarding as a "shadow of good things to come" (Hebrews 10:1), all diligent Bible students know that it contains much that is veritably precious, in the setting forth by type and picture, of the principles of the doctrines underlying redemption, atonement, forgiveness, justification, sanctification, substitution, access, service etc..

Though this covenant was made to depend upon the faithfulness of Israel, God foretold their failure and the suffering that would follow, including their scattering among all people and nations (Deuteronomy 28:58-68). History has confirmed the divine prediction as to the failure, the sorrow and the dispersion. This leads us on to the consideration of the next declaration.

6. God's declaration to Israel concerning their return to the land (Deuteronomy 30:1-10)

This looks forward to Israel's final possession of the land as originally promised to Abram and specified in Genesis 15:18-21. Nothing will hinder this blessing. Even Israel herself will be willing in the day of His power, regardless of what the modern Jew, or foe of Zionism may think or say. Neither Arab, Communist, Fascist, Roman Catholic, modernist or any other can or will prevent the time when Israel will be regathered into their own land to possess it for ever. At verse 3 of Deuteronomy 30, in the words "will return and gather thee", is the first prophetic hint of the 'second coming' of Christ, and of Israel's "gathering together unto Him" (2 Thessalonians 2:1). It is at the time of the Lord's return to earth that this declaration will find its true fulfilment. There are many other prophetic statements which underline and emphasize this declaration, see for instance Jeremiah 23:5-8; Ezekiel 37:21-28.

If you have just read, as we hope you have, the two passages referred to, you will appreciate that the predictions concerning the King who is to reign over them in the land, lead us to the consideration of the seventh of the eight occasions we earlier listed (idem page 104) as being important agreements, arrangements or covenants between God and man:

7. God's covenant and oath to David concerning the establishment of the kingdom (2 Samuel 7:4-17; 23:5; Psalm 89:2-4, 20-37; Acts 2:30).

By the terms of this covenant and oath, David is promised a royal lineage, a throne, and a kingdom, all of which are to endure for ever, and these are referred to at Isaiah 55:3 and at Acts 13:34 and "the sure mercies of David". Notwithstanding the fact that God reserves the right to interrupt the actual reign of David's sons or kingly descendants, if chastisement is required (verses 14, 15; Psalm 89:30-37) the perpetuity of this promise cannot be broken. From the day that this covenant was made and confirmed by oath (Acts 2:30) unto the birth of Christ, David did not lack for a son to sit on his throne (Jeremiah 33:19-21), and Christ, "Son of man", "Son of God", "Son of David", being the rightful heir, and the One who will yet sit upon that throne (Luke 1:31-33), completes the fulfilment of the promise to David that a son would sit upon his throne for ever.

It is fitting at this point that we should pause to draw together some of the threads of lines of truth which have so far emerged from our study, noting particularly such as have reference to God's chosen people and the outworking of His purpose through them.

We have seen that the first declaration to Adam was superseded by the second, and that the effects of the second declaration to Adam, as also those of the covenant with Noah, are in force for mankind generally to this present day.

The Abrahamic covenant and promises, through which Israel were singled out to be God's own earthly people, guaranteed to them an everlasting entity as a nation (Genesis 17:7; Jeremiah 31:36), and an everlasting possession of the land of Canaan (Genesis 13:15; 1 Chronicles 16:15-18; Psalm 105:9-11). To Abram, the Messiah had been announced, more or less clearly, as the promised *seed* (Galatians 3:16); to Moses, the Messiah is revealed as the coming *Prophet* (Deuteronomy 18:15-19); to all of the Mosaic age, through the "covenant of priesthood" (Numbers 25:10-13; Jeremiah 33:21; Malachi 2:4-10) and through the general teaching of the tabernacle services and sacrifices, Messiah is revealed as Priest. Now to David He appears, in addition, as *King*, and this Davidic covenant guarantees to Israel an everlasting throne (2 Samuel 7:16; Psalm 89:3, 4, 34-37), an everlasting King (Jeremiah 33:20, 21), and an everlasting kingdom (Daniel 7:14).

All that was required for these promises and covenants to find complete fulfilment, was the faithful response and willing co-operation of those whom God had chosen to be His representative people upon earth. Tragically, it was just in these features that they utterly failed. They were constantly faithless and disobedient, often rebellious, sometimes idolatrous; they miserably broke the disciplinary and educative covenant of the law and thus brought upon themselves the threatened curses and troubles. Has God then been thwarted in His purpose and plan? No! That could not be. In order that the plans and purposes of God with and through His chosen people should be made possible, He declares to them the terms of another covenant – the last of the eight declarations that we set ourselves to consider.

8. God's promise, purpose and prediction of the new covenant (Jeremiah 31:31-37).

Before we turn directly to this new covenant, we must get a clear picture of the background, although this will mean a measure of repetition. The "old" or "first" covenant of the law, was, as we have stated on page 110, in great measure passing and preparatory. It was necessary because Israel, although the elect nation, like the other peoples and nations of the earth, was sinful, disobedient and unbelieving. The Law was necessary because of these transgressions, and was intended to discipline and educate the nation in order that it might take the place God had planned, so making possible the implementing of the promises and covenants made with Abraham and David. Israel miserably failed and refused to be disciplined and taught. They broke the covenant of the law and suffered the consequences which God had foretold. They were besieged, persecuted, scattered and taken into captivity whilst their land was despoiled under the heels of oppressors.

Now it is upon such background that there comes the definite word of the Lord through the prophet Jeremiah (Jeremiah 31:3), "I have loved thee with an everlasting love; therefore with loving kindness I have drawn thee". What amazing love! Indeed "God is Love" (1 John 4:8). Through the prophet He says "Because of my everlasting love I will build thee again ... I will bring them from the north country and gather them from the coasts of the earth ... a great company shall return thither" (i.e. to the lands as promised to Abraham), "Behold, I will sow Israel and Judah with the seed of man ... I will watch over them to build and to plant" (Jeremiah 31:4-28). Yes! God will keep His promises, but in that day of His power, Israel will not be regathered under the old covenant of the law, which having already broken they would break again. No! God has some "better" method to bring into operation (Hebrews 7:19, 22; 8:6; 9:23, etc.). "I will make a new covenant with the house of Israel, and with the house of Judah", not on the old terms, for "I will put my law in their inward parts and write it in their hearts ... and they shall all know me ... for I will forgive their iniquity and will remember their sin no more" (Jeremiah 31:31-34).

These terms of the new covenant promise the forgiveness of Israel's former shortcomings and sins, and guarantee that the discipline and education of the law will be effective, so that "in those days", yet to come, Israel, His people, will be the "great nation" through whom "all the families of the earth shall be blessed" (Genesis 12:3), and over whom great David's greater Son will reign in righteousness (Jeremiah 33:14-17; Psalm 47; Zechariah 14:9, 16).

"But", you may ask, "just how is this going to be made possible, how can God write His law in their inward parts and in their hearts?". Ezekiel 36, amongst other prophetic passages, answers this clearly. Read from verse 21, "I had pity ... I will sanctify my great name. I will take you from among the nations and gather you out of all countries and will bring you into your own land ... Then ... will I cleanse you. A new heart will I give you ... *and I will put my spirit within you and cause you to walk in my statutes,* and ye shall keep my judgments and do them, and ye shall dwell in the land ... and ye shall be my people and I will be your God" (Ezekiel 36:21-28). Thus it will be that the new covenant will be made effective. The new covenant is the covenant of the Spirit, and in His Spirit's power God will utterly, completely, fulfil all His Word.

In concluding this section we desire to comment on the fact that there are many who consider and teach that the new covenant is 'the covenant of grace' which, they say, God has made with all who believe in Christ in this present day and age.[17] Now we say, without fear of contradiction, that to seek to apply the new covenant to believers *today,* is a serious mistake which leads to other mistakes and causes confusion; mistakes and confusion which prevent the believer from entering into and enjoying the blessings and privileges which God would make known to those who will accept and believe that He, in His Word, says what He means and means what He says. God said that He would make the new covenant with Israel and Judah (Jeremiah 31:31; Hebrews 8:8). He does not say that He will make it with any other nation or people. People of other nations, i.e. the Gentiles, could only be brought into the sphere of the new covenant as "wild olive branches, "grafted" into Israel's "good olive tree" (Romans 11:17-24). This was only possible because the promise of the forgiveness of sins was revealed as being for both the covenant people, Israel, and also for people of other nations. It was the revelation of this fact which perturbed Peter, and so "astonished" the Jews, at the time of the conversion of Cornelius, for as Peter then stated, the word of God had been "*sent unto the children of Israel*" and not to Gentiles and until that time it had been counted "an unlawful thing for a man that is a Jew to keep company, or come unto one of another nation" (see Acts 10, also note 18).

Nevertheless, Gentiles could not enter into those terms of the new covenant which spoke of the national restoration of Israel, and of the chosen people's elevation to the promised position of a "kingdom of priests". In these respects the Jewish Christians had much advantage over their Gentile brethren at that time (Romans 3:1, 2). Such Gentiles as were brought into the sphere of new covenant blessing during the Acts period, and those Gentiles who will yet be brought within its sphere when the promised kingdom is in operation, were blessed, and will be blessed on the ground of God's previous covenant and promise to Abram (Genesis 12:3), and then only on the basis of the forgiveness of sins, and because, in the Acts period, and in that time to come, Israel stood, and will then again be standing as "the people of God". The position of Gentiles enjoying anything of the new covenant blessing during the Acts period is clearly stated in Romans 11, a careful study of which will shew that the Gentile believers *were then* in an inferior position to the Jewish believers. Gentile believers are *not* being dealt with in this way today, for Israel is not standing as a nation before God, therefore Gentiles cannot be "partakers", or partners, with them, of "spiritual things" (Romans 15:27).

At the end of the Acts "the salvation of God" was taken from Israel (Acts 28:28), and the "tree" of Israel was "cut down", or is "withered away" (Matthew 3:10; Matthew 21:17-22; Luke 13:6-9 as betokened by the destruction of Jerusalem at A.D. 70. The new covenant, promised for and made with the nation of Israel, cannot now be in operation, and will not be in operation until, at the second coming of Christ, Israel as a people will be gathered again to their own land, and will become the "kingdom of priests" through whom the covenant blessing will flow out to other nations. In this connection, notice that the Gentile nations and peoples are, according to prophecy, to be subservient to the chosen nation when the kingdom under new covenant terms becomes a reality) Isaiah 60:5, 6, 10-14; 61:5, 6 etc.). If, therefore, the new covenant is in operation *now*, something must be wrong somewhere, for the Gentile nations are in no way subservient to Israel. No! The truth is that the new covenant is *not now* in operation.

The place of, and teaching concerning, the Covenants in the New Testament.

The man-made and artificial (though in many ways useful) designation of the two major parts of our Bible as 'Old Testament' and 'New Testament', causes many to have the idea that there was not only the break of about 400 years in the recorded history of the chosen people, but that there was also a break and change in both the doctrinal and dispensational positions as between the Old and New Testaments. The opposite is actually the case, for there is an unbreakable link and continuation of both doctrine and purpose. The doctrine of the Old Testament is joined to, and intensified by, the teaching of the New Testament. In the main, those to whom the teaching and ministry are directed are just the same in both Testaments. Old Testament teaching was directed to the chosen people, Israel, with the promises and prophecies of blessing through them to the other nations. The truth and teaching of the New Testament is first of all to that same nation and people (Matthew 10:5, 6; 15:24; Romans 15:8; Acts 2:5, 14, 22, 36; 3:12, 25; 11:19, etc.), and the beginnings of the out-workings of the promises and prophecies of the spreading of the blessing are seen, as many Gentiles are brought within the sphere of the covenants, or as Paul states it, are "grafted into the good olive tree", i.e. Israel (Romans 11).

We have said that there is a definite and unbreakable link between the Testaments. This is clearly seen in relation to the truth of the covenants that we have been considering. In the last written prophecy of the Old Testament we read, "The Lord whom ye seek shall suddenly come to His temple, even the messenger of the covenant whom ye delight in: behold, He shall come" (Malachi 3:1). In the fulness of time Christ came, "to perform mercy promised to our fathers and to remember His holy covenant; the oath which He sware to our father Abraham" declares Zacharias (Luke 1:72, 73).

The Lord Jesus, as "the messenger of the covenant", and as "the minister of the circumcision" (Romans 15:8), ministered to the covenant people, "the lost sheep of the house of Israel" (Matthew 15:24), and He directed the twelve chosen apostles to minister in exactly the same sphere (Matthew 10:5-7). They obeyed His instructions, as seen in the Gospel records, and as seen in the Acts, where they continued to minister to the "circumcision", i.e. Israel. Even as the sphere of ministry widened, the "twelve", and those who received their "gospel of the kingdom" (Matthew 24:14), and "gospel of the circumcision" (Galatians 2:7, 8), continued to minister "to note but unto Jews only" (Acts 11:19). This is also seen in the written ministries of Peter, James, John and Jude, who wrote to the Jews of the dispersion (1

Peter 1:1, 2 Peter 3:1; James 1:1, etc.). Paul also, though not of "the twelve", during his first ministry, which extended from his conversion and up to the closing of the Acts (including those epistles written by him during the Acts) exercised the "ministry of the new covenant" (2 Corinthians 3:6), and always took his message "to the Jew first".

Let us study this movement more closely. The Lord Jesus, as "the messenger of the covenant" (Malachi 3:1) and in order "to confirm the promises made unto the fathers" (Romans 15:8), was "born King of the Jews" (Matthew 2:2); was recognised as "the King of Israel" (John 1:49); was offered to Israel as "King of the Jews" (John 18:39, etc.), for He was, as we have seen (idem p. 116), the rightful heir to David's throne. "By the determinate counsel and foreknowledge of God" (Acts 2:23), the "King of the Jews" (Matthew 27:37; John 19:15) was rejected and crucified. At the Passover supper, just prior to His arrest, He referred to the sacrifice He was about to offer, and declared that the blood He was to shed was "the blood of the new covenant" (Matthew 26:28; Luke 22:20).

As we have earlier pointed out, every true covenant was attested by sacrifice, and under the Old Testament economy there was also a ceremonial "cutting" or "dividing" of the sacrifice, and a "passing between the pieces (or parts)" (Genesis 15:17; Jeremiah 34:18, 19). The rejected messenger, Himself the King, became the sacrifice, His blood became the token, and His flesh received the "cutting" (see Colossians 2:11; Isaiah 53:8), to seal, ratify and inaugurate the new covenant for Judah and Israel.

After the crucifixion and resurrection of Israel's King, Peter, on the day of Pentecost, offers the new covenant to the chosen people, using the "keys" to open to Israel the door of "the kingdom of heaven" Matthew 16:19; see Daniel 2:44), which, by their failure of a national repentance, they refused to enter. In his offer, Peter refers to the implementing of "the promise of the Father" (Acts 1:4), by giving of the Spirit as prophesied by Joel (Acts 2:4, 17, 38; Joel 2:28) – the Spirit, in whose power and operation the kingdom and new covenant were to be made effective, as we earlier pointed out (page 117-118). He speaks of Christ, as King, being raised to sit on David's throne (Acts 2:30, 31); he speaks of "the remission of sins" (verse 38) as promised for Israel (2 Chronicles 7:12-14), and covenanted to them by the terms of the new covenant (Jeremiah 31:34[18]).

In Acts 3, after the significant miracle of the healing of the lame man, (an enacted parable of what would be Israel's national experience if they would be repent, as called upon to do, and accept and enter into the proffered kingdom under new covenant terms), Peter, preaching still to

Israel, (Acts 3:12), points to the one who had been crucified and raised; he again calls for repentance (verse 19); he promises the speedy return of Jesus Christ as King, to set up the kingdom as spoken of by the Old Testament prophets (Acts 3:19-21; 2:30-36). He links all this with the *"prophet"* about whom Moses spoke (Acts 3:22), Deuteronomy 18:15-19), and with the covenant made with Abraham, which centered in and dependent upon the "seed" (Acts 3:25).

Now notice particularly to whom the calls for repentance and promises of blessing were addressed. "Jews, out of every nation under heaven" (Acts 2:5, 8-11); "Men of Judea and Jerusalem" (Acts 2:14); "Men of Israel" (Acts 2:22); "All the house of Israel" (Acts 2:36); "Ye men of Israel" (Acts 3:12). They were "men and brethren" (Acts 2:29); the descendants of "our fathers, Abraham, Isaac and Jacob" (Acts 3:13, 25), and "the children of the prophets and of the covenant" (Acts 3:25). This is surely, absolutely and distinctly Israelitish ground – what room is there here for teaching that Pentecost was the birthday of the "church" which continues to this present day? Oh! The confusion that is caused by not simply believing that God through His servants and messengers means what He says, and says what He means.

This unbreakable link with the Old Testament covenant truth continues throughout the whole of the Acts – yes! Right to Acts 28, where we have Paul testifying before the leaders of the Jews of the dispersion at Rome, and telling them "that for the hope of Israel", i.e. the covenant hope in respect of "land", "King", and "Kingdom", he "was bound with this chain" (Acts 28:20), while he seeks to "persuade them out of the law of Moses and the prophets" (Acts 28:23). Thus the Acts concludes on very much the same note as it commences. "Wilt thou at this time restore again the kingdom to Israel?", ask the apostles at chapter 1 verse 6, and Paul, testifying in the same strain, and founding his expositions and persuasions on the law of Moses and the prophets, declares "For the hope of Israel I am bound" (Acts 28:20) – exactly the same hope as expressed in the question of Acts 1:6.

Again we ask, is there any room here for the "church" of today, "the church which is His body" (Ephesians 1:22, 23; Colossians 1:24), which has no links at all with Israel's earthly kingdom, being concerned with a sphere of blessing "far above all" (Ephesians 1:21) where the members are already "seated in Christ Jesus" (Ephesians 2:6); "the church which is His body" which has no "covenant" promises behind it (Ephesians 2:12)?

The same covenant truth can be traced all through the epistles written by Peter, James, John and Jude, in the exercise of their ministry to the circumcision and the dispersed of the circumcision: it is also found quite prominently in those epistles written by Paul before the end of the Acts, when he was exercising the "ministry of the new covenant" (2 Corinthians 3:6).

Significantly, all the names and features connected with Israel's covenants – i.e. the Abrahamic, Mosaic, Davidic, and new covenants, are practically absent from those epistles written *after* the close of the Acts. Such references as there are in Paul's later epistles are mostly of a negative character so far as the covenants are concerned, and no positive covenant teaching can be derived from, or connected with, any of them. We trust that a study of the following list of names and features connected with the "covenants of promise" will help the reader to appreciate the statement just made. (These are set out on the chart displayed below.)

	Books connected with Israel's Covenants		Epistles written by Paul *after* the end of Acts. Ephesians, Philippians, Colossians, Philemon, 1,2, Timothy & Titus
Name or Feature	**# of Times Used**	# of Times Used	**# of Times used & References**
ABRAHAM	**46**	29	**Not once**
ISAAC	12	7	Not once
JACOB	**18**	5	**Not once**
ISRAEL-ITE-ISH	58	20	(2) Eph. 2:12; Phil 3:5.
SEED (ref. to the promise)	**10**	17	**(1) 2 Ti 2:8.**
LAND (ref. to land of promise)	7	1	Not once
Circumcise-d-ion-ing	**14**	32	**(9) Eph. 2:11;Phil 3:3,5;Col 2:11;3:11; 4:11;Titus 1:10.**
MOSES	59	20	(1) 2 Ti 3:8.
LAW	**55**	125	**(8) Eph .2:15;Phil 3:5,6,9;1Ti 1:7,8,9;Titus 3:9.**
DAVID	53	5	(1) 2 Ti 2:8.

JEW-S-ISH	**about 170**	**29**	**(2) Col 3:11; Titus 1:14.**
COVENANT-S, and TESTAMENT	7	25	(1) Eph. 2:12.
KING (ref. to Christ)	**37**	**0**	**(2) 1 Tim 1:17; 6:15.**
KINGDOM +	32	2	(1) Eph. 5:5 Kingdom of Christ and of God.
KINGDOM OF HEAVEN	**31**	**0**	**(1) Col 1:13 Kingdom of His Dear Son.**
KINGDOM OF GOD	61	3	(1) Col 4:11 Kingdom of God. (1) 2 Tim 4:1 His Kingdom. (1) 2 Tim 4:18 His Heavenly Kingdom.
+The Kingdom, A Kingdom, His Kingdom, Kingdom of the Father, Thy Kingdom, My Kingdom, My Father's Kingdom, Kingdom of our father David, Everlasting Kingdom			

[See *Appendix: Helpful Charts* for a variation of this chart plus another which gives further information.]

The statement by Paul recorded at Ephesians 2:12 is the key to unlock any difficulties in respect of the significant omissions of covenant truth from Paul's later epistles. There, i.e. in Ephesians 2:12, he categorically states that the Gentiles (the members of the nations or races other than the chosen nation, Israel), "are" (i.e. have been and are) "aliens from the commonwealth" (polity, manner of administration) "of Israel, and strangers from" (unacquainted or unconnected with) "the covenants of promise". The "covenants of promise" are those made by God with: -

1. Abraham, Isaac and Jacob ("the fathers"), wherein are promises respecting "the land", "the great nation", "the seed" etc..

2. Moses, on behalf of Israel, wherein are promises of the nation being constituted a "kingdom of priests", and of earthly enrichment and advancement, as rewards for obedience in law keeping.

3. David, wherein are promises concerning the everlasting king, throne and kingdom.

4. Israel and Judah, in the new covenant, wherein are promises of the forgiveness of former failures and sins; promises of empowerment by the Spirit, in order that the requirements of God shall be assured of fulfilment: promise that Israel, as the elect nation, should truly be His people and He their God, and promise of the miraculous, spiritual and abiding knowledge of God.

There remains to us the study of the scriptural position in respect of the covenants today, which we will set out in the next part.

The place of the declarations and Covenants today.

A. The Declaration after the fall, and the Covenant with Noah and his sons.

The whole world of men, since early days, has been, and still is, suffering under the terms of the declarations made by God, immediately after the fall, to the serpent, to Eve and to Adam (Genesis 3:14-19). The statement concerning Eve's "seed" (verse 15), has already had its initial, foundational fulfilment, through the death of Christ on Calvary. The final result of His unique work will not be manifested until the "seed" of the serpent (the anti-christ and beast of the Revelation) is dealt with, and the serpent himself is destroyed (Revelation 20:10).

New Testament teaching at 1 Timothy 2:11-15; 1 Corinthians 11:3-12; Ephesians 5:22, 23; Colossians 3:18. etc., testifies to the continuance of the conditions enunciated at Genesis 3:16, concerning the manner of life imposed upon all women from Eve's day. Secular history gives abundant proofs of the severity, often bestiality, with which this condition has been inflicted by sinful men, and despite the considerable alleviation consequent upon the spread of Christianity, the enlightenments of modern civilization, and the raising of the status of women in many spheres, the conditions of the statement to Eve still remain, and "the man is the head of the woman" for "the woman is of the man" and "the woman is for the man" (1 Corinthians 11:3-12).

The effects of Adam's original "transgression", "offence" and "disobedience" (see Romans 5:12-21), are felt by all men everywhere. Thorns and thistles, weeds and wild growth, spring readily from the ground that is cursed. If left to themselves, previously highly cultivated food-producing trees, shrubs and plants tend to revert to the 'wild' or 'bramble' state. Work, as the necessary adjunct to life, is universally recognised (2 Thessalonians 3:10-12).

With the transmitted knowledge of good and evil, the propensity to sin has passed like a virus through the whole human race, and the resultant penalty, first announced to Adam, "thou shalt surely die", has "passed upon all men for that all have sinned" (Romans 5:12). The ever increasing cemetery grounds are silent yet stem reminders of the truth that "dust thou art and unto dust shalt thou return" (Genesis 3:17-19).

As we have stated concerning the course and destiny of the human family in section 3 of this chapter, the continuance of the beautiful, spectacular rainbow in the heavens caused by the light from the sun being refracted, reflected and dispersed as it passes through the myriad drops of falling rain and thus made visible as a coloured arc, is still token to God in respect of His gracious covenant promise to "all flesh" (human and other living creatures) that the "waters shall no more become a flood to destroy" – as they did in Noah's day – "all in whose nostrils was the breath of life, and every living substance" (Genesis 9:15; 7:21-23).

Many find difficulties here, saying that Noah's flood could not have encompassed the whole of the earth's globe, and further, that such floods as have periodically brought dire destruction and death to tremendous areas of the valley of the Yang-se-kiang river in China, and similar flood conditions in other parts of the world, must have approximated both the extent, and the results of the flood of Noah's day, therefore that the covenant promise has been broken! But a careful reading of the Scriptures reveals:

> 1. That in those days the landmass of the earth was all in one place (Genesis 1:9, 10).
>
> 2. That as was the case for some many years after the flood, so also before it, men were all of one speech and language, and as a consequence the whole human family was congregated in one, possibly comparatively small, portion of that land mass. Archaeologists have found indisputable evidence of Noah's flood in the region which is now known as the valleys of the Euphrates and Tigris rivers. (See *The Bible Comes Alive* and *The Bible is True* both by Sir Charles Marston, also *The Bible as History* by Werner Keller).
>
> 3. That is was not for many years after the flood, when the new human family, springing from Noah and his sons, had reached large proportions, that, because of the renewal of Godlessness and lawlessness the Lord saw fit, a) first to confound the then common

speech and language, b) then to scatter the progenies of Shem, Ham and Japheth the one from the other, (Genesis 11:1-9,[19]), c) finally to "divide" the earth, in the days of Peleg (Genesis 10:25; 11:16-19), who lived at the time of the building of the tower of Babel. It was thus, through the "dividing" of the earth (Genesis 10:25) by what must have been a terrific seismic disturbance (which would account for many of the remarkable geological 'faults' in the earth's crust), that the geography of the globe, as we know it today, was for the most part brought into being.

A consideration of these biblical statements and facts supplies the answers to all the problems in respect of the flood, and preserves intact the gracious covenant promise given to Noah and his sons, and through them to "all flesh: even unto this present day.

B. The Covenants of promise

As we have set out above, it is beyond dispute that the covenant with "all flesh" through Noah, and the declaration to Adam after the fall, are both still in force today. But what of the other covenants and declarations we have previously considered. Are they still being actively forwarded today? Just what happened in respect of those far-reaching promises to Abraham, to Israel through Moses, to David, and to Israel through the prophets?

Those who will accept and believe what they read in the inspired Scriptures, will clearly see, as we have earlier declared, that these "covenants of promise" were in the forefront of the outworking of the counsel of God *right to the last chapter of the Acts.* Remember too, that the historical period covered by the Acts includes such truth and teaching as is contained in the epistles written during that time, those epistles being from Peter, John, James and Jude, who ministered to "the circumcision" (Israel) both in their homeland and in dispersion, along with the first seven epistles of Paul to the Galatians, Thessalonians, Hebrews, Corinthians and Romans, while he was ministering the "new covenant" (2 Corinthians 3:6) and "reconciliation" (2 Corinthians 5:18), going always "to the Jew first" and afterward to the Gentiles, and endeavouring to bring them together in the purpose of God as promised to Abraham (Galatians 3:8, 9, 14 – read whole of Galatians 3).

It is also well to note that all through the same period, covered by the Acts and the epistles as stated above, the "signs", as promised to and by Moses and the prophets, as being for Israel and to Israel (Deuteronomy 4:33-40; Isaiah 28:11; Jeremiah 32:20), miracles, accompaniments of the outpouring of the Spirit (Joel 2:28; Mark 16:15-18; Acts 2:17 etc.), also continued unabated (Acts 2:43; 4:30; 5:12;8:13; 14:3 etc.; Romans 15:18, 19; 1 Corinthians 14:22; 2 Corinthians 12:12; Hebrews 2:3, 4 etc.).

But what happened after the closing period covered by the Acts? Within a short time the invading hordes of Titus encompassed Jerusalem and destroyed it, even as foretold by the Savior (Matthew 23:34-39; Luke 19:41-44; 21:20-24) and Israel's "tree" was "cut down" (Luke 13:6-9), or "withered away" (Matthew 21:17-22).

This historical act of the destruction of Jerusalem was the outward and visible token of the truth spoken a few years earlier by Paul, as recorded in Acts 28:28, that the "Salvation of God" was taken from Israel and "sent unto the Gentiles". That statement is the great and only reason why there is no positive mention of covenants, or the names and features connected with the covenants, in that portion of the Scriptures written by Paul *after* Acts 28. See the chart just above, and notice that any positive connection with the covenants of promise (to Abraham, through Moses, to David, or in relation to the new covenant) is completely missing from Paul's later epistles.

As added evidence consider this also. Miracles, signs and other miraculous features likewise ceased at the same time. Abundant and conclusive proof of this can readily been seen by noting what happened in this direction to Paul himself. At Acts 19:12 we read that "handkerchiefs and aprons" taken from Paul's body, were sufficient to overcome disease and evil spirits; at Acts 20:9, 10 we read of the miraculous restoration of Eutychus; at Acts 28:3-6 the incident in respect of the death-dealing viper, and at 28:8, 9, of the healing of the father of Publius, and many others.

It is clear that Paul performed miracles and healings right to the end of the Acts period, thus proving, and carrying out the promise voiced correspondingly clearly evident that *after* Acts 28 there is a complete change, for at Philippians 2:25-30 we read of the serious illness of Epaphroditus, even when staying with Paul, who clearly made no attempt to use miraculous powers to heal or cure him.

Then again, at 1 Timothy 5:23, Paul instructs Timothy about physical weakness – why did he not send a handkerchief or other means of transmitting healing and strengthening? Moreover at 2 Timothy 4:20, the record of the sickness of Trophimus is added testimony to the fact that miraculous powers must have ceased.

If you have followed this study thus far, there will hardly be need to ask why these evident changes took place. The answer is clear and plain to those who will believe what is written. The "covenants of promise", and all the miraculous accompaniments – which were God's tokens to the fact that He was dealing with and through His own chosen people – fell into abeyance and ceased to operate from the time of the decisive statement through Paul, when the Jews "departed", or more accurately "were dismissed", or "divorced", thus becoming "Lo-ammi – not my people" (Acts 28:25-29; Hosea 1:9).

From the call of Abraham up until the end of Acts, Israel were, says God, "My people" (Romans 11:1, 2; 1 Peter 2:10). They were God's "key" people, and in accordance with the "covenants of promise" He was seeking to work out the purpose of grace for "all the families of the earth", in which Israel was to have the pre-eminent place. But Israel, as a people, refused to co-operate; refused to "repent" or "turn" as requested. Not only had they the most prominent part in the crucifixion of their "King"; not only did they consistently refuse the offers of mercy and forgiveness, and the possibility of "perfect soundness" as pictured in Acts 3:1-16, but they persecuted the apostolic messengers, and did all they could to hinder the purpose of God to bring blessing to the Gentiles, which, says Paul in 1 Thessalonians 2:14-16, was a "filling up of their sins", and that "the wrath of God is gathering over their heads".

Thus finally, about thirty five years after the crucifixion of Christ (thirty five years of continued offers of grace and blessing to this stubborn nation), it was clear that was God was "stretching forth His hands to a disobedient and gainsaying people" (Isaiah 65:2; Romans 10:21, and read all Romans 9, 10 and 11 to see what was Israel's position up to the end of the Acts), and the wrath of God, which had been gathering over their heads, finally fell. The 'key' people "received Him not" (John 1:11) and as intimated by Paul the opportunity of "hearing, seeing and understanding", was taken from them (Acts 28:26-28), and as we have stated before, "the salvation of God" was "sent unto the Gentiles".

It logically follows that all the covenant purposes and plans in which Israel as the 'key' people were to take prior place, could not possibly be worked out or made good. Such purposes and plans will not be taken up again and worked out until "the times of the Gentiles are fulfilled" (Luke 21:24). Then the "covenants of promise" will again be to the fore, when Jerusalem is utterly freed from Gentile domination, and a rebuilt city will be the centre for the regathered Israeli people.

C. Truth for Today – Not connected with or dependent upon any covenants.

Until such true re-gathering of Israel takes place, and the "covenant" purposes are then continued, certain other specific purposes of God are being brought to fruition.

1) Through the declaration of the world-embracing love of God[20] and by means of the "whosoever" invitation *made plain in the Gospel which John wrote after the close of the Acts*, God is calling out "other sheep, not of Israel's fold" (John 10:16). These "others" are vaguely hinted at by the prophet Isaiah (Isaiah 56:8), and, we believe, will be the "guests" at the marriage supper as spoken of in the parable by the Lord (Matthew 22:1-14). This "whosoever" invitation through John accords with, and is proclaimed on the basis of "the gospel of the grace of God" as intimated and proclaimed by Paul (see Acts 13:38, 39; Romans 3:20-28 etc.; Ephesians 2:8-9), with its basic doctrines of justification by faith alone, and redemption through "His blood", and thus answers the need of all men for "life" in place of the "condemnation" and "death" that have spread to all, consequent upon Adam's "transgression", "offence" and "disobedience".

2) Running parallel with this offer of full and free salvation for all, is a *further special ministry, addressed to believers, through those epistles written by Paul after the end of the Acts.[21]*. In these epistles the truth concerning "the mystery" (Ephesians 3:3) is made known, a special purpose of the "exceeding riches of His grace", which had not previously been revealed in any way, either by type or teaching, prophecy or preaching, throughout the Old Testament or in the New Testament up to the end of the Acts. This special purpose, the "administration of the grace of God" given to Paul for us Gentiles (Ephesians 3:1, 2 etc.), is to "build up the body of Christ" (Ephesians 4:12) and to reveal Christ as "the head over all things to the church which is His body" (Ephesians 1:22, 23). We say that this truth was not previously hinted at, for Paul claims that this special revelation was originally given exclusively to him – see Ephesians 3 where in verse 2 we read of the "administration ... given me to youwards"; verse 3 "by revelation ... made known unto *me*"; verse 8 "Unto *me* ... that *I* should preach among the Gentiles", and at Colossians 1 where in verses 24-27 he voices the same claim. Coupled with this is the further claim that this special truth "had been *hid in God* from the beginning." (Ephesians 3:9); *"In other ages"* it *"was not made known"* (Ephesians 3:5); it was *"the mystery which hath been hid from the ages and the generations, but now ... made manifest"* (Colossians 1:26). Moreover Paul further claims, at Colossians 1:25; that this revelation and ministry to and

through him, was given "to fulfil the word of God", that is, to 'fill full' or 'complete' the revelation of the redemptive purposes.

This most blessed truth of "the church ... His body" had been kept secret – "hid in God" – until revealed to and made known by Paul. Even when declared it was, and still is, "the mystery", in that it is made known only to those who, because of His foreknowledge, God has "chosen in Christ *before the foundation of the world*, according to the good pleasure of His will" (Ephesians 1:4, 5).[22]

Neither of these two present purposes of God are dependent upon Israel, or upon the covenants made with Israel, in any way. Those who believe the gracious gospel of love and grace which is personified in "Christ the Son of God" are made partakers of "life through His name" (John 20:31), without any reference to covenants, or Israel. Likewise, those saved ones who give acknowledgement to the truth of "the mystery", are blessed, not "with faithful Abraham", as was the case *before* Acts 28:28 (see Galatians 3:7, 9, 14, 29), but are blessed "in heavenly places in Christ" (Ephesians 1:3), and are given the hope, not of the covenant promised "Jerusalem which is from above" (see Galatians 4:22-31; Hebrews 11:8-16), the Bride-city which is to come "down out of heaven" (Revelation 21:10-27), or of participation in an earthly kingdom, but they are directed to consider and look for the "hope of His calling" (Ephesians 1:18 etc.), which is "the high calling of God in Christ Jesus" (Philippians 3:14), "far above all" (Ephesians 1:20, 21), and which will be fully and gloriously realised "when Christ who is our life shall appear and we shall appear with Him in glory" (Colossians 3:4; Titus 2:13).[23] *No* mention here of covenants, of Abraham, Moses, David, or of Israel, in any shape or form.

We are tempted to continue pointing out the wondrous blessings connected with the revelation of "the mystery", but our space limit has already been passed. We must conclude our study, praying that the truths concerning the covenants of the Scripture have been sufficiently disclosed to point the interested reader along the path of blessing which opens when it is fully realised that the present ministries of the "whosoever believeth" gospel message to the unsaved, as presented through the gospel of John, which was written *after* the end of the Acts, and the truth presented to "the saints and faithful" in those seven epistles of Paul which were also written *after* the end of the Acts (i.e. Ephesians, Philippians, Colossians, Philemon, 1 and 2 Timothy and Titus), are completely severed from all the national features and dispensational truth relating to those with whom the "covenants of promise" were made. The special truths connected with the outworking of "the purpose of the ages" (Ephesians 3:11) for this present time, are directed specifically to the whole world of men – Gentiles, who are "strangers from the covenants of promise" (Ephesians 2:12).

May "the eyes of our understanding be enlightened, that we may know the hope of His calling, the riches of the glory of His inheritance in the saints, and the exceeding greatness of His power to usward who believe", that we may "press toward the mark of the prize of the high calling of God in Christ Jesus"; (Ephesians 1:18, 19; Philippians 3:14).

The Lord's Table

A Scriptural Study

And it came to pass, when Jesus had finished all these sayings, he said unto His disciples, "Ye know that after two days is the feast of the Passover, and the Son of man is betrayed to be crucified" ... Now the first day of the feast of unleavened bread the disciples came to Jesus, saying unto Him. "Where wilt thou that we prepare for thee to eat the Passover?" And He said, "Go into the city to such a man, and say unto him 'The Master saith, My time is at hand; I will keep the Passover at thy house with my disciples'". And the disciples did as Jesus had appointed them; and they made read the Passover.

Now when the even was come, He sat down with the twelve. And as they did eat, He said, "Verily I say unto you that one of you shall betray me". And they were exceeding sorrowful, and began every one of them to say unto Him, "Lord, is it I?" And He answered and said, "He that dippeth his hand with me in the dish, the same shall betray me. The Son of man goeth as it is written of Him: but woe unto that man by whom the Son of man is betrayed! It had been good for that man if he had not been born". Then Judas, which betrayed Him, answered and said, "Master, is it I?" He said unto him, "Thou hast said".

And as they were eating Jesus took bread, and blessed it, and brake it, and gave it to His disciples, and said "Take, eat; this is my body." And He took the cup, and gave thanks, and gave it to them, saying, "Drink ye all of it; for this is my blood of the new testament, which is shed for many for the remission of sins. But I say unto you, I will not drink henceforth of this fruit of the vine, until that day when I drink it new with you in my Father's kingdom".

And when they had sung a hymn, they went out into the Mount of Olives (Matthew 26:1-2; 17-30).

The Lord's Table – scope of study

In this study of the Lord's Table we intend to consider every relevant reference throughout the scriptures, so that our faith and consequent practise may rest upon the scriptures of truth, and not on tradition, church history, custom or sentiment. We will deal with the subject under two principal lines of enquiry:-

A. The Roots of the Lord's Table in the Old Testament.

This, in the main, will be a consideration of the prominent and important phrases and words used in the New Testament records of this 'ordinance', which link it with the Old Testament.

B. The Records of the Lord's Table in the New Testament.

Each scripture passage in the New Testament where mention made of this ordinance, or from which any teaching concerning it is to be gathered, will be examined. To deal with the subject in this fashion will be, we are sure, scrupulously fair, and should give the interested reader or student all the necessary information to enable him to form his own opinion as to whether our conclusions in this matter are correct. Our terms of reference demand a wide enquiry, consequently we will have to omit much which is of a secondary nature, and leave te interested student to pursue such secondary matters as he so desires.

A. The Roots of the Lord's Table in the Old Testament.

Even a quick glance through those portions of the scriptures in the Gospels of Matthew, Mark and Luke, and in Paul's first Epistle to the church at Corinth, where details of this ordinance of the Lord's Table are recorded, will make evident five prominent phrases, which we must take into consideration before we can hope to form any clear picture of its real significance, or come to any firm conclusion as to its place in our worship in these present days. The prominent phrases are: -

1. The Passover
2. The New Testament
3. "My Blood"
4. The Kingdom
5. The Twelve

Each of these phrases will take us back to the Old Testament Scriptures.

1. The Passover

"In two days the feast of *the Passover* (Matthew 26:2); "Prepare for thee to eat *the Passover* (26:17); "I will keep the Passover" (26:18); "Made ready *the Passover*" (26:19; see also Mark 14:1, 12, 14, 16; Luke 22:1, 7, 8, 11, 13, 15; John 11:55; 12:1; 13:1 and 1 Corinthians 5:7, 8). Now please note particularly from Matthew 26, "keep the Passover", "made ready the Passover", (verses 18, 19) "He sat down with the twelve", (verse 20 "as they did eat"; (verse 21) "as they were eating" (verse 26). What was it that was made ready, what as it they were eating? Why! *the Passover*. At Mark 14:18, 22 and at Luke 22:8, 11, 15, the same words are employed, so that "in the mouth of two or three witnesses" it is established beyond doubt that it was whilst partaking of the articles prepared for the Passover; during the actual celebration and eating of the Passover, that the incidents lifted out and now called "The Lord's Table", "The Lord's Supper", "The Last Supper", "The Communion", "The Eucharist" and/or "The Mass"; took place.

"The Bread" and "the Cup" were part of "the Jews Passover" (John 11:55), and not an addition to the Passover as some say. Granted, a significance additional to the original meaning attaching to this particular "bread" and "cup" was given to them by that which the Lord said about them on that occasion, but nevertheless it remains that what was done by Him, in taking the bread and cup, was the usual procedure at each Passover, and this we hope to display more clearly later in our study.

As these particular incidents were a part of the Passover, a short study of the origin, and of some of the features of this feast is called for, as this will shed light on several points relative to the Lord's Supper.

On the night that God took the children of Israel out of Egypt, the first observance of this commemorative feast was held. Explicit detail is given in Exodus chapter 12, which chapter should just now be carefully read. Having read Exodus 12 we are ready to ask and answer some questions about this special feast.

a. *What was the Passover?* "This day shall be a memorial", "observe this in (or throughout) your generations", "Observe this ordinance for ever" (Exodus 12:14, 17, 24). Here there is a threefold command. This meal was to be "a memorial", i.e. an act of remembrance "through your generations" "for ever", i.e. a perpetual reminder.[24]

b. *Who was to eat of it?* "All the congregation of Israel" (Exodus 12:3 etc.) "No stranger ... no uncircumcised person" (Exodus 12:43-49). No uncircumcised person, i.e. no Gentile (unless ceremonially circumcised when becoming a Jewish religious proselyte).

c. *Where was it to be observed?* "When *ye be come to the land* which the Lord thy God giveth thee ... *ye shall keep this service"* (Exodus 12:25 see also Deuteronomy 16:1-8). After the initial observance in Egypt, and one special observance commanded in the wilderness (Numbers 9:1-5), the Passover was to be observed in, and was specially reserved for "*the land*", i.e. Canaan, or Palestine.

d. *Why was it to be observed?* "What mean ye"? ... "It is the Lord's Passover ... passed over our houses ... smote Egyptians and delivered our houses" (Exodus 12:26, 27), "To be observed *for bringing them out from Egypt*" (Exodus 12:42, see also 13:3; 13:8-10). It was to be observed because of a deliverance, a "bringing out from" "bondage"

e. *When was it to be observed?* "This day ye came out in the month Abib" (Exodus 13:4, see also 23:15; Deuteronomy 16:1). "In the tenth day of this month ... take ... a lamb ... keep it until the fourteenth day of the same month ... and Israel shall kill it ... and they shall eat ... that night ... the Lord's Passover" (Exodus 12:3-11). It was to be observed *once each year on the 14th day of the month Abib* (later named Nisan, Nehemiah 2:1, Esther 3:7).

2. The New Testament.

"This is my blood of the new testament" (Matthew 26:28; Mark 14:24; Luke 22:20; 1 Corinthians 11:25). This phrase "the new testament"; must not be confused with the title given to the books of the scripture from Matthew to Revelation.[25]

In seeking to understand just what "the new testament", as spoken of here by the Lord, really is, we must first ask ourselves, "What did those disciples to whom the Lord addressed these words, understand Him to mean?" It is not recorded that they queried the statement in any way, therefore they must have understood what He was meaning. Likewise, later, when Paul, writing to the believers at Corinth, used the same phrase as recorded at 1 Corinthians 11:25, he did not in any way seek to explain it, thus it must have been clearly understood by them also.

Meaning of the word "testament"

In the commonly used *Authorised Version* scriptures, the word used by our Lord, and translated "testament" occurs 33 times. The *Revised Version* alters ten of the *A.V.* renderings "testament", to "covenant" (including those in the verses we are studying), and not once does it change "covenant" to "testament". It is safe to say, therefore, that the disciples to whom the Lord spoke and the believers at Corinth to whom Paul wrote, understood this phrase as *new covenant*". Moreover because they were Jews, [26] with a knowledge of their own scriptures, (our present Old Testament), they would immediately be reminded that they were keeping the commemorative feast of the deliverance from Egypt which led to the making of the 'old' or 'first' covenant (2 Corinthians 3:14; Hebrews 8:7, 13; Exodus 24:3-8). This 'old', or 'first' covenant, was the covenant of the law which was broken even before it was properly received. (Exodus, chapters 32-34, in chapter 34 the broken covenant was renewed.)

What is the "New Covenant"?

But what was this 'new covenant' of which the Lord spoke? To answer this we must refer again to the 'old' covenant, for though that was renewed to Israel, it was soon broken again, and as a consequence the curses and troubles threatened upon disobedience and non-compliance fell upon them – but before the final blows fell, God made known through some of the prophets, in particular through the prophet Jeremiah, that He would enter into a 'new covenant' with His chosen people, by and under which the former disobedience and unbelief would be dealt with and more than compensated. It is important that you should here read Jeremiah, from chapter 29 verse 24 to chapter 31 verse 40, for this passage shows that God promised to bring the rebellious and scattered people of Israel back to the originally covenanted blessings and land, by a greater deliverance than that of the Exodus from Egypt, and in this connection He makes a solemn declaration, specifically naming it the "New Covenant" (Jeremiah 31:31).

The terms of the New Covenant

The exact terms of this new covenant are stated in Jeremiah 31:27-34, *which please read.* Note especially "Behold the days come saith the Lord, that I will sow ... Israel and Judah with the seed of man ... so will I watch over them to build and plant ... Behold ... I will make a new covenant with ... Israel and ... Judah ... not according to the covenant which I made with their fathers ... which they brake ... but this shall be my covenant ... I will put my law in their inward parts and write it in their hearts ... for they shall all know me ... for I will forgive their iniquity and will remember their sin no more." The prophet Ezekiel reveals that the terms and promises of this covenant are to be made effective and operative by the power of the Spirit, - see Ezekiel 36:24-28, *which please read*, noting "a new spirit will I put within you ... I will put my spirit within you, and cause you to walk in my statutes, and ye shall keep my judgments and do them." This new covenant is also named the "Everlasting covenant" (Jeremiah 32:40; Ezekiel 16:60), and "a covenant of peace" (Ezekiel 34:25).

The parties of the "New Covenant"

The scripture places it beyond all question that *this covenant was made by God with Israel and Judah* (Jeremiah 30:3; 31:31, 33), *and not with the Gentiles.* Paul categorically states that the covenants, old and new, belong to Israel (Romans 9:4), and in the Epistle to the Hebrews he twice quotes its terms as belonging exclusively to that same chosen people (Hebrews 8:6-13; 10:16-18), whilst in Ephesians 2:11, 12 he states that the Gentiles are "strangers from the covenants of promise".

3. "My Blood"

"This is my blood of the new testament" (Matthew 26:28; Mark 14:24). "This cup is the new testament in my blood" (Luke 22:20; 1 Corinthians 11:25). The wondrous truth of redemption by blood is the keystone of the bridge of the doctrines of grace which spans the great distance between God and man.

The "Blood" throughout the Scriptures

It is not necessary for us to list the many references, or to quote even some of the many verses, from both Old and New Testaments, where mention of the "blood" is made. Unmistakable, the red line runs throughout the scriptures, from Genesis 3:21 where by the slayings of animals, blood must have been shed, to provide the necessary coverings for Adam and Eve, to the scenes set in the future, as revealed to and recorded by John in the Revelation, when those redeemed ones sing praise to the "Lion-Lamb" Who prevailed to open the book (Revelation 5:1-10). But the glorious truth that our Lord became the "one sacrifice for sins", shedding His blood and so making possible the redemption and salvation of *all*, must not blind our minds to other facts, and prevent us from seeing that other purposes were also effected in and through the same precious blood.

The Blood and the New Covenant

Amongst those other purposes is this of which the Lord Himself speaks. As the 'old' or 'first' covenant of the law was ratified by blood, when Moses sprinkled "both the book of the covenant and all the people" (Exodus 24:8; Hebrews 9:18-20), and Israel pledged obedience to the enactments and requirements of that law (Exodus 24:3), so also the greater, perfect and, more far-reaching new covenant was likewise sealed and ratified *to Israel*, by the blood of the one who is named "the messenger of the covenant" (Malachi 3:1), and that blood was the divine pledge and seal which ensures that Israel as a nation and people shall yet perform all the purpose of God for them on earth, and will be a true priestly kingdom, under, and in the empowerment of the Spirit, as promised by the new covenant, to mediate between God and the other nations. What the sprinkled blood of animals could not affect, "the blood of the new covenant" does and will ensure (see Hebrews 8 and 9).

In this connection note that the Lord did not say, "My blood ... shed for *all* men ... for the remission of sins" (Matthew 26:28), but limits the effect of the blood of the new covenant to "many" – a smaller number than "all", for the "cup" represented the ratifying blood of the new covenant which was made only with the "many" of Judah and Israel, and was effective to bring about the redemption, deliverance, forgiveness and empowering of those with whom the covenant was made. The limited number "many" is used in Isaiah 53:11, 12, and again refers to Israel, for the prophet is dealing with the work of "my servant" (Isaiah 52:13; 53:11), in relation to the re-instatement of the "divorced" nation (50:1), whose parents were Abraham and Sarah (51:2), and whom he addresses as "Jacob" (49:5), "tribe of Jacob" (49:6), "Israel", "Zion" and "Jerusalem".

4. The Kingdom

"I will not drink henceforth of this fruit of the vine, (representing the blood of the new covenant), until I drink it new with you in my Father's kingdom" (Matthew 26:29; Mark 14:25; Luke 22:16, 18, 29-30).

From the terms of the covenant and promises made by God to and with Abraham, in preparation for the 'chosen people', it can be clearly seen that a kingdom was in view. See Genesis 12:2 "I will make of thee a great *nation*; Genesis 13:14-17 "*all the land* ... to thee will I give it and to thy seed after thee ... *the land* ... for I will give it unto thee"; Genesis 17:6 "And I will make *nations* of thee and *Kings* shall come out of thee", (see also Genesis 17:16; 35:11). Here we have promises concerning "Nation", "Land" and "Kings", and when eventually the great company of former slaves had been delivered from Egypt, the Lord promised them, through Moses, "... if ... then ... ye shall be a kingdom of priests" (Exodus 19:5, 6)[27].

The Kingdom in Scripture

We cannot here enter into a detailed study of "the kingdom" as found in the scripture, but would ask the reader to consider the following brief notes. The prophet Daniel says "The God of Heaven *shall set up a kingdom*" (Daniel 2:44, see 7:18, 27).

The Psalmist, also prophetically, states "Yet have I set *my King* upon My holy hill of Zion" (Psalm 2:6). When in the "fulness of time" Christ was born, the first question asked concerning Him was, "Where is He that is born *King of the Jews?*" (Matthew 2:2). As King, Christ promised the twelve, "Verily ... ye which have followed me ... shall sit on twelve thrones" (Matthew 19:28), and again "I appoint unto you *a kingdom* ... that ye may eat and drink in *my kingdom* ... and sit on thrones judging the twelve tribes of Israel" (Luke 22:29-30). Christ was crucified as King (Matthew 27:29; Mark 15:26; etc). The leading question asked by the disciples just prior to the ascension was "Wilt thou ... *restore the kingdom* to Israel?" (Acts 1:6). The promise, given through Peter on the day of Pentecost and after, was of the restitution of things about which the prophets had spoken, coupled with a call for repentance, which if sincerely shown would eventuate in the return of the King, "Christ to sit on his (i.e. David's) throne" (Acts 2:30. read *all* Acts chapters 2 and 3).

This Kingdom still future

This promised kingdom has not yet come into being, nor can it be constituted apart from the *national repentance of the people of Israel.* The "Church" of the present day cannot be the kingdom, for the kingdom as promised by and revealed in the scriptures, must be centred in "the land", i.e. the Promised Land, the "Holy Land". The true church of the present day, i.e. "the church which is His body" (Ephesians 1:22-23), whilst recognising the kingly authority of the Savior and Head (as seen in 1 Timothy 6:15), does not look to Him as "King". He is not "King" of the church, but "Head" of the church corporate, and "Lord" over the individual members.

A pertinent question

We have already seen that the "supper" as partaken by the Lord and His disciples was connected with the Kingdom (see again Matthew 26:29; Mark 14:25; Luke 22:16, 18, 29-30). This kingdom is Israel's kingdom, thus we ask "What part have Gentiles in a feast which is connected with Israel's deliverance, as promised under, new covenant power and blessing, and which will find its full fellowship in the earthly Kingdom of Israel in the land of promise?"

We have one other prominent phrase to consider: -

5. The Twelve

"He sat down with the twelve" (Matthew 26:20; Mark 14:17; Luke 22:14). "The twelve" are definitely a representative number, as a reference back to the usage of this number in the Old Testament conclusively proves. For instance, at Genesis 49:28 we are gold of the twelve tribes of Israel (named according to, and being the descendants of the twelve sons of Jacob, the original Israel (Genesis 32:27-28). At Exodus 24:4; 28:21; 39:14, we read of twelve pillars, and twelve precious stones, being used to represent the twelve tribes. At Leviticus 24:5, 6, twelve cakes (the Shewbread or Presence Bread (Exodus 25:30), and at Joshua 4:3, twelve stones out of the bed of the river Jordan, are used for similar purpose. But coming nearer to our point of study are the references at Deuteronomy 1:23; Numbers 13:1-16; Joshua 3:12 and 4:2, where we read of one man from each tribe, singled out as representing that tribe.

The principle of the use of 'twelve' to represent all Israel is well established. Thus the twelve who sat at the Passover table with the Lord represented all Israel in the presence of their Redeemer King (Isaiah 59:20; John 1:49, etc.), who through His sacrifice, was to make possible the implementing of the promise of the Kingdom, in the spirit and power of the new covenant, to which He referred. The words of the Lord as reported at Matthew 19:28 and Luke 22:30, give further point to this fact, and reveal that the twelve were chosen to exercise executive authority in the kingdom which was to be set up. (In this connection see Revelation 21:14.)

Summary of first part of study

Before we pass on to consider the New Testament records of this, ordinance, of the Lord's Table, let us summarise the matter we have already considered. We have found that the Lord's Table has its roots deep down in Israelitish soil. (1) It is part of the "Jews Passover", and "the twelve", representing the twelve tribes of Israel, were under the presidency of the "King of Israel". (2) "The cup" was used to represent the ratifying blood of the new covenant, which was promised for and made with the house of Israel and the house of Judah. (3) The Passover feast was originally a memorial *looking back* to the deliverance from Egypt and the old or first covenant, so by the King's specific usage and direction, this little part of the Passover, relating to "the bread" and "the cup", were to be singled out and henceforth used by believing Israel (as represented by those present with the Lord), to be the memorials of His sacrificial death ("body given – blood shed" Luke 22:19, 20), when the blood to ratify the new covenant was poured out, becoming a token – as the blood of the first

Passover lambs had been a token (Exodus 12:13) – by which the inheritors of the kingdom could *look forward* to the time when their King would return (see 1 Corinthians 11:26 "Till He come"), and national deliverance be granted them, in order that they may function as a kingdom of priests in the glorious Kingdom of Righteousness.

Application of findings

Having thus dug to the roots we can surely say that the 'Lords Table' has nothing to connect it with the church of this present time, composed as it is of Gentiles who are not expected to keep the Passover[28], who have no covenant relationship with God (Ephesians 2:11, 12), who have no promise or hope of an earthly kingdom; are not represented by "the twelve", not being of the twelve tribes of Israel, and look not to the Lord as "King" but as "Head". Conversely the "Lord's Table" has *everything* to connect it with Israel, its covenants and its kingdom.

Despite its entirely Israelitish and "kingdom" background, there may be teaching in the New Testament which will connect this ordinance with the Gentiles who form the church of this present time. So now we must turn to our second line of enquiry.

B. The Records of the Lord's Table[29] in the New Testament

As a boy of twelve years of age Jesus observed His first Passover (Luke 2:41-42), and His last observance was a short while before His arrest, trials and crucifixion. Read Matthew 26:17-30; Mark 14:12-26; Luke 22:1, 7-39; John 13 and 14. In the passages from Matthew, Mark and Luke note particularly "the bread" and "the cup". As both these were actually a part of the Passover ritual, it will greatly help if we can learn just where they were placed, and the significances attaching to all the various parts of the ritual as observed at the time of Christ's life and immediately after.[30]To this end let us study: 1) The articles used for Passover celebration. 2) The order of service as observed by Christ and mentioned by Paul.

The Passover

After synagogue prayers, (during which the women folk of the family or group concerned prepared the actual meal to be partaken as "the feast", and duly set the various articles to be used, at their customary places on the table), all assembled for the celebration.

1. Articles on the Table

a. Dishes of unleavened bread.

b. Three special cakes of unleavened bread, Note: - *Leaven* the emblem of sin. Israel's deliverance was from both the bondage of Egypt and from that which lay behind all bondage, i.e. sin. Unleavened bread symbolizes a life, (bread representing life) free from sin. *Three* cakes, representing said the Rabbis, (i) Priest (ii) Levite (iii) Common Israelite (i.e. all Israel), were placed in a special dish, and covered by another dish, upon which was:

c. An animal shank bone (representing the Passover lamb), and a hard-boiled egg (representing perfection. Shank bone and egg together standing for "a lamb ... without blemish" Exodus 12:5).

d. Bunches of herbs – of bitter taste if possible – various herbs being used, (representing the hyssop (Exodus 12:22) also the bitterness of bondage).

e. A mortar or paste made of crushed nuts, (representing clay for brick making).

f. Dishes of salted water (representing Red or Salt Sea).

g. Cups or wine glasses – each participant had his own cup or cups, filled as needed from the wine-jar or wine-skin. (Four special or ceremonial 'cups' were taken during the ritual, see Exodus 6:6-7 "Bring", "Rid", "Redeem", "Take").

2. Order of Service and Meaning

According to Rabbi Gamaliel, and others who were contemporary with Christ and Paul, upon assembly all partook of:

i. The first cup of wine – "cup of sanctification" – followed by ceremonial washing of hands, ("clean hands" Psalm 24:4).

ii. Herbs, dipped in salted water and eaten, (Note:- at this point there was dissension amongst the disciples, Luke 22:24, and the "feetwashing" by the Lord, John 13:4 etc.).[31]

iii. The middle one of the three special unleavened cakes was then taken by head of house (or president of feast), broken in two and hidden away, usually behind cushions, (representing Israel and Judah in captivity, or under the heel of oppressors).

iv. Question by children (Exodus 12:26), and recited answer by head or president.

v. Singing of 1st part of "the Hallel" (parts of Psalms 113 and 114).

vi. Second cup of wine then taken. "Cup of salvation or redemption".

vii. Second eating of herbs, this time dipped into the nut paste along with unleavened bread (representing the bitterness and bondage of Egypt. This called "the Sop", John 13:26, 27, 30. Judas departed immediately after taking this).

viii. The actual meal or "Feast" was then taken. Fish, soup, meat, and a sweet dish, in that order. *Now note*:- as the actual meal was finishing, "as they were eating" (Matthew 26:26; Mark 14:22), Jesus "took bread". This was the continuance of this symbolic ritual which was always taken up again at this point. This "bread" was the previously.

ix. Broken and hidden cake recovered, (see iii. above), (representing Judah and Israel delivered from bondage and vassalage), broken again into smaller pieces so that each present might by eating identify himself with the restored, delivered nation. Some Rabbis said it equally represented the manna ("hidden manna" Revelation 2:17?) which was the unfailing provision in the wilderness, (see Matthew 26:26; Mark 14:22; Luke 22:19; 1 Corinthians 11:24).

It was this "bread" that was given an added significance by the Lord Who, as He broke it into smaller pieces, said, "This is my body, broken for you", thus identifying Himself with the nation which was to be re stores, as such restoration could only be through Him, and further, making Himself the anti-type of the manna, as He had previously taught "I am the bread of life" etc. (see John 6:26, 27, 32-35, 47-58; also 1 Corinthians 10:3 "spiritual meat"). He was thus by symbol teaching them that it was to be by His "broken body" – i.e. sacrifice – that the new covenant would be implemented, and the deliverance, redemption, and restoration of the broken nation effected.

x.   The Third cup, "of blessing", was then taken (1 Corinthians 10:16) – representing, said the Rabbis, the life giving water from the rock (exodus 17 and 1 Corinthians 10:4 "spiritual drink ... spiritual rock ... that rock was Christ". See also John 4:13-14; 7:37-39; water symbolic of the life giving spirit).

It was this representation of the water from the rock that was given added significance by Christ, when He said, "This is my blood of the new covenant" (Matthew 26:29; Mark 14:24; Luke 22:20 and 1 Corinthians 11:25). The 'old' or 'first' covenant of the law had failed, - but now Christ "the messenger of the covenant" (Malachi 3:1) is about to shed His blood, not only to effect redemption, but to make possible the new covenant, the "better covenant" (Jeremiah 31:27-34; Hebrews 7:27; 8:6), and by His sacrifice and blood-shedding the giving of the Spirit would also be made possible, in whose power the restored, redeemed Israel would be empowered to keep the terms of this new covenant, in taking the "bread" and the "cup" and giving them the added significations, Christ was revealing Himself as "the minister of the circumcision i.e. Israel – to confirm the promises made unto the fathers" (Romans 15:8). After the third cup:

xi.   Prayers were recited, (special verses, Psalms 79:6 and 69:25; Lamentations 3:66).

xii.   The Fourth cup of wine ... the "cup of praise" was then taken, after this,

xiii.   2nd part of "Hallel" sung. Psalms 115-118 (shortened) and Psalm 136. This was the "hymn" Matthew 26:30). The whole ritual was concluded by

xiv.   Recital of special poem, by head of house or president of feast, ending, if celebration was away from Jerusalem, with the wailing cry, taken up by all "next year in Jerusalem!"

"Bread" and "Cup" were part of the Passover.

From this order of service it can readily be seen that the "bread" and "cup" (numbers ix and x above), were most definitely parts of the Passover ritual, and the special added meanings were given by the One Who was the promised King and Redeemer of Israel (Isaiah 44:6; 41:14; 54:5 etc.), henceforth to be observed by the believing Christian Jews, who would still keep the feast as Moses had commanded, and who, through the obedience of Christ, would thereupon enter and partake of "the powers of the age to come" (Hebrews 6:5), and enjoy "the heavenly calling" (Hebrews 3:1). Note again here what the Lord said about the unending character of this feast, (Matthew 26:29; Mark 14:26; Luke 22:16, 18, 29, 30), "Ye may eat and drink at my table in my kingdom", which promise agrees with the prediction of Ezekiel 45:21, that the Passover will be observed in the millennial city.

Having set forth the place of the "bread" and "cup" in relation to the complete Passover ritual, we will now proceed to examine certain phrases and words in the New Testament records.

The Lord's Table connected with the Kingdom

The command accompanying the taking of the bread and the cup "do this in remembrance of me" (Luke 22:19, 20; 1 Corinthians 11:24, 25), is linked by Christ, who gave the command, with a promise, "I appoint you a kingdom that ye may eat and drink at my kingdom and sit on thrones judging the twelve tribes of Israel" (Luke 22:29, 30). A similar promise had been given to the same men not long before, when the Lord said "Take no thought for your life ... seek ye the kingdom ... Sell that ye have ... For it is the Father's good pleasure to give you the kingdom" (read whole passage Luke 12:22-40).

This promise is identical with that stated at the supper. "Give you the kingdom"; (Luke 12:32), "Appoint you a kingdom" (Luke 22:29). The men to whom the promise was given, truly believed and actually obeyed the injunction, not only thereafter specially "remembering" the Lord when they partook of the Passover, including the particular "bread" and "cup" as specified. but they also sold their possessions and lands, "*all* that believed – sold their possessions" (Acts 2:44, 45; Acts 4:34-37, and see what happened to Ananias and Sapphira, Acts 5:1-11). We say without fear of contradiction, that scripturally the "Lord's Table" and "the kingdom" are inseparably linked. Those to whom the kingdom was promised sat at the Passover, and partook of "bread" and "cut"; those to whom the kingdom was promised were enjoined to "Sell"; and they obeyed. If you think that you should obey the command concerning commemoration, you should also obey the command to "Sell that ye have and give alms". We would consider the one command to be just as binding as the other.

The Lord's Table in John's Gospel

It is significant that this particular Passover occasion preceding the crucifixion, at which the "bread" and "cup" were given special prominence, is practically omitted from the Gospel of John. Significant indeed when it is appreciated that John's Gospel was written with the needs of all men in view, and makes its appeals and gracious offers to "whosoever" and "the world".[32] Because of its "worldwide" scope John deemed it necessary to explain and interpret many Jewish words employed, and Jewish customs mentioned, in order that the non-Jewish readers to whom it was directed, might the better understand.[33]

Now it is evident, in the face of the many interpretative and explanatory notes scattered throughout the whole gospel, that if it was intended that the Jewish Passover, or such little part of it now commonly known as the Lord's Table or Supper, should be observed continually by the "whosoever" Gentile believers, out of "the world", then most certainly John would have made sure to have written concerning it, and further, would have been careful to interpret and explain its Jewish terms. But as we have said, he almost passes it over in silence, recording absolutely nothing concerning "bread" and "cup": referring only to the fact that the supper was eaten (John 13:1, 2): to the incident of the "Sop" (John 13:21-30) – which significantly, John evidently did not think of sufficient interest or importance to need explanation for Gentile readers – and the fact that they arose from the table (John 14:31).

The Lord's Table and the "feet washing"

One matter, not actually a part of the Passover, but a matter which had been overlooked by the twelve as they assembled, is recorded in detail – we refer to the act of the feet washing (John 13:4-17), which act should be continued and observed by us who are Gentiles, if the acts relating to "bread" and "cup" – "If I ... have washed your feet ye also ought to wash one another's feet ... I have given ... an example ... ye should to as I have done ... happy are ye if ye do ..." (John 13:14-17). Now as this injunction to "wash one another's feet" is in the Gospel specifically stated to be for "whosoever" and "the world", we would judge that if any particular rite should be continued and observed by us Gentiles "the feet washing" should take prior place. However, it is widely taught that it is the inner, spiritual significance of this act that is to be remembered and kept by us, that is, the recognition that humility and self-effacement is true God-honouring service. With this we heartily agree, but would add that if the "feet washing" command is thus to be spiritualised then the commands concerning "bread" and "cup", given at the same table, to the same men, at the same time, should also be spiritualised. And this we find is exactly what Christ taught.

Christ's teaching concerning his "flesh" and "blood"

In John 6 the Lord is reported as teaching "Verily ... except ye eat the flesh of the Son of man, and drink His blood, ye have no life in you ... for my flesh is meat indeed and my blood is drink indeed" (John 6:53–58). You rightly ask, as did the Jews to whom He spoke at the time, "How"? (John 6:52), "How shall we eat and drink of Him? By partaking of 'bread' and 'cup'?" "No!", says our Lord, "It is the spirit which giveth life, the flesh (bodily, outward action) profiteth nothing" (John 6:63).

In other words He teaches "spiritualise the eating and drinking of me, for fleshly eating and drinking of my flesh and blood is impossible (see John 6:52), and even if it were possible would not profit you in any way, but the *words* I speak to you, the *teaching of truth* which can and should be assimilated by faith, those words, that teaching is spiritually profitable and life giving".

We Gentiles would be wise to accept Christ's own teaching on this subject and to recognise that to partake in any outward ceremony or act, which is, after all only of the flesh, such as eating of the "bread" and drinking of the "cup", will profit us nothing, but that a spiritual assimilation of Christ and His fullness, and an humble acknowledgement of His headship over the members of "the church which is His body", will most assuredly enrich us and glorify Him.

The "Lord's Table" in the Epistles

The only *direct* references to the "Lord's Table", outside the Gospels are in 1 Corinthians,[34] but there are allusions to a feast or meals which in those days were evidently associated with, or made the occasion of, the celebration of what the Corinthian believers, and possibly believers in assemblies at other places, mistakenly thought was a celebration of the "Lord's Table". (We hope to demonstrate this in succeeding pages). The allusions to the feast or meals referred to are to be found in the Acts, and the epistles of James, Peter and Jude, as well as in 1 Corinthians.

Heathen feasts and necessity for the "Feasts of the Lord"

Before we seek to exhibit and explain the matter stated above, we must set the background. Practically all the heathen religions keep feasts (usually with a sacrificial implication and most often accompanied by licentious and obscene behaviour) as part of, or connected with, their rituals – a practise which pertained to early days and persists in the present days. It was to counter the possibility of Israel being ensnared into unholy and unclean fellowship with idols and demons, through participation in the idol feasts and offensive behaviour of the nations through whose territories they had to pass, and in whose territories Israel eventually found a home, that the Lord ordained the various religious feasts to be observed by the redeemed nation, for they were called to be an "Holy" nation, separate and "different" (Exodus 11:7)

That such provision was necessary, is seen in the fact that whilst Moses was communing with God at the top of the holy mount, the children of Israel, in a state of idolatry, "sit down to eat and drink" at a feast before the calf idol (Exodus 32:6; 1 Corinthians 10:7), "and rose up to play", i.e. with lascivious dancing and singing that led to immorality and brought the judgment of God upon them (Exodus 32:25-29).

A Repetition

In the earlier part of our study we have seen that the *true* Passover was ordained for "the land", and was to be observed annually upon a set day. It was a memorial of the deliverance from Egypt and is thus connected with the "old" or "first" covenant of the law. Further, we have seen that the "bread" and "cup" were definitely parts of the Jewish Passover ritual, but that the Lord gave to these two particular symbols a special added significance in respect of the "new covenant", under which Israel was to enjoy an even greater deliverance, and to receive the Spirit's empowerment to enable them to keep and observe all God's requirements.

"A Memorial of a memorial"

Now as the Passover, (including "bread" and "cup") could only be properly observed in Palestine – "the land" – and as special feasts were in those days the common accompaniments of religious exercises, the Jews *outside* Palestine, such as those at Corinth, Thessalonica etc., substituted for the true observance what we might call "a memorial of a memorial". (Even as the orthodox Jews *outside* Palestine also do to this present day when they keep the Passover.)

Upon such a background it was an easy matter therefore, for the believing Christian Jews at Corinth to link a substitute observance to such occasions of communal feasting or partaking of meals together, as indicated by the "love feasts", and the "breaking of bread from house to house", of which we read in Jude verse 12; 1 Corinthians 11:17-22; 2 Peter 2:13. (see also Luke 24:30; Luke 24:35; Acts 2:42; 2:46; 20:7; 1 Corinthians 10:16).

But these "love feasts" and other social occasions gave rise to excesses and abuses – gluttony, drunkenness and class distinction were to the fore (1 Corinthians 11:17-22; James 2:2-5; 2 Peter 2:13; Jude verse 12), so that what purported to be a memorial of the new covenant blessings and grace, as made possible by the sacrifice of the "messenger of the covenant" upon the cross, became nothing but a travesty. "This" says Paul "is not the Lord's supper" (1 Corinthians 11:20), and in respect of the whole sorry business – for such it was – he says "I praise you not" (1 Corinthians 11:17; 11:22), and takes the opportunity to restate what he had previously taught the Jewish Christians at Corinth ("that which I delivered unto you" 1 Corinthians 11:23), claiming that he had received special revelation concerning it ("I received of the Lord" 1 Corinthians 11:23).

The Lord's Table and the Corinthian believers

We intend to consider the verses in 1 Corinthians 11, in which the "Lord's Table" is set forth, as fully as space will allow, and would ask the reader to approach this with prayer and patience, - prayer that understanding might be given, and patience because a certain amount of repetition will be necessary.

a. A matter of importance

First, it is of the utmost importance to be sure as *to whom these words in 1 Corinthians 11 were really addressed.* Reference to 2 Corinthians 3:6 and 2 Corinthians 5:18 reveal that at that time the apostle was engaged upon the ministry "of the new covenant" and "the ministry of reconciliation". as we have seen, (idem p.p. 136-138) the new covenant was made with and belongs to Israel and Judah (Jeremiah 31:31), and so in his "ministry of the new covenant", Paul addresses himself *to* Jews. "The ministry of reconciliation" was exercised in order, (1) to reconcile a stubborn and unrepentant Israel to God, (2) to reconcile "the world" (2 Corinthians 5:19), i.e. the Gentile nations, to God, and (3) to reconcile Jew's with Gentiles, at a time when the Jews were still the "elect", "chosen" people of God, and held a position of "advantage" (see Romans 3:1, 2; 9:4, 5) over the Gentile believers who *were then* but *"wild olive"* branches "grafted" into Israel's olive tree, and thus stood only because Israel still stood, and were in danger of forfeiting such blessings as they enjoyed. (Read Romans 11 very carefully, noting verses 15-24, particularly verses 20, 21, 22). From this it will be seen that we will have to study carefully to determine *to whom* the words of 1 Corinthians 11 were really addressed.

b. Jews and Gentiles in the Corinthian Assembly

The assembly at Corinth was a mixed assembly, being composed of Jews (Acts 18:4, 5), possibly led by Crispus, a former chief ruler of the synagogue (Acts 18:8), and Gentiles ("many Corinthians" Acts 18:8), possibly originating from many places, Corinth being a cosmopolitan city. These two sections were common to most of the assemblies of that time, and the main distinction between the two is indicated clearly at Acts 21:20-25 where we read of "Jews which believe, *zealous of the law*", i.e. the Mosaic Law (Acts 21:20), and "Gentiles which believe" (Acts 21:25), *who did not observe Jewish customs or consider themselves bound in any way by the Mosaic Law,* having been instructed to observe "the decrees", which had been formulated by the council at Jerusalem (Acts 15), for the guidance of the Gentile believers. (Read all Acts 15 and see Acts 16:4 where the formulated requirements are called "the decrees"). These very "decrees" became a cause of "enmity" between the two parties (Ephesians 2:14, 15), for they plainly directed that the Gentile believers were to be exempted from circumcision, Mosaic law-keeping and feasts etc. The "advantage" of the Jewish section, to which we referred above, was evidenced by the outward fleshly rite of circumcision, it being the God-given sign of the Abrahamic covenant (Genesis 17:9-14; 1 Corinthians 7:17-20), and Paul records concerning the Jews *at that time,* whether believing Christian Jews or otherwise, that their advantage consisted in the fact that "to them belonged the adoption, the glory, the covenants, the giving of the law, the service of God, the fathers, and of whom in the flesh, Christ came" (Romans 9:4, 5).

c. The Gospel "to the Jew first"

At that time, i.e. throughout the period covered by the historical events of the Acts (from Pentecost to Paul's imprisonment in Rome, which period includes the written ministry of Paul as contained in the epistles to Galatians, 1 and 2 Thessalonians, Hebrews, 1 and 2 Corinthians and Romans, as well as the ministry to the circumcision exercised through the epistles of Peter, James, John and Jude), *at that time* we repeat, the gospel was "to the Jew first" (Romans 1:16; 2:9; 2:10)[35], because they definitely held prior place in the outworking purpose of God, so that *at that time* "Salvation" was "of the Jews" (John 4:22).

d. Gentiles but "wild olive branches"

The believing Jews were named by Paul "the Israel of God" (Galatians 6:16), and they were likened by him to an "olive tree" (Romans 11:17), into which the Gentile believers *of that time*, as "wild olive branches" were "grafted" and so made partakers of the "root and fatness" of Israel, the true olive tree (Romans 11:17-28), and thus partakers of "Israel's spiritual things" (Romans 15:27). *At that time* Israel still stood as the "elect" "people of God", and to them still belonged "the covenants" etc. (Romans 9:4, 5).

Jewish national and racial exclusivism was very strong as is evidenced by Peter's reaction in relation to Cornelius. (Read Acts 10:10-29). It was *at that time* counted an unlawful thing for a Jew to have fellowship with a Gentile (verse 28). At Galatians 2:11-21 we have further evidence of the cleavage between Jews and Gentiles, even though they were Christians, in the behaviour of the Jewish brethren from Jerusalem who stirred up trouble at Antioch, bringing fear to Peter (verse 12), and causing even Barnabas to be affected (verse 13).

Such was the position when Paul wrote his epistles to Corinth: the two sections, "circumcision" and "uncircumcision", were plainly evident; the "middle wall of partition ... the law of commandments contained in ordinances, "(decrees)", stood between the two Christian companies (Ephesians 2:14-15) whom Paul, by his "ministry of reconciliation", sought to bring together, so that they might realise that they were "all one in Christ Jesus" (Galatians 3:28) despite outward distinctions.

e. 1 Corinthians – an Epistle of answers

A careful reading of 1 Corinthians will show that, as stated in note 26, this epistle was in answer to one sent to Paul by the Assembly at Corinth (1 Corinthians 7), in which a variety of questions from both sections had been asked. In one part of 1 Corinthians he answers questions from the Jewish section of the assembly and in another part he answers questions from the Gentile section, whilst some parts of his answering epistle are to both sections.

Undoubtedly the original epistle made this quite clear, but it is partly apparent even in our *Authorised Version*. To the Jewish Christian believers he writes as one of them and addresses them "Brethren ... *our* fathers" (1 Corinthians 10:1). To the Gentile section he writes, "Ye know *ye* were Gentiles" (1 Corinthians 12:2), whilst in the opening salutation he addresses them together as "the assembly of God ... saints" (1 Corinthians 1:2).

Some might be wondering why we have seemingly digressed into this line of teaching, but it has been necessary in order to make clear the following: - *that much of 1 Corinthians cannot be applied to, or considered to be binding upon, Gentiles today, as it was not even applicable to, or binding upon, the Gentiles in the assembly to which it was originally sent. If it was not applicable to those Gentiles **then**, why is it considered to be binding upon Gentiles **now**?* With this in mind we shall examine those parts of the epistle relevant to our inquiry.

Passover and Lord's Table in 1 Corinthians.

At 1 Corinthians 5:7, 8 Paul refers to "Christ *our* Passover", and again we see that Paul *as a Jew*, includes himself with the others as he continues, "let us keep the feast", and draws spiritual teaching from it. Now, as we have earlier seen, the Mosaic instructions prohibited uncircumcised Gentiles from partaking of the Passover (Exodus 12:43-49) and further, under the 'decrees' formulated by the leaders of the Church at Jerusalem (Acts 15; 16:4; 21:21-25), the Mosaic requirements were endorsed for the Jewish Christians, and Gentile Christians were excluded from participation in the Jewish feasts and ceremonies.

Moreover, is it conceivable in the face of the rigid Jewish national exclusivism as mentioned on the previous page, and despite the 'decrees' from the Jerusalem conference, that Paul, who at that time prided himself as being "an Israelite, of the seed of Abraham of the tribe of Benjamin" (Romans 11:1), and who, as "a Hebrew of the Hebrews, as touching the law" was "blameless" (Philippians 3:5-6); who at that very time of writing this epistle to Corinth was under obligation to an Old Testament vow (Acts 18:18); who at Acts 23:6 still retained his standing as a Pharisee and who at Acts 25:8 alleges that he had not at all offended against the law, and as late as Acts 26:22 maintained that in all his ministry up to that time, he had said "none other things than those which Moses and the prophets did say should come", ... is it direct uncircumcised Gentiles to observe and partake of the Passover and to encroach upon the Jewish religious privileges, so giving the Jews a cause of offence? Though actually charged with such Jewish law-breaking (Acts 21:28; 23:29; 24:6; 25:7), in his defence he stoutly maintains complete innocence (Acts 24:13, 16; 25:7, 8, 10-11), and could have been acquitted and set at liberty had he not appealed unto Caesar (Acts 26:31-32).

No! Paul did not address his teaching and exhortations about the Passover (1 Corinthians 5:7, 8) to the *Gentile* Christians at Corinth, the truth is that he addresses himself to the *Jewish* Christian section of the assembly.

Continuing, at 1 Corinthians 10:1-11, Paul, again including himself as a Jew along with those to whom he was writing, refers to "our fathers", who he says, "were under the cloud and passed through the sea ... baptised unto Moses ..." etc. The "fathers" did not belong to the Gentiles, but to "the Israelites ... whose are the fathers" (Romans 9:4, 5).

Paul writing to the Jewish Christians.

It should be quite clear from a consideration of the foregoing that Paul was indeed addressing himself to the Jewish Christian section of the Corinthian assembly throughout the succeeding passage. At verse 16 he refers to "the cup of blessing which we bless", again including himself with the Jewish brethren, for it was the Jews, not the Gentiles, who blessed "the cup of blessing", which was the third cup of the Passover ritual, as we have pointed out (idem. p. 144), for let us repeat, the Passover was forbidden to uncircumcised Gentiles.

Still in verse 16 Paul refers to "the bread which we break", i.e. the special unleavened Passover cake, and after citing the spiritual implications goes on to compare the Jewish commemoration with the idol sacrifices and feasts observed by unbelieving Gentiles, and gives warning that believers should exercise care, considering the consciences of others, when attending any social function where perchance meat which had previously been offered to idols might be provided.

In this connection he uses the phrase "The Lord's Table" (1 Corinthians 10:21) or "the table of the Lord" (which phrase throws us back to Malachi 1, where the equivalent is twice used in verses 7 and 12), and contrasts it with what he terms "the table of devils" or demons. (See and read whole section 1 Corinthians 10:7-33).

Still answering questions from the Jewish section of the assembly, in chapter 11:1-16 Paul gives guidance in respect of being covered or uncovered during worship, for it was the Jewish (and Roman) custom to worship with covered head, and the Greek with uncovered, thus the Jewish Christians desired to know just what to do for the best.

"Love Feasts" and the true "Lord's Table"

We feel that we now come to the crux of our study so far as the New Testament records of this 'ordinance' are concerned, for a true understanding of 1 Corinthians 11:17-34 puts the whole matter beyond dispute. Continuing to write to the Jewish section, as we shall see, Paul reprimands them concerning the "Love Feasts" – at which evidently all partook, whether Jewish or Gentile believers, and seemingly under the mistaken notion that, by including a ritual of the breaking of some "bread" and the drinking of some "cup", they were obeying the Lord's command as given at the pass over supper before His arrest and consequent sacrifice.

"But" writes Paul "when you gather on these occasions it is impossible for you to be eating the 'Lord's Supper' (1 Corinthians 11:20), for in the first place there are serious divisions amongst you (verse 18), secondly, those meals, though 'Love-feasts', degenerate into occasions of drunkenness and gluttony, whilst some of the poorer members, because of their poverty are neglected, and left with hunger unsatisfied (verse 21, 22 and 34).

Furthermore, because of these excesses and profanities, many of you are suffering physical sickness and weakness, and many have been judged by death (verses 27-32). "This cannot be the Lord's Supper", writes Paul, "for He revealed to me what I delivered to you" – (and remember he is still addressing his words to the Jewish section, whose prerogative it was to keep the Passover) – "The Lord Jesus, the night in which He was betrayed, took bread ... this do *ye* ... in remembrance of me" (1 Corinthians 11:23-25).

When was this to be done? Why, on the annual anniversary of "the night in which He was betrayed", i.e. at the Passover celebration.

Who was to do it? "Ye" ... and those to whom Christ spoke, as we have seen, were representative of "all Israel". Yes! It is Israel who has to "do this" ... not the Gentile.

What was to be eaten? "Bread" (verse 23). "*This* bread" comments Paul (verse 26), that is, the special Passover cake or bread, the bread similar to that which He took "the night in which He was betrayed".

What was to be drunk? "The cup" immediately after the actual Passover mean (verse 25). "*This* cup" (verse 26), comments Paul, that is, "The cup of blessing" (idem. p. 144, x), the 3rd cup of the Passover ritual – the cup similar to that which the Lord took "the night in which He was betrayed".

"*This* bread" and "*This* cup", to which the Lord gave the added significances in respect of His sacrifice, which was to be the basis for the outworking of the new covenant (verse 25) for Judah and Israel (Jeremiah 31:31). Paul further comments "As often as ye eat ... and drink, ye do shew the Lord's death, till He come".

How often did they rightly, scripturally do this? Not as they had mistakenly been doing, when they linked what they supposed to be a celebration of the "Lord's Supper" with the garish "Love-Feast", and other occasions of communal meals. "No! not that!" says Paul "That is not the Lord's Supper" (1 Corinthians 11:20).

The true Lord's Supper.

"The true Lord's Supper is to be celebrated year by year at Passover time, and if you do this" continues Paul (1 Corinthians 11:26) "Ye do shew the Lord's death". *At that time* throughout the period covered by the Acts, the Jewish Christian had this "advantage" (Romans 3:1,2) over the Gentile Christian, in that by partaking of the Passover as directed, and realising the truth of the added significances attaching to "bread" and "cup", he had the opportunity of bringing home to the unbelieving, though "orthodox" Jews, some of whom would be sitting with him, and partaking with him at the same Passover celebration, something of the real meaning of the "new covenant", by "setting forth", or "shewing forth", in the use of the "bread" and "cup" as illustrations, the fact that the promised "new covenant" had been made possible by the obedience of Christ, and ratified by His broken body and shed blood. Such testimony should be given, directs Paul, and we can imagine what must have transpired when the children present at the Passover asked the customary question, "What mean ye by this service?", and the Jewish Christian present took advantage of the occasion so to "preach Christ".

The Lord's Table "till he come"

One last direction is given by Paul, who says the testimony should be borne each Passover time "till He come" (1 Corinthians 11:26).

There are considerations here which would take much more space to set forth than we have to spare, but this much must be stated, that *at that time* the return of the Lord *as King, to set up the promised kingdom under new covenant terms*, was a lively expectation – an expectation that was not realised, because it depended upon the national repentance of Israel.

The "coming" conditioned by Israel's repentance

The first prophetic word concerning "the second coming" (as it is loosely termed), is in Deuteronomy 30:1-3 where we read, "It shall come to pass .... when these things are upon thee, the blessing and the curse which I have set before thee ... thou shalt call them to mind ... among the nations ... whither the Lord ... hath driven thee, and shall *return and obey* ... that then the Lord shalt *turn* thy captivity *and will and will return and gather thee* from the nations whither the Lord hath scattered thee". (This is undoubtedly the scriptural basis of Paul's phrase at 2 Thessalonians 2:1 "The coming of the Lord and our gathering together unto Him".)

"Return", "Turn again", and "Turn", are words of exhortation and invitation addressed to Israel throughout the Old Testament scriptures (the interested reader could see 1 Kings 8:33, 34; 2 Chronicles 30:6-11; Jeremiah 25:1-9; 2 Chronicles 36:13 and other passages). Israel, as a nation, refused to "turn", thus eventually all twelve tribes suffered captivity, and Gentile rule overtook "the land", and will not be completely broken until "the stone cut without hands" (Daniel 2:34), - the heavenly kingdom (foretold from the early days and seen in vision by Nebuchadnezzar and Daniel), is set up and "the times of the Gentiles are fulfilled" (Luke 21:24).

The offer of this kingdom along with a call for "turning" or "repentance", was proclaimed by John the Baptist, and by Christ and the twelve. Moreover, after the sacrifice of Christ, "the messenger of the covenant", who shed the blood which ratified the new covenant, *the same offer* is carried into the Acts, the epistles written during the Acts, and the ministries of Peter, James, John and Jude in their office as "ministers of the circumcision", and thus presented afresh to Israel under new covenant terms.

The "hope of Israel" throughout the Acts

That the return of the Lord to set up the "new covenant" Kingdom was a lively expectation all through this period can be plainly seen. Immediately upon the ascension of the Lord, the angelic messengers underlined the teaching and promises that He had previously given, when they encouraged the wondering and bewildered disciples with the words, "This same Jesus ... shall so come ..." (Acts 1:11), "Shall come". For what purpose? Why, to set up the Kingdom, the restoration of which was uppermost in their minds, as revealed in the question they asked, "Wilt thou ... restore ... the kingdom to Israel?" (Acts 1:6). Tis was Israel's great hope, and it persisted right to the end of the period covered by the Acts, for Paul, in Rome, called the Jews together and "testified the kingdom", claiming "that for *the hope of Israel* I am bound with this chain" (Acts 28:16-24).

Scriptural proof of the "lively hope"

We have twice stated the "hope of Israel", or expectation of the return of the Lord as "King to sit on his (David's) throne", was *at that time* a lively hope, and in support of this please see the following (along with the references already quoted). Matthew 24:36,42,44; John 21:22, - words of Christ hinting possible speedy return. Acts 3:19,20 "He shall send Jesus"; Romans 13:11,12 "Salvation near ... day at hand"; 1 Corinthians 7:29 "Time is short", therefore unless absolutely necessary, do not marry; 1 Thessalonians 4:15 "we", Paul *at that time* expected to be "alive unto the coming"; 1 Corinthians 10:11 "The ends of the age are come" upon us, says Paul; 2 Thessalonians 2:1-7; 3:10-13. Some evidently ceased working, thinking Christ's return imminent; Hebrews 1:2 "These last days"; 10:25 "the day approaching"; 10:37 "a little while ... He shall come"; James 5:1-3 "Rich ... heaped treasure for last days"; 5:8 "nigh"; 1 Peter 4:7 "end at hand"; 2 Peter 3:3-14; 1 John 2:18 "It is the last time"; Jude 18 "mockers" a sign of "the last time".

Lack of space prevents comment on these passages, but it is evident even from a cursory reading of them, that those who wrote and spoke thus, and those to whom this truth was ministered or written, expected that the Lord would return quickly to "restore the kingdom to Israel" (Acts 1:6), and so to bring in new covenant blessing and grace. Thus the believing Christian Jews were directed to observe the Passover with the added significances attached to "This bread" and "This cup", "until" the soon expected coming of the King should be a fact. Thereupon, the annual feast would change character a little, it being partaken again in the presence of the King as He stated (Matthew 26:29; Mark 14:25; Luke 22:16,18,29-30; and see Ezekiel 45:21).

The "coming" deferred

But that soon expected 'coming' was not realised, the King did not return, - has not yet returned, though more than nineteen hundred years have passed! Why? Simply *because Israel as a people would not respond or repent.* "His own received Him Not" (John 1:11), so that after many opportunities had been given them, the offer of the kingdom and the implementation of the new covenant was temporarily withdrawn, as seen from a reading of Acts 28:23-29, where after Paul had "expounded and testified the kingdom of God ... out of the law of Moses and the prophets", only *some* believed.

Thereupon Paul utters the words which temporarily closed the door to this people Israel: "The salvation of God" ... is taken from you "and sent unto the Gentiles". Then "the Jews departed", they were "sent away", "dismissed", or "divorced", and all the kingdom and new covenant purposes and hopes were suspended. The historical evidence of this was the destruction of Jerusalem in 70 A.D. (as prophesied by the Lord, Matthew 23:34-39; Luke 19:41-44; 21:20-24) which is a sure indication that Israel's national privileges and spiritual advantages were brought to an end, and the Jew's were further dispersed "until the times of the Gentiles be fulfilled".

A new hope revealed through Paul

At the time of this temporary withdrawal of Israel's opportunities, Paul was given the revelation concerning "the church which is His body" – truth not before revealed in any way – making known purposes of grace completely unrelated to either Israel's kingdom or covenants. This truth of the "mystery" pertains to this present time, and in relation to *it* a new hope is given.

The Lord's Table not related to the "hope" of the church which is his body"

The hope or expectation of "the church which is His body" is not the "coming" of Christ as King to set up a Kingdom, for as stated earlier in this study, Christ is not "King" of the church, but "Head" and "Lord" – No! It is not His "coming" for us, that we might take part in a "gathering together" of Israel "unto Him" (2 Thessalonians 2:1; Deuteronomy 30:3), either in "the air" (1 Thessalonians 4) or as participants in an earthly kingdom. No! Not His "coming" for us, but our "going" to be with Him in glory. This, says Paul is "That blessed hope ... the appearing of the glory of the great God and our Saviour Jesus Christ" (Titus 2:13), and we, i.e. the members "of His body", are taught "when Christ who is our life shall appear, then shall ye also appear with Him *in glory*" (Colossians 3:4).

The "bread" and "cup" of the Lord's Table do not point forward to, or have anything to teach about, this "appearing" *in glory*, but as we have sought to point out, the Lord's Table has unbreakable connections with His "coming" to fulfil the expectations of Israel, its kingdom, and its covenants.

The considered findings of our study

Thus we must conclude our study. We have together dug to the roots of this subject, and found that it is planted deeply into distinctly Israelitish soil. We have together studied all the New Testament references to it, and can assuredly state that the words used, and that the teaching related to this "ordinance" at every phase, link the "bread" and "cup" of the Lord's Supper to Israel, and to Israel's hope of the kingdom under new covenant terms, and conversely, plainly and completely sever it from the Gentiles who form "the church which is His body", and from the hope of that church.

We realise that the conclusions arrived at may annoy, even anger – many to whom the "ordinance" of the Lord's Table means so much, therefore we desire to set it on record that we have not written any of this study in order that those who see and think differently from ourselves may be annoyed and angered: neither have we written in a spirit of censoriousness, or to arouse conflict.

This study has been undertaken out of a deep desire to honour the Lord by setting forth what we clearly see, and sincerely believe, to be the truth of this matter, as revealed in and through His inspired word. No! do not be annoyed and angered, but rather make it a matter for bible searching, prayer and surrender. It is not the prerogative of the writer to dictate what another shall believe, but with such simplicity as may be, and with sincerity of heart and mind, to seek to make plain what the Bible teaches. Believing friend, do you believe *just what others have said about* the word of God, or, *what the word of God says for itself?*

Many partake of the Lord's Table because they sincerely believe that the Lord commanded it. Oh yes. He did command it, but He also commanded many other things which are never obeyed by those same believers. Read the Gospels through carefully and note the many instructions. If the Lord's command about the Table is to be obeyed by all believers today, what about those other commands? Can what you say you believe, and what you practise, be subjected to the searchlight of the truth of the *whole* word of God? If it can be, then well and good, but if not, then let the inspired, unbreakable truth be your critic, teacher and guide. Not one of us can be "approved unto God" (2 Timothy 2:15), unless we are willing to "search the scriptures" and see "whether those things" we believe and practise are really according to that inspired word (Acts 17:11). We must be willing to "prove the things that differ" (Philippians 1:10 *R.V.* margin), if we really aspire to be "workman needing not to be ashamed, rightly dividing the word of truth" (2 Timothy 2:15).

We send forth this writing with the prayer that it may be used of the Lord to enable at least some to see the true place of the "Lord's Table", and perchance help them to "see what is the fellowship of the mystery ... to the intent that now unto the principalities and powers in heavenly places might be known by the church the manifold wisdom of God" (Ephesians 3:9-10).

Another Look at the Gospel of John

Preface

The writing here presented, was conceived more than thirty years ago and in due course a manuscript was sent to Christian publishers but was returned as unsuitable. Now at last it is with thanks to our God and Savior, that the manuscript, having been resurrected from a large suitcase full of notes, prepared messages and writings, (collected during a ministry of over 50 years), has been examined and very kindly rearranged by two Christian friends. Also we understand that its production is being made possible by other interested friends who wish to remain anonymous. To these and any others who may have had any part in its production, we wish to express our very sincere thanks, along with the hope and prayer that it may lead to a better and clearer understanding of this important portion of the divinely inspired Word of God.

Ernest H. Streets

****

Introduction

The Scripture known as *The Gospel According to St. John* has been the foundation and background of a countless number of evangelistic and devotional messages.

> For God so loved the world, that He gave His only begotten Son, that whosoever believeth in him should not perish, but have everlasting life. (John 3:16)

> He that believeth on the Son hath everlasting life: and he that believeth not the Son shall not see life: but the wrath of God abideth on him. (John 3:36)

> Verily, verily, I say unto you, "He that heareth my word, and believeth on Him that sent me, hath everlasting life, and shall not pass into condemnation; but is passed from death unto life." (John 5:24)

The Holy Spirit has been pleased to use the above words, and various others, as a means of opening the eyes of many enquirers and of causing conviction to rest upon them and spiritual enlightenment to favour them. Every part of each of the twenty one chapters, as also every other part of the inspired Scriptures, has been used at some time or another to minister teaching, help and comfort to the believers and salvation to the seekers. Partly because of this, but chiefly because of the fact that the writing is manifestly different from the other three accounts of the earthly life and ministry of our Lord, this document has often been called the *spiritual gospel*, as distinct from the accounts penned by Matthew, Mark and Luke who look at and report His work and teaching from very much the same viewpoint. Because of this, the writings of Matthew, Mark and Luke are termed *synoptic;* (*syn* = together, *optic* = to see – hence they see together.)

It cannot be said that John's Gospel is any way opposed to the others, or that he disagrees with them. No! It is that he reports so much of what the Lord said which the other three do not mention and his *application* of the incidents and sayings of Christ that the others do report is not the same. The Synoptic Gospels dwell chiefly on our Lord's work in Galilee and Perea, the region beyond the Jordan. They report sayings and events which were contained within a period of little more than a year of ministry, although they intimate in various ways that the work and witness was of longer duration and extended to Judea also. Of this Judean ministry John gives many details, particularly of the Lord's words and teachings, so that about two-thirds of his narrative is entirely new, and his reports of those matters which are also to be found in the Synoptic Gospels are given with such important additions or omissions as to place them in entirely new light.

The Synoptics present a threefold view of Christ, each connected with the then immediate *earthly* kingdom aspects and consequences of His ministry, and they are almost entirely confined to the narrow Israelitish outlook. Matthew presents the Lord as King, Mark as Servant and Luke as Man. John lifts the whole concept of the Lord's life and ministry by equating Him with "The Word – Who was with God, and Who was God ... in the beginning." John thus presents Him as Son of God, Who was given for the whole world – the whosoevers.

It is the duty, and privilege, of the sincere Bible student to discover, if he can, the reason for the manifest difference between John and the Synoptics; to explain, and thus determine, *the original reason why John wrote his Gospel* and be able to appreciate its real value.

In an endeavour to help those who are uncertain respecting many points, we shall set out various observations, queries and suggestions. Although we have it in mind to leave some issues as inconclusive, we suppose that from what we write, and from the manner in which we set down our suggestions, it will be evident which way our studies are inclining us. We feel, however, that much more sifting of evidence, much more patient study and much more weighing of the *pros* and *cons* is necessary before anything approaching conclusiveness is attained.

As we commence, we must try to forget, if we can, the precious truths revealed in the later Scriptures but which are already known to us. We feel that we are far too prone to read into certain earlier parts of the New Testament, those truths which are only to be found in the later epistles. Or that we are apt, in our minds at least, to *spiritualise* certain statements and truths found in such writings as the Gospel of John in order to make them fit into, or more closely associate with, the revelation of the mystery only revealed after Israel had lost its national privileges at Acts 28:26-28 and which is the burden of Ephesians and Colossians. This is not necessary. In His own good time, when "the mystery of God is finished", He will integrate the separate parts of "the purpose of the ages" and be victoriously manifested as "all in all", (1 Corinthians 15:24-28). Each part of "the purpose of the ages", as revealed by and in the Scriptures, can stand securely on its own and does not need to be bolstered up by applying *spiritualised* truth from other parts. In this connection we must recognise and allow place for the fact that there are many lines of teaching in the outworking of truth, connected with each calling revealed in Scripture, which are more or less parallel. This is because each calling is, of necessity, linked in some way or other with the wonderful work of the Lord, as accomplished by His death and resurrection, and each calling finds the fulfilment of its hope in and through him. Because the work of Christ is the basis for each calling and because each finds its hope in Him, this gives us no warrant for confusing their issues. Are we not exhorted to "rightly divide the word of truth" (2 Timothy 2:15) and to "test the things that differ", (Philippians 1:10, margin)?

The date of John's Gospel

The date of the writing of this Gospel of John can only be inferred. Traditional sources affirm that it was written at Ephesus towards the end of the first century A.D., almost 30 years after Paul had completed his course and 25 years after Jerusalem had been laid waste by Titus in 70 A.D. We wonder if this is really so. Traditional sources have at different times proved unreliable. Not that the actual time of writing makes for much difference in any case, but we feel that there are strong indications of a date much earlier than generally thought.

It is fairly certain that the Gospel was written by John after the recording of the Revelation, as we shall show shortly, but when was the Revelation written? Was John's banishment to Patmos during the persecution in the reign of Nero, 54-68 A.D., or during the persecution in the reign of Domitian, 81-96 A.D.? In this matter, the testimony of tradition is about equally divided. We cannot go into details but give a few points from the rather strong arguments which favour the earlier date.

> (1) The references to Jerusalem and its temple, as made in Revelation 11:1-3, seem clearly to imply that the siege of 70 A.D., which reduced the city to rubble, had not taken place when John wrote.

> (2) The prominence given to the Lord's speedy return in Revelation 1:1,3 & 22:6, 7, 10, 12, 20 (as *parousia* or *apocalypse*). The nearness of the return finds abundant expression in the Scriptures written before the close of Acts, *but* not in those written *after* the setting aside of Israel at Acts 28:26-28. (See, for example, "the coming of the Lord draweth nigh" James 5:7-9; "The end of all things is at hand" 1 Peter 4:7; "For yet a little while, and he that shall come will come, and will not tarry" Hebrews 10:37; "the time is short" 1 Corinthians 7:29; "The night is far spent, the day is at hand" Romans 13:12. These are similar to the sentiments of Revelation chapters 1 and 22.)

Each of these points gives strong support to an early date for the writing of Revelation.

We must note particularly in Revelation 10:11 John is told "Thou must prophecy again, before many people and nations and tongues and kings." The Revelation itself was not a prophecy *to* or *for* "people, nations, tongues and kings" for the whole of it is expressly stated to be to the seven churches in Asia (Revelation 1:4, 11; 22:16) whose locations are specified. Therefore not even the remaining portion of Revelation, after the statement of 10:11, could be the promised further prophecy.

The first epistle of John is plainly written to some group of believers and the other two little letters given under John's name are "to the elect lady" and "to Gaius", so they cannot be the promised prophecy. This being so we ask if the Gospel of John fulfills the promise, remembering that scriptural prophecy is "*spokesmanship* for God involving *forthtelling* the truth as much, if not more than, *foretelling* the future?

It cannot be denied that John's Gospel has a *very wide audience* in view, *the world* and *whosoever*, and that these terms surely include "all people, nations, tongues and kings" and thus correspond with the statement of Revelation 10:11. It is also the first scriptural document to plainly state that God loved the whole world, (3:16).

If the promised further prophecy is not the Gospel of John we are driven to conclude either that the promise was broken or that the further prophecy was given but not included in the canon of Scripture, in which case the promise that the further message would be for so wide an audience could hardly have been fulfilled. We need not entertain such God dishonouring thoughts for the Gospel does fill all the necessary conditions so that we need not make conjectures.

With these observations as background we again ask "Is it certain that John wrote his Gospel late in the first century A.D.?" Consider these points.

> (1) If the Revelation was written in Patmos, or soon after the Patmos experience, at an early date before the setting aside of Israel in about 63 A.D., would 30 or more years have elapsed before the implementing of the promise of Revelation 10:11? Possibly yes, but rather unlikely.

> (2) In his Gospel John displays an intimate detailed knowledge of both Palestine in general and Jerusalem in particular. Land and city evidently meant much to him. Scripture portrays and speaks of John as "the disciple whom Jesus loved", but nevertheless the Lord names him, along with his brother, Boanerges – son of thunder (Mark 3:17). Other incidents in which John figures reveal him as loyal and devout, yet also forthright, perhaps quick-tempered, and we would say a keenly nationalistic Jew. Despite this, throughout the Gospel, he does not even so much as hint that Jerusalem with its temple has been destroyed, which took place in 70 A.D. On the contrary, his descriptions of places and his interpolated explanatory notes (undoubtedly supplied for other than Jewish readers) are all framed in such a way as to lead the reader to suppose that the places mentioned could still have been visited. Surely had this Gospel been written towards the close of the first century, 20 or 25 years *after the destructive siege of the city* by one who knew it so well, he would have at least included

some little explanatory note to the effect that the places to which he referred had been laid waste.

(3) Positive evidence that Jerusalem could still be visited and viewed at the time of writing the Gospel seems to be given at 5:2 and perhaps at 19:17. At 5:2 John states "... there *is* at (or *is* in) Jerusalem a pool which *is* called Bethesda *having* five porches." If written after the sack of the city, would he not have written "... there *was* at Jerusalem a pool which *was* called Bethesda which *had* five porches"? At 19:17 he writes of "... the place of a skull which *is* called Golgotha." Evidently the place could still easily be identified and was most probably continuing in use as a place of executions when John wrote.

Such present tense references would hardly have been likely at the close of the first century for Josephus (*Wars of the Jews*, Book VII Chapter 1) records that the entire city, excepting for three towers which were spared for use as Roman army barracks and stores, was completely devastated even as foretold by the Lord (Luke 19:41-44). So thorough was the destruction, that although a comparative few of the populace and those who had gathered into the city might have survived the rigours of the terrible siege, the fires, the systematic destruction, the killings and the subsequent deportations ensured that Jerusalem did not have further historical mention for years, and did not become a place of habitation of any size until 130 A.D. The greater number of those remaining in Jerusalem after 70 A.D. were shipped to Egypt and others sent as slaves to the provinces, (Josephus, *Wars of the Jews*, Book VI Chapter 9 and see Deuteronomy 28:68, Hosea 8:13 & 9:3). A few might have found refuge in underground vaulted chambers and places.

Each of these points lessens the support to the late dating of the Gospel which is a record of part of the earthly ministry of the Lord who, upon earth, was "a minister of the circumcision for the truth of God to confirm the promises made unto the fathers: and that the Gentiles might glorify God for His mercy" (Romans 15:8-12).

This Gospel was part of the written ministry of one-who was called by the Lord (Matthew 4:21, 22); who took part in the initial kingdom ministry (Matthew 4:22, 10:1-42); who, up to the time of the writing of the epistle to the Galatians, was recognised as one of the leading apostles (Galatians 2:9, a pillar) engaged in the ministry of the circumcision (Galatians 2:7-

9). **Nowhere in the New Testament is there the least indication that John was ever called to exercise any other ministry.**

"But isn't his Gospel written *to the world, to the whosoevers?*" you may ask. We would reply that as John received the commission, along with the other original apostles, to go only to "the lost sheep of the house of Israel" (Matthew 10:6) and, as we have already noted, was later confirmed in ministry "unto the circumcision" (Galatians 2:9) with no hint that this commission and confirmation was ever changed or in any way enlarged, this Gospel of John could not specifically be *to the world, to the whosoevers.*

We suggest that a careful reading reveals that the Gospel of John was most definitely a *circumcision* or *new covenant* document, written basically *to* and *for* the covenant people, Israel, but *with the wider witness of Israel* to the whole world very much in the foreground. This is in agreement with the *missionary* commissions given by the Lord prior to his ascension.

> Go ye therefore, and teach all nations, baptizing them in the name of the Father, and of the Son, and of the Holy Ghost: teaching them to observe all things whatsoever I have commanded you. (Matthew 28:19, 20)

> Go ye into all the world, and preach the gospel to every creature. (Mark 16:15)

> Repentance and remission of sins should be preached in his name among all nations, beginning at Jerusalem. (Luke 24:47)

> And ye shall be witnesses unto me both in Jerusalem, and in all Judea, and in Samaria, and unto the uttermost part of the earth. (Acts 1:8)

The purpose of John's Gospel

In the first chapter of this Gospel we soon come to an important statement at verse 11. He, the Word, Who made all things (verses 1-3) "came unto His own and His own received Him not". His own world "knew Him not" (verse 10). His own place, Bethlehem, the city of David, did not realise that He had come. His own people did not receive Him.

This verse 11 has been cited as referring either to His rejection by the Jewish people in the land, which did not come to a head until the crucifixion, or to the rejection of the message of Christ offered to the Jewish dispersion during the book of Acts, which did not come to a head until Acts 28:24-28.

However, the context of John 1:11 contains the statement that "the Word was made flesh and dwelt amongst us" (verse 14). This emphasizes the fact of the birth of the Lord. Both His mother Mary and his legal father Joseph were of David's line. Because of the decree of Caesar Augustus, Joseph and Mary – who was ready to give birth – travelled from Nazareth to Bethlehem because they were "of the house and lineage of David"; (see Matthew 1:1-16 and Luke 2:4 & 3:23, 38, first the kingly line and then the natural line. Joseph was legally reckoned to be the son of Heli, through betrothal and subsequent marriage to Heli's daughter Mary).

When the two arrived at the place where David had been born, "there was no room for them at the inn" (Luke 2:7). The innkeeper must have been a relative and every other soul in David's city that night must have been of David's line, but not one offered better accommodation for them than the place at the inn where the animals were kept. Thus He was born "king of the Jews" (Matthew 2:2) and from the very beginning of His human life was "despised and rejected of men" (Isaiah 53:3), even by His own close relatives.

Before chapter one finished we read that John the Baptist stated that the role of his ministry was that the "Lamb of God, which taketh away the sin of the world ... should be *made manifest to Israel*" (John 1:29-31) and we read of Nathaniel rightly addressing Him as "Rabbi, Thou art the Son of God; Thou art the *King of Israel*" (John 1:49)

In chapter 3, verses 1-10, Nicodemus was disturbed and perturbed by the Lord when He stated that the experience of being born from above (or born again) is necessary in order to see or to enter the Kingdom of God. The Lord expected this "master of Israel" to know this by his own reading of the prophets, (i.e. Ezekiel 37:2-14; Isaiah 66:8).

As we see it, this Gospel of John is a continuation of the kingdom and covenant literature, in particular containing the details of the life, ministry and teaching of the King, through whose sacrificial blood the *new covenant* had been ratified. It is a continuation of the kingdom and covenant literature in relation to the wider missionary activity in which *the twelve* in particular, and the people of Israel in general, could have engaged as a result of the equipment specially given to them at Pentecost time, seven weeks after the crucifixion and resurrection.

According to God's revealed plan, the evangelizing of the nations in relation to the kingdom and covenant purposes is most definitely the responsibility of Israel. The "gospel preached before unto Abraham" (Galatians 3:8), specifically stated that "in thee (i.e. in Abraham and his seed) shall all nations (families of the earth) be blessed," (Genesis 12:3, 18:18, 26:4 etc.). Later it was revealed, particularly through the prophet Isaiah, that, the chosen people would be the vehicle of the blessing as promised, through their *witness* to the other nations and peoples.

> Let all the nations be gathered together, and let the people be assembled: who among them can declare this, and shew us former things? Let them bring forth their witnesses, that they may be justified: or let them hear, and say, "It is truth." *Ye are my witnesses* ... and my servant whom I have chosen: that ye may know and believe me, and understand that I am He: before me there was no God formed, neither shall there be after Me. I, even I, am the Lord; and beside me there is no Saviour. I have declared, and have saved, and I have shewed, when there was no strange god among you: therefore *ye are my witnesses* ... I am God. (Isaiah 43:9-12)

Earlier we stated how the Lord, prior to His ascension, commissioned His disciples to be *witnesses* to the wider world, (note Matthew 28:18, 19; Mark 16:15; Luke 24:47 & Acts 1:8 quoted earlier). In view of this we suggest that John's Gospel is the record of "all things whatsoever" Christ had commanded His disciples to teach as *witnesses* to the nations (Matthew 28:20). As the principal minister of the circumcision (Romans 15:8) and as the "faithful and true witness" (Revelation 3:14; compare with John 8:14 etc.), Christ had instructed those whom He had gathered round Him and whom He was to leave on earth to continue the circumcision witness and ministry, in those truths necessary to ensure that all the "promises made with the fathers" might be confirmed and eventually fulfilled.

> Now I say unto you that Jesus Christ was a minister of the circumcision for the truth of God to confirm the promises made unto the fathers: and that the Gentiles might glorify God for His mercy; as it is written, 'For this cause I will confess to thee among the Gentiles, and sing unto Thy name.' And again he saith, 'Rejoice, ye Gentiles, with His people.' And again, 'Praise the Lord, all ye Gentiles; and laud Him, all ye people.' And again, Esaias saith, 'There shall be a root of Jesse, and He shall rise to reign over the Gentiles; in Him shall the Gentiles trust.' (Romans

15:8-12)

As can be seen from the above verses, these promises "made unto the fathers" embraced and included the Gentiles who, through Israel's witness, would be brought to praise and glorify God. But Scripture makes it apparent that the twelve, as well as the other disciples, were "foolish" in that they were "slow of heart" to believe all that the prophets had spoken (Luke 24:25). Despite the fact the Lord "opened their understanding that they might understand the Scriptures" (Luke 24:45), they nevertheless failed to engage in the wider witness but continued, almost exclusively, to go "to none but the Jews only" (Acts 11:19).

After the passing of time, and in accord with the statement of the Lord concerning the ministry of the Holy Spirit (John 14:26), John gradually had brought back to his "remembrance" (Greek *hupomim* = to remind gradually, Young) the things which the Lord *had* said – backed up by certain things that He *had* done – to prepare and teach the twelve in respect of the world-wide witness and message. We believe that this Gospel of John was the result.

It seems to us that in this writing of John is the content of the message which *missionary* Israel could have taken to the world had they, as a people, responded to the appeals for repentance made at Pentecost and in the days and years which followed, to the end of Acts. Had they, as a people, thus repented, they would doubtless have been instructed by the apostles who, similarly to John through the ministry of the Spirit, would have *gradually remembered* the teaching of Christ as to the role that a repentant, restored Israel should plays as *witnesses* before and to the Gentile world.

Note how *witness* figures largely in John's Gospel. The word in its two main forms occurs no fewer than 47 times. *Witness* originally indicated both the testimony borne and its most likely result of martyrdom. This word markedly links the Gospel with Revelation, where the witness or testimony bearers are the *overcomers* who "loved not their lives unto the death", thus becoming martyrs, (Revelation 12:11). We are strongly of the opinion that this Gospel was necessary in order to prepare the way for that *witness* which will be sustained by repentant, restored Israelites, many of whom will be the *overcomers*, giving their testimony as world missionaries when the time for that ministry comes. Meantime, we who are members of the Church which is His Body should recognise this Gospel of John as being originally written to give the message for such Israelitish missionaries to take to the whole world, most likely *after* the present purpose of God shall have been completed; when the kingdom and covenant purposes which were deferred about the time of Acts 28:28, will be resumed. If this view is correct it means that the dispensational place of this Gospel is mainly in a yet future day, in a period prior to, and also perhaps through, the millennium.

By the time John wrote his Gospel it had become apparent that Israel as a force were failing to repent, and their opportunity of national repentance was fast declining. "Blindness in part" had happened to them; only "a remnant according to the election by grace" were faithful and the rest were hardened, as Paul stated in Romans 11:25. So it is that John opens his Gospel against the background of an unrepentant and failing Israel, and he records that from His very earliest days, as prophesised by Isaiah, "the Saviour of the World" (John 4:42), was despised and rejected of men (Isaiah 53:3). *His own* rejected Him and in the end insisted upon His crucifixion, crying out "His blood be on us and on our children" (Matthew 27:25). Looking back from the time of his writing this account, John goes on to indicate, however, that despite such widespread national rejection, *the door was not yet completely closed*, for "as many as" individually had "received Him – believing on His name" had been granted power as children of God and had received of "His fulness ... grace for grace," (John 1:12-18).

From this point, with reference to Elias who was to come before the *day of the Lord* and the millennial kingdom (compare Malachi 4:5, 6 and Matthew 17:10, 11, and Isaiah, who prophesied concerning the greatness and blessings of the promised kingdom,) and with a record of Nathaniel's pointed testimony to Christ as King of *Israel* (John 1:25, 49), John goes on to trace those aspects of the Lord's teaching and to recount those incidents of His ministry which form the basis of "The gospel of the kingdom" which Israel had, at the time of John's writing, failed to take to the whole world as instructed by Christ, (see Matthew 24:14; 28:19; Mark 16:15; Luke 24:47; Acts 1:8). With the missionary commands evidently still ringing in his ears, and having been reminded under the ministry of the Spirit, John proceeds to indicate that his fellow countrymen would not, indeed could not, be *witnesses* for God to the whole world until they had been made to understand, just as Nicodemus, who was a master of Israel, needed to understand. Thus as a nation they must be born by water, i.e. baptism, and by the spirit, as John the Baptist had proclaimed, ("born of water and of the spirit", John 3:5, links with Mark 16:16). As a nation they must be born from above by the Spirit's operation, before the kingdom could be seen or entered, even by themselves let alone those who were outside Israel's fold. The much used gospel statement at John 3:16 is the outcome of the teachings of the necessity of being born again – (see Isaiah 66:8) – linked with the operation of the Spirit as *wind* or *breath* – (see Ezekiel 37, where the bringing together and bringing to life of the dried up dead bones of the nation is accomplished by the same *breath*. Note too that Ezekiel 37 concludes with a reference to the effect of Israel's resuscitation upon *the heathen*, i.e. the other nations, who would be brought to know God's wondrous works, verse 28).

In chapter 4 John records the conversation with the Samaritan woman which reaches its climax in the observation concerning spiritual worship.

Israel was needing to be taught, as this woman was then being taught, that narrow nationalistic and ceremonial conceptions would have to be swept away before *salvation*, of which the Jews were than and will again be custodians (verse 22) ministering the life giving water (verses 5-15) to all the world. As a sequel to this revelation to the Samaritan woman, Christ, looking ahead, saw "the fields (the world) white already to harvest," (the harvest as "the end of the age" – the *sunteliea* leading on to the millennial period; e.g. Matthew 13:38, 40). We have not the space to continue giving all applications of the Lord's teaching along this line as is contained throughout the Gospel. (e.g.; in Chapter 15 Christ speaks of Himself as *the true vine*, Israel as a vine having failed, and the disciples and believers as branches, branches that must *abide* or *continue* (verses 1-7 for fruitfulness in the world) verses 16-19).

Together, with the worldwide aspect attached to the Lord's teaching, John records eight specifically selected signs (20:30-31) which, among other things, set forth Israel's then present and continuing importance and their blindness (5:1-15 & 9:1-41), from which they could be delivered if they would but respond; their need of Christ's presence when upon the agitated sea of this world, if true witness was to be given (6:15-21 & cf 16:33): the result of their witness and ministry, in that a great multitude would be satisfied in the kingdom of God (6:1-14). The sign at Cana teaches that the Lord's glory will be manifest at the marriage (2:1-11 & 3:29), pointing forward to the great marriage to come (Revelation 21) and the sign of the draught of fish and the breakfast on the shore (21:1-14) points forward to the satisfaction to be enjoyed by Israel as the principal participants of the feast in His presence at the fruition of the covenant purposes.

These eight signs, each of which was specifically selected for Israel the *sign* people, were specially recorded, we are told, in order that belief in Jesus as *Christ (Messiah) the Son of God* might be engendered (20:30-31). Not, Mark you, in Jesus as Head, but as the divine *Messiah* (1:41; 4:25 etc.

& cf. Daniel 9:25), the God anointed One Who was to come, Israel's Prince, leader and peculiar hope in and through Whom all the kingdom and covenant promises were to be fulfilled. This stated purpose for the recording of the eight signs, as well as the general teaching of the Lord as recorded in this Gospel, seems to us plainly to indicate that the message of John's Gospel is primarily concerned with kingdom, covenant and circumcision matters, and will find its place and fulfilment at the time when the kingdom and covenant purposes are resumed.

This does not mean that the Gospel of John cannot be of use today. Indeed, no! It is part of "all Scripture given by inspiration and is profitable ... that we may be thoroughly furnished" (2 Timothy 3:16, 17). It is important to note that in each of the Gospels one of the main themes is the person of the King Who is portrayed in His humiliation as well as in His special relationship to Israel. We can only understand and appreciate Him in His exaltation in the heavenly places in relation to our understanding and appreciation of Him while in the flesh. Also there is much in John's Gospel that is illustrative of truth necessary for each part of the purpose of God. Much runs parallel with truths that are the special portion of the members of the church which is His body but we need to be careful not to confuse the issues by trying to make the truths of this Gospel equal to those of the message of the mystery, whose truths are only to be found in the epistles Paul wrote after the blindness of Israel at Acts 28:26-28.

Some may ask if John's Gospel is not to be used as basic to the evangelistic message for today, "Where in scripture do we find the basis of the gospel of our present salvation?" Plain statements of the saving truth affecting Gentiles of this present phase of the purpose of God are found in abundance in the epistles written after Acts 28:26-28. For example:

> He hath made us accepted in the beloved. In Whom we have redemption through His blood, the forgiveness of sins, according to the riches of His grace. (Ephesians 1:6-7

> But God, who is rich in mercy, for His great love wherewith He loved us, even when we were dead in sins, hath quickened us together with Christ, (by grace ye are saved;) and hath raised us up together, and made us sit together in heavenly places in Christ Jesus; that in the ages to come He might shew the exceeding riches of His grace in His kindness towards us through Christ Jesus. For by grace are ye saved through faith; and that not of yourselves: it is the gift of God: not of works, lest any man should boast. (Ephesians 2:4-9)

Who hath delivered us from the power of darkness, and hath translated us into the kingdom of His dear Son: in Whom we have redemption through His blood, even the forgiveness of sins. (Colossians 1:13, 14)

And you, that were sometime alienated and enemies in your mind by wicked works, yet now hath He reconciled. In the body of His flesh through death, to present you holy and unblameable and unreproveable in His sight. (Colossians 1:21-22)

For there is one God, and one Mediator between God and men, the man Christ Jesus; Who gave Himself a ransom for all. (1 Timothy 2:5, 6)

God Who hath saved us, and called us with a holy calling, not according to our works, but according to His own purpose and grace, which was given us in Christ Jesus, Who hath abolished death, and hath brought life and immortality to light through the gospel. (2 Timothy 1:9, 10).

For the grace of God that bringeth salvation hath appeared to all men. (Titus 2:11)

These, and similar statements to be found in the epistles written by Paul, the apostle to the Gentiles, after the end of Acts, find their foundation in the basic sacrifice of our Lord Jesus Christ, and are amplified by the doctrines that are built upon that *one sacrifice for sin*; i.e. redemption by blood and justification by faith as elaborated in Paul's epistles to the Romans and Galatians, which doctrines are illustrative and typified in a multitude of ways throughout the Old Testament scriptures, particularly in and through the early history of the people of Israel. This great field of truth is rich enough to provide material for all gospel preaching in this present age, and the kingdom and new covenant teaching need only be referred to as *illustrating* certain facets of present day gospel truth, or for building up the general pattern of God's dealing with believers, or men generally, as necessary.

Let us re-iterate that it seems that this Gospel of John falls into the same category as those of Matthew, Mark and Luke, in that all four set forth truth about the *King*, the *kingdom* and the *gospel of the kingdom,* but John is markedly different in a very important way. The Synoptics record the message of the kingdom and its gospel *for the house of Israel*, while the

King was present upon earth and the kingdom was *at hand*, while the Gospel of John records the background of the message of the *gospel of the kingdom* in relation to its world-wide application as taught by the Lord, and as it should have been *preached* by missionary Israel "in all the world for a witness unto all nations," and as it will *yet* be proclaimed by Israel prior to "the end" (Matthew 24:14). It is in this way that this Gospel will be the fulfilment of the promise given to John as recorded at Revelation 10:11, and from this point of view it is a prophecy forthtelling and foretelling the message and witness concerning the kingdom which is yet to be given by Israel, when they set forth the Lord as their Messiah, through Whose name is life for all who believe.

The purpose of God

Perhaps it will be as well to give a synopsis of that part of the purpose of God which includes Israel's witness. From the record of Genesis 2 and 3 it is quite evident that there was the possibility of Adam eating of the tree of life and thus living forever; i.e. possessing natural physical life for an undefined period of time. (We propose to discuss the terms *for ever, eternal, everlasting* etc. later in this study.) But sin entered, man fell and although Adam lived for over 900 years, eventually he and all mankind since have fallen prey to death, outstanding exceptions being Enoch and Elijah. Nevertheless, provision was made to keep, or guard, the tree of life from wrong usage, (Genesis 3:22-24), thus picturing and proclaiming God's intention that despite man's fall, He would make possible the partaking of the life giving fruit of the tree so that eventually man could have life *forever;* that man would be able to enjoy a continuance of natural physical life on earth without fear or dread of the consequences of the original disobedience.

In order to make this and other facets of the purpose of the ages possible, God first chose Abraham and made him the progenitor of an elect people whom He could use as His *witnesses* first to the inhabitants of the land (Exodus 15:14; Numbers 14:13, 14), and later to the whole earth (Deuteronomy 28:9, 10; Isaiah 43:10-13, 44:8), by making them the living illustration of His gracious intentions for all mankind. In the process of the unfolding of this design, God made Himself known to Abraham as *El Olam*, the everlasting God or, more literally, the God of the Age, (Genesis 21:33). Later in Israel's history, David prayed "Thou has confirmed to Thyself Thy people Israel to be a people unto thee *for ever*" (2 Samuel 7:24), again *olam*, and we would render this "a people unto Thee for the age."

At Isaiah 44:7 we read of the ancient (*olam*) people. Therefore Israel are "the *age* people". To these elect *age* people God made a promise of a certain tract of land which was theirs "for ever" (Genesis 13:15), as an "everlasting possession" (Genesis 17:8; 48:4). With Israel God entered into an "everlasting covenant" (Genesis 17:13). The one promise God gave in the Ten Commandments was to the effect that "thy days *be long* upon the land which the Lord thy God giveth thee" Exodus 20:12). The promise for obedience to the requirements of God as to be the enjoyment of *life* as opposed to *death* (Deuteronomy 30:15-20), that their days should be *prolonged* upon the land because God was their life. This was interpreted by the psalmist as "life for evermore" (Psalm 133:3) and he speaks of those who are blessed as inheriting the earth to "dwell for evermore" (Psalm 37:2-27).

Furthermore Israel were promised a throne and a kingdom *for ever* (2 Samuel 7:13-16), which kingdom Daniel saw in a vision (Daniel 7:27). They were to be ruled by "David their prince (ruler or captain) *forever*" (Ezekiel 37:24). Thus in "the age to come", Israel is to be made "an eternal excellency, the joy of many generations" (Isaiah 60:15).

In this last verse, and in the references above, the words *for ever, eternal ancient, everlasting and evermore* are variant English renderings of the Hebrew word *olam*, which has the basic meaning of "age enduring". Had we space to spare we could multiply references which would make it quite clear that Israel, the age people, have been promised a golden age during which, as God's elect privileged nation, and as a lesson for all other peoples, Israel will be "high above all nations" (Deuteronomy 26:18, 19; 28:1) "the head and not the tail" (Deuteronomy 28:12, 13). They will shew to all the world the benefits of submission to the rule and righteousness of God, and will lead those other people, tongues, nations and kings to an acknowledgement of God and into the enjoyment of the same *everlasting life* or *life for evermore.*

In the book of Revelation we read that after the golden age, the thousand years during which Christ reigns in righteousness (Revelation 20:2-6), and after the final deception of the nations by Satan has been dealt with (Revelation 20:7-9) and the judgment settled (Revelation 20:10-15), God's original intention will be realised. The illustration of *the age people* living throughout the millennial period will have served its purpose and an even more abiding reality of life will then be enjoyed. The former heaven and earth will pass away. A new heaven and earth will be brought into being (Revelation 21:1) and among the many blessings and benefits "there shall be no more death" (Revelation 21:4). The "water of life" shall proceed "out of the throne of God" and "the tree of life" will be available for all, its leaves perfecting the healing of the nations. There will be a complete reversal of the Edenic curse (Revelation 22:1-5). Life, as forfeited by Adam, will again be possible (perhaps unending physical life), to be enjoyed by those who will people the new earth.

But we must go back to the Gospel of John and see, if we can how it fits into the overall scheme. The principal line of teaching running from beginning to end of the Gospel is concerned with *life*. The word for life is *zoe* and occurs 36 times. Its cognate *zao*, to live, occurs 17 times. From its general New Testament usage it is evident that it is an inclusive word which covers living existence in all its forms and at all levels, from Divine life down to the lower animals and vegetable forms of life. In several places it is used in conjunction with *eternal* and *everlasting*.

In John 1:1-4 we read "the Word was God ... in Him was *life*". "The Word became flesh ... the only begotten of the Father" (1:14). At 10:10 we read the Lord's statement "I am come that they (i.e. the sheep of this, Israel's, fold) might have life", and in order that this might be possible He said "I lay down my *life* for the sheep" and for "the other sheep ... which are not of this fold" (10:15, 16). Towards the end of the Gospel, at 20:31, we read that those who believe "that Jesus is the Christ, the son of God" will have "*life* through His name". By reference to the general teaching of the Gospel, this believing "that Jesus is the Christ" involves believing that "the Word was *life*", that "the Word became flesh", that the Word, as "the shepherd of the sheep", gave His *life* that it might be assimilated by those for whom it was given (John 6:50-58). On some 17 occasions in this Gospel *life* is defined as being *eternal* or *everlasting*. Can we find out just what this might mean?

Ainoios is the adjectival form of the noun *aion* which in the New Testament is rendered world, age, ever and never. From these variant renderings of the noun it will be appreciated that the adjective will of necessity be a difficult word to assess. In classical Greek Herodotus, Euripides and other use *aion* as meaning "the length of life" and "the life principle", which carries a man through the years no matter how few or how many their numbers might be. It was also employed to define a generation or an epoch, and finally "a very long space of time".

In Hellenistic Greek times *aionios* was used to express the supposedly never ending royal power of Rome as personified in their Emperors, who were often treated as gods. In Plato's *Law* he writes that *aionios* is the possession of gods and not of men. The principal facts emerging from the classical and secular usage of *aionios* is that it is a word of deity as contrasted with humanity, of quality rather than quantity, of essence and character of being more than length of time. Milligan says that it described "a state wherein the horizon is not in view". Thus it is a word which transcends time and distance.

In the New Testament Scriptures *aionios* is employed in connection with life, redemption, inheritance, habitations, covenant, hope and salvation. It is used of the kingdom and of the gospel, of the fire of punishment and of the punishment itself; of judgment and destruction. A careful assessing of its varied usages will reveal that to take it as meaning "lasting for ever" is either not definite enough (when used of God and things of God) or perhaps going too far (when used in conjunction with man and the things of man).

In order to arrive at its Scriptural meaning, the *context of each usage must be taken into consideration*, as well as the *basic meaning*, remembering that in the final analysis it is the word which can only really be applied to God. To confine its meaning to "lasting for ever" is to oversimplify and misunderstand the truth it would convey. We would try to sum up its scriptural meaning thus: - when *aionios* is used, according to its context, it signifies that which befits God's character and nature of love, holiness, goodness, truth and justice to give, make, promise or inflict, as the case may be. In some instances this might involve "unending" or "lasting for ever" as humanly understood, but always remember that such interpretation expresses only part of its meaning. What we have written concerning the Greek *aionios* we would repeat concerning its equivalent Hebrew word, *olam* and would say that both have a touch of mystery in their make up as well as in their meaning.

The place of John's Gospel

Now we feel that our enquiry has, for the time, proceeded far enough and in conclusion we suggest that the message of the Gospel of John is a circumcision, kingdom and New Covenant message, basically *to* and *for* the covenant people. It sets out the means whereby their failure as witnesses to the world could be overcome – i.e. by their accepting *aionios* (age-enduring) life via the new birth accomplished by the power of the Holy Spirit and by their assimilation of Christ. This experience of "*life* through His name" would be the illustrations of the witness they would bear, which *life* is to be shared by all of the *whosoevers* who hear and receive the testimony to the Christ, the Messiah, in preparation for the *one thousand years*.

Seen thus, the dispensational place of the Gospel of John is in a time different to the purpose concerning the Church which is His Body. It could have had its fulfilment in the Acts period if the twelve and the other disciples had followed the commission of the resurrected Christ (Matthew 28:18, 19; Mark 16:15; Luke 24:47; Acts 1:8). Now it awaits that future period when the kingdom on earth which is again actively anticipated, prepared for and proclaimed by those who are to be missionaries of that particular *good news*. We suggest that John's Gospel is:

> (1) the background of the message of the kingdom upon the earth which is yet to be:

> (2) possibly the content of the message to be used by the kingdom missionaries in their ministry to the whole world:

> (3) the prophetic message, backed by the illustration of the restored *age enduring* people Israel, of the *everlasting life* that is to be enjoyed in and through the vase phases of the Divine purpose which lies beyond the Millennial age. Vast ages when "there shall be no more death" (Revelation 21:4) and when the servants of God and of the Lamb "shall serve Him and see His face" (Revelation 22:3, 4) and when God will be "all in all" (1 Corinthians 15:18).

Appendix: Helpful Charts

	The Gospels, The Acts Epistles of Peter, James, John, Jude & Revelation	Paul's Epistles written *before* end of Acts, Galatians 1 & 2 Thessal, Hebrews, 1 & 2 Corin Romans	Epistles written by Paul *after* the end of Acts. Ephesians, Philippians, Colossians, Philemon, 1 & 2 Timothy & Titus
Name or Feature	**# of times Used**	**# of Times Used**	**No. of Times Used and References**
ABRAHAM	46	29	Not Once
ISAAC	12	7	Not Once
JACOB	18	5	Not Once
ISRAEL-ITE-ISH	58	20	2 (Ephesians 2:12; Philippians 3:5)
SEED (Referring to land of Promise)	10	17	1 (2 Timothy 2:8)
LAND (referring to land of Promise)	7	1	Not Once
Circumcise-d-ion-ing	14	32	9 (Ephesians 2:11; Philippians 3:3,5; Colossians 2:11;3:11;4:11; Titus 1:10)
MOSES	59	20	1 (2 Timothy 3:8)
LAW	55	125	8 (Ephesians 2:15;Philippians 3:5,6,9; 1 Timothy 1:7,8,9; Titus 3:9)
DAVID	53	5	1 (2 Timothy 2:8)

JEW-S-ISH (approx.)	170	29	2 (Colossians 3:11; Titus 1:14)
COVENANT-S, AND TESTAMENT	7	25	1 (Ephesians 2:12)
KING (referring to Christ)	37	-	2 (1 Timothy 1:17; 6:15)
KINGDOM +	32	2	1 (Ephesians 5:5) Kingdom of Christ and of God
KINGDOM OF HEAVEN	31	-	1 (Colossians 1:13) Kingdom of His Dear Son
KINGDOM OF GOD	61	3	1 (Colossians 4:11) Kingdom of God 1 (2 Timothy 4:1) His Kingdom 1 (2 Timothy 4:18) His Heavenly Kingdom
+The Kingdom, A Kingdom, His Kingdom, Kingdom of the Father, Thy Kingdom, My Kingdom, My Father's Kingdom, Kingdom of our father David, Everlasting Kingdom.			

This first chart, on pages 172 & 173, is a slight modification of the one given earlier in this book and pages 114-115.

The second chart, on the next two pages, *The Three Divisions of the New Testament* is by Michael Penny and comes from his book *The Beginning and end of ... The Acts of the Apostles.*

The Three Divisions of the New Testament
Note: All numbers in this table are approximate

Word / subject	*The Gospel Period*	*The Acts Period*			*The Post Acts Period*
	The Gospels	The Acts of the Apostles and the earlier letters			The Later Letters
	Almost exclusively Jewish	To the Jew first, and also to the Gentile			All believers equal. No such thing as Jew or Gentile
			Letters to Jewish Christians	Paul's earlier letters to Jewish & Gentile Christians	Paul's later letters to Christians
	Matthew Mark Luke John	The Acts of the Apostles	Hebrews James 1,2 Peter 1,2,3 John Jude Revelation	Romans 1,2 Cor Galatians 1,2 Thess	Ephesians Philippians Colossians 1, 2 Tim Titus Philemon
No. of Chapters	**89**	**28**	**56**	**59**	**28**
Abraham	34	7	13	19	0
Isaac	7	4	5	3	0
Jacob	14	8	3	2	0
Israel / Israelite	31	21	6	18	2
Moses	43	19	13	9	1
David	38	11	5	3	1
Jew (s), Jewish	72	81	2	27	2
Total so far	**239**	**151**	**47**	**81**	**6**
Jerusalem	87	62	4	10	0
Covenant (s)	4	2	18	9	1

Priest (s)	99	27	40	0	0
Law (*nomos*)	24	19	21	94	6
Fast (s) fasting	21	5	0	3	0
Sabbath	56	10	0	0	1
Heal (ed), healing	72	14	15	4	0

About the author

Ernest Streets was born in London in 1905. On leaving school he worked first in a factory and then in a solicitor's office, before entering Glasgow Bible Training Institute. From there he conducted various weekend evangelical campaigns in Scotland, one being held in Cowdenbeath, a small coal-mining town in Fife. The following year he returned to Cowdenbeath for the whole of the summer with a marquee. At the end of 1927, following a great summer of revival and aided by another student from the Bible Training Institute in Glasgow, one who had been born in that town, together they founded the Cowdenbeath Gospel Mission. Ernest Streets became its pastor in 1927 and was its only pastor. In 1990 the Mission was forced to close its doors, and in 1991 Ernest Streets fell asleep in Christ. He lived his life "looking for that blessed hope, and the glorious appearing of the great God and Saviour Jesus Christ" (Titus 2:13), and now he awaits that moment, "When Christ who is our life shall appear, then shall ye also appear with him in glory" (Colossians 3:4).

Michael Penny

Further Reading

Approaching the Bible
Michael Penny

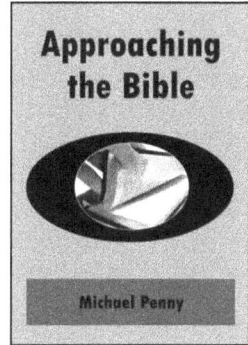

If you have enjoyed reading this publication then this book by Michael Penny clearly explains the rationale behind some of Ernest Streets' teaching. It does so in an easy to read style and with easy to understand method, and it does an excellent job of following the advice of Bishop Miles Coverdale (referred to by Ernest Streets), which was contained in the first Bible printed in English. That advice was based on asking such questions as:

- "Who" were these words written to, or "Who" were they about?
- "Where" is this to take place?
- "When" was it written or "When" is it about?
- "What", precisely, is said?
- "Why" did God say it, do it, or will do it?

After asking such questions, we then will have a better understanding of what the Scriptures say and make a better application to our lives,

****

For further details of this book, and the ones on the next page, please visit **www.obt.org.uk**

Copies can be ordered from that website and also from

The Open Bible Trust,
Fordland Mount, Upper Basildon,
Reading, RG8 8LU, UK.

They are also available as eBooks from Amazon and Apple and as KDP paperbacks from Amazon.

The Miracles of the Apostles
Michael Penny

Ernest Street's referred to 'These Signs' of Mark's Gospel. To encourage the nation of Israel to repent the Apostles were given power to perform 'The Signs' and various wonders. But what did 'These Signs' signify to Israel?

In this book Michael Penny describes the nature of each miraculous sign. Each one is clearly defined and its purpose explained. The miraculous signs discussed include:

healing and judgement,
visions and voices,
knowledge and wisdom,
tongues and interpretation,
visitations and revelations,
wonders in heaven above and signs on the earth beneath.

This book deals with every type of miraculous signs performed by the Apostles, leaving each miracle in its biblical context, the author explains the significance and reason behind each type of miracle.

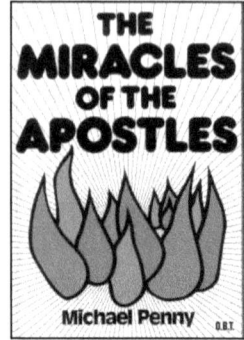

40 Problem Passages
Michael Penny

There are far more than *40 Problem Passages* in the Bible but by using the Rules for Bible Study advocated by Miles Coverdale, and thoroughly explained in *Approaching the Bible*, Michael Penny equips the reader with a method by which many more difficult passages can be understood and successfully applied to life today.

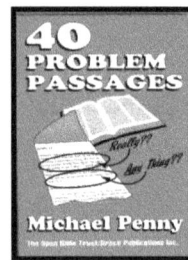

¹ In this connection it is well to note that it says in Galatians 2:7, 'the gospel *of* the circumcision 'and' the gospel *of* the uncircumcision'. Not the *same* gospel being proclaimed through different sets of messengers to the Jews (circumcision) on the one hand and to the Gentiles (uncircumcision) on the other, but *different messages* (though based on the same 'sacrifice for sins') for Paul says in Galatians 2:2 that 'by revelation' he went to Jerusalem to 'communicate unto them', i.e. the apostles and leaders at Jerusalem *'that* gospel which I preach among the Gentiles', a gospel so different from the gospel preached by the others, that it occasioned: 1) The writing of the epistle to the Galatians, with Paul's fighting defence of both *his* apostleship and *his* gospel (see Romans 2:18; 2 Timothy 2:8) and in which he voices a curse upon any, be it angel or even himself, who would seek to impose 'another gospel', i.e. the gospel of the circumcision, upon these Galatian believers who had responded to and been blessed under his 'gospel of the uncircumcision' (see Acts 15:1-5; Galatians 1:8-9). 2) The Council at Jerusalem, as reported at Acts 15, when the whole matter was thoroughly considered, guiding principles adopted, and the 'decrees' for the Gentile believers were formulated (read Acts from 15:1 to 18:4).

² Those who desire to study this more closely should note:

1) John's usage of *'parousia'* in connection with the Lord's return (1 John 2:28).

2) The possible nearness of the realization of that return, 'it is the last hour' (2:18).

3) Miraculous knowledge (2:20; 2:27; and cf 1 Corinthians 12:8).

4) The test for spirit utterance (1:1-3; and cf 1 Corinthians 12:3).

5) Immediate answers to prayer (5:14, 15 & Acts 1:24-26; 4:29-33; 12:5-14; etc.

6) The 'sin unto death' (5:16-17; cf Acts 5:1-11; Matthew 12:31, 32)

Each of these features is connected with 'the circumcision' and 'the kingdom'.

³ The ministries 'to the circumcision' and 'to the uncircumcision'. During their proclamation 'the circumcision' were privileged and held prior place, having then 'much advantage and profit' as stated at Romans 3:1, 2.

⁴ Romans 11:11; 11:17; 11:25 also makes it plain that Israel still stood as a nation before God. Only "*some* branches broken off", only "blindness *in part.*

⁵ [5] During Paul's 1ˢᵗ and 2ⁿᵈ missionary journeys and until when at Ephesus during the 3ʳᵈ missionary journey, he made the Jewish synagogue, (if there was one in the place being visited) his preaching centre. – Acts 13:11; 11:1; 17:1; 17:17; 18:1; 18:19; 19:8. – and gave his gospel 'to the Jew first'. The movement towards a 'Gentiles only' ministry was made

when Paul "departed from" the synagogue at Ephesus "and separated the disciples, disputing daily in the school of one Tyrannus" (Acts 19:9) but unto the end of his first ministry he acted upon the principle "to the Jew first", as we see when right at its close, on his arrival at Rome, he first "called together the chief of the Jews" (Acts 28:17), to meet with him at his place of detention, and to place before them what proved to be the last opportunity of repentance and acceptance of such blessing and grace and God, even then, was still willing to bestow upon Israel had they but repented, and accepted it.

[6] "Speaking with tongues" is known as '*glossolalia*' by the psychologists. Various forms of this phenomenon are actually far older than Christianity; instances are to be found in all primitive religions – (from earliest times and even into this present day) – where ritualistic orgies in honour of some deity usually concluded with a display of incoherent babblings, trances, convulsive fits, or other strange and startling manifestations of subconscious tension or demonic possession. The true "speaking with other tongues" of the Acts period, was a "sign", specially given by God, operative in the power of the Spirit, to give witness to Israel (Isaiah 28:11; 1 Corinthians 14:21, 22).

[7] Not, as Matthew 28:19 records Christ as directing, "in the name of the Father, and of the Son, and of the Holy Ghost". Have you ever stopped to ask why there is no record of this formula having been used throughout the history of the Acts period?

[8] See Appendix 1 – To The Jew First.

[9] See Appendix 2 – Scriptural Proof of the "Lively Hope"

[10] The opposite is also true, - the sudden unlooked-for death or falling into severe sickness and weakness, of those who outwardly appeared perfectly robust.

[11] Except the Didache, or Teaching of the Twelve, which is supposed to be about the middle of the second century, but which shows how soon the corruption of the New Testament "Christianity" had set in.

[12] The teaching that man is the possessor of an 'immortal soul' cannot be found on the page of Scripture. On the contrary, in His grace God prevented the possibility of man living "for ever" sin (Genesis 3:22-24), and in that same grace safeguards the way to "the tree of life", thus pointing forward to the One "who only (alone) hath immortality" (deathlessness), and through Whom alone man will realise and enjoy "the promise of life" (see 1 Timothy 6:14-16; 2 Timothy 1:10).

[13] See Isaiah 11:6-8 and Romans 8:19-22 for other teaching which links the destiny of the lower creation with that of man.

[14] "Everlasting covenant". This expression occurs 14 times throughout the scriptures, as follows: - Genesis 9:16; 17:13; 17:19; Leviticus 24:8; 2 Samuel 23:5; 1 Chronicles 16:17; Psalm 105:10; Isaiah 24:5; 55:3; 61:8;

Jeremiah 32:40; Ezekiel 16:60; 37:26; in the Old Testament, and Hebrews 13:20 in the New Testament.

[15] In this respect see how that at first God speaks of the "seed" of Abram under the metaphor of "the dust of the earth", Genesis 13:16, indicating an earthly purpose. When the actual covenant is made God speaks of the "seed" under the metaphor "the stars", Genesis 15:5, indicating a heavenly purpose. After the typical sacrifice and resurrection of Isaac, both heavenly and earthly aspects are mentioned together at Genesis 22:17, under the metaphors of "the stars of the heaven" and "the sand upon the sea shore", for it is only through the sacrificed and resurrected Christ, who is the actual "seed" (Galatians 3:16;), that these two parts of the purpose concerning Israel can and will be effected.

[16] The word "believed" comes from the root, whence we derive our 'Amen'. As it were, Abram said "Amen" to the Lord. Amen in Scripture never means 'May it be' but is always the strong assertion 'It shall be' or 'It is'.

[17] No covenant is mentioned under the name 'covenant of grace' in the Scriptures.

[18] In dealing with and thinking about this subject of the forgiveness of sins, it is most often overlooked that the wonderful message of the forgiveness of God extended to *all men* everywhere, on the basis of grace alone, though perhaps hinted at in the Old Testament and also by Christ, was not made known or proclaimed *until after the conversion of Paul*. Prior to Paul's conversion, forgiveness was stated and offered to the chosen people only. In this connection it is startling to realise that the first reference to the love of God in the New Testament, according to the order of the books as in our Bibles, if at John 3:16! More startling still when it is appreciated that John's gospel was certainly the last of the four gospels to be written! Chronologically, it would appear that Paul's message that "God commendeth His love toward us, in that, while we were yet sinners, Christ died for us" (Romans 5:8; the "us" being "all" men, for "all have sinned" Romans 3:23), is the first of such statements in the New Testament, and again it must be remembered that the epistle to the Romans was written towards the end of the historical period covered by the Acts.

[19] This was probably caused by the preparatory movements which would possibly presage the "dividing" of the earth.

[20] In this connection, see again the second half of note 18.

[21] Paul had two distinct ministries. The Epistles written by Paul *after* the close of Acts are: - Ephesians, Philippians, Colossians, Philemon, 1 and 2 Timothy and Titus.

[22] In this connection, see that the covenant and kingdom purposes and truths are revealed and dated as "*from or since* the foundation of the world", (Matthew 13:35; 25:34; Luke 11:50 etc.) and the members of the

"church – His Body" are linked with a choice made "*before*" the foundation of the world" (Ephesians 1:4), these being two quite distinct time periods.

[23] The "appearing", or 'manifestation', - must not be confused with the "coming", which points forward to Christ's 'presence' on earth as King. An "appearing – in glory" "far above all" cannot possibly be the same as a meeting with the Lord "in the air" (1 Thessalonians 4:17) or participation in the consequent millennial reign.

[24] According to Ezekiel 45:21 the Passover will be observed in the millennial sanctuary, and in this connection, mark the Lord's words recorded at Matthew 26:29; Mark 14:25; Luke:16, 18, 30.

[25] It is true to state that the Old Testament books are largely taken up with the "old" or "first" covenant, and the results of Israel's disobedience of its terms, and the New Testament books are, for the most part, a record of the offer of the new covenant, and the results of Israel's refusal to repent and accept its terms. Therefore, the whole Bible is largely an Israelitish or Jewish book, dealing with the covenants between God and His chosen people, Israel.

[26] It must be remembered that the assembly at Corinth was composed of a company of Jewish believers (Acts 18:4, 5) possible led by Crispus, a former chief ruler of the synagogue (Acts 18:8), and a company of Gentile believers (Acts 18:8 "Corinthians"). The Jewish section had "advantage" over their Gentile brethren (Romans 3:1, 2; Romans 9:4, 5). Various questions from both companies had evidently been posed to Paul, and 1 Corinthians contains his answers. The section in which the phrase "new testament" occurs, is a section written to the Jewish believers, (see 1 Corinthians 10:1 "Our fathers"). We will give more detailed consideration to the differences that existed at that time between the Jewish and Gentile believers, when dealing with the records of the Lord's Table in the New Testament.

[27] It is this promise which Peter quotes in his first epistle (1 Peter 2:5-9), when writing to the "elect" "strangers", - i.e. the chosen people, Israelite "strangers", because scattered from their homeland by persecution (Acts 8:1; 11:19). This promise cannot be applied to Gentiles; they never have been called to be a special "nation", or promised a "land"; in which they could be constituted a "Kingdom of Priests".

[28] Read Acts 15 carefully, and note the letter recorded in verses 23-28 where it is made plain that the Gentile believers of that very early day of "Church" history (even before the revelation of "the church which is His body" was made known through Paul), were exempted from any thing Israelitish – circumcision, law-keeping, feasts including Passover – and were only expected to keep the "decrees" of Acts 15:29 (see Acts 16:4; 21:20-25).

29 'The Lord's Table'. This phrase has its roots in the Old Testament, see Ezekiel 41:22; Malachi 1:7, 12. "Lord's Table" in 1 Corinthians 10:21; "Lord's Supper" 1 Corinthians 11:20; "Communion of the blood ... and body of Christ" 1 Corinthians 10:16; "My table" Luke 22:30; "Supper" John 13:2, 4; 21:20.

30 We are indebted to the Glasgow Bible Training Institute lectures by the late Principal D. M. McIntye D. D. and the late W. M. Christie for particulars of Passover procedure, and significances of articles used.

31 John 13:2 "Supper being *ended*" a mistranslation, see *R.V.* "and during supper", or lit. "supper being come – or brought in".

32 For further notes as to the place of John's Gospel in the unfolding revelation of the truth of God, see the next chapter.

33 See John 1:38; 1:41; 2:13; 5:1; 6:1; 6:4; 7:2; 9:7; 10:22; 11:55; 19:13; 19:17; 20:16.

34 If the "Lord's Table" was really of such importance as is attached to it by nearly all parties, denominations and sects of Christendom in the present day, the necessity for its observance would surely have been found enforced and enjoined in other of the epistles.

35 "To the Jew first". See Luke 24:47; Acts 1:8; 2:14; 2:22; 2:36; 3:12 (Jerusalem, Judea, Israel); Acts 3:25, 26 "unto you (Jews) *first*"; Acts 11:19 "unto Jews only"; Acts 13:45, 46 "The Jews saw ... filled with envy ... contradicted. Then Paul said, 'It was necessary that the word of God should *first* have been spoken *to you*.'" Until well through the 3rd missionary journey Paul always used the synagogue, (if there was one in the place being visited) as his preaching centre, - see Acts 13:14; 14:1; 17:1; 17:17; 18:4; 18:19; 19:8 – and gave his gospel to "the Jew first". He acted upon this principle to the end of the Acts, as we see when he called the Jews together to his place of detention in Rome (Acts 28:17), to place before them what proved to be the last opportunity of repentance and acceptance of such blessing and grace as God, even then, was still waiting to bestow upon them.

www.ingramcontent.com/pod-product-compliance
Lightning Source LLC
Chambersburg PA
CBHW071532040426
42452CB00008B/984